From Force to Persuasion

Perspectives in Process Studies Series

Process Studies refers to a transdisciplinary field of study inspired by thinkers like Alfred North Whitehead, Charles Hartshorne, John B. Cobb Jr., David Ray Griffin, and many others. It's a perspective that has influenced many people around the world. The process-relational perspective is a framework for conceiving reality according to the principles of deep relationality, harmony, intrinsic value, and change. The implications of taking these principles seriously are far-reaching. From cosmology and metaphysics to ecology, psychology, religion, and beyond, the Perspectives in Process Studies book series engages a wide range of topics from a process-relational lens, harmonizing fragmented disciplinary thinking in order to develop integrated and holistic modes of understanding.

Series Editor:
Wm. Andrew Schwartz

From Force to Persuasion

Process-Relational Perspectives on Power and the God of Love

Edited by Andrew M. Davis

CASCADE Books · Eugene, Oregon

FROM FORCE TO PERSUASION
Process-Relational Perspectives on Power and the God of Love

Perspectives in Process Studies Series

Copyright © 2024 Wipf and Stock Publishers. All rights reserved. Except for brief quotations in critical publications or reviews, no part of this book may be reproduced in any manner without prior written permission from the publisher. Write: Permissions, Wipf and Stock Publishers, 199 W. 8th Ave., Suite 3, Eugene, OR 97401.

Cascade Books
An Imprint of Wipf and Stock Publishers
199 W. 8th Ave., Suite 3
Eugene, OR 97401

www.wipfandstock.com

PAPERBACK ISBN: 978-1-6667-8442-8
HARDCOVER ISBN: 978-1-6667-8443-5
EBOOK ISBN: 978-1-6667-8444-2

Cataloguing-in-Publication data:

Names: Davis, Andrew M. (1987–), editor.

Title: From force to persuasion : process-relational perspectives on power and the God of love / edited by Andrew M. Davis.

Description: Eugene, OR: Cascade Books, 2024. | Perspectives in Process Studies Series. | Includes bibliographical references and index.

Identifiers: ISBN 978-1-6667-8442-8 (paperback). | ISBN 978-1-6667-8443-5 (hardcover). | ISBN 978-1-6667-8444-2 (ebook).

Subjects: LCSH: Process theology. | God (Christianity)—Omnipotence. | Good and evil—Religious aspects—Christianity. | Political theology. | Religious pluralism. | Eschatology.

Classification: BT83.6.F70.2024 (print). | BT83.6 (epub).

VERSION NUMBER 07/31/24

Unless otherwise noted, Scripture quotations are taken from the New Revised Standard Version Bible, copyright © 1989 National Council of the Churches of Christ in the United States of America. Used by permission. All rights reserved worldwide.

Quotations marked NRSVue are from New Revised Standard Version Updated Edition, copyright © 2021 National Council of the Churches of Christ in the United States of America. Used by permission. All rights reserved worldwide.

Scripture quotations marked (NIV) are taken from The Holy Bible, New International Version® NIV® Copyright © 1973, 1978, 1984, 2011 by Biblica, Inc. Used with permission. All rights reserved worldwide.

Quotations designated (NET) are from the NET Bible® copyright ©1996, 2019 by Biblical Studies Press, L.L.C. http://netbible.com All rights reserved.

Quotations marked (JPS) are reprinted from *Tanakh: The New JPS Translation according to the Traditional Hebrew Text*. Copyright © 1985, 1999 by The Jewish Publication Society with the permission of the publisher.

In Memory of David Ray Griffin (1939–2022)

Contents

Series Foreword / Wm. Andrew Schwartz | xi
List of Contributors | xiii
Acknowledgments | xvii
Introduction / Andrew M. Davis | xix

Part One: Rethinking Divine Power

1. Omnipotence as a Philosophical Mistake / Daniel A. Dombrowski | 3
2. Reconsidering Omnipotence / Anna Case-Winters | 14
3. Omnipotence Is Not Born of Scripture / Thomas Jay Oord | 24
4. Love, Trust, and Divine Vulnerability / Wm. Curtis Holtzen | 49

Part Two: From the Spirit to the Polis

5. Integrative Spirituality / Patrick J. Mahaffey | 67
6. The Whole-Making Numinous / Sheri D. Kling | 78
7. Carl Schmitt's *Political Theology* / Matthew David Segall | 94
8. Prehending Political Potentials / Timothy C. Murphy | 125

Part Three: To Pluralism, Axiology, and Apocalypse

9. The Buddha's Pedagogical Power / John J. Thatamanil | 143
10. The Elephant Is Loving / Bruce G. Epperly | 157
11. God, Value, and Ontological Gratitude / Andrew M. Davis | 172
12. Power, Apocalypse, and the God of Love / Catherine Keller | 186

Appendices: Prehending the Past

Appendix A: Two Conceptions of Power / Bernard Loomer | 197

Appendix B: Worship and Theodicy / David Ray Griffin | 230

Index | 253

Series Foreword

Perspectives in Process Studies

The goal of this book series is to make accessible big ideas that are too often marginalized. By big ideas I mean ambitious, comprehensive, and fundamental questions about life, truth, meaning, and more. From cosmology and metaphysics to ecology, psychology, religion, and beyond, the Perspectives in Process Studies series has been developed to engage a wide range of topics from a process-relational lens, harmonizing fragmented disciplinary thinking in order to develop integrated and holistic modes of understanding.

Process Studies refers to a transdisciplinary field of study inspired by thinkers like Alfred North Whitehead, Charles Hartshorne, John B. Cobb Jr., David Ray Griffin, and many others. It's a perspective that has influenced many people around the world. The process-relational perspective is a framework for conceiving reality according to the principles of deep relationality, harmony, intrinsic value, and change. The implications of taking these principles seriously are far-reaching.

By recognizing that all things flow, the process perspective represents an alternative to static ontologies of being. Interdependent moments of experience replace independent substances as the final real things upon which the world is made. By extending subjectivity to all living entities, process thought deems the natural world intrinsically valuable. Therefore, the process perspective is fundamentally an ecological perspective. Process thought naturalizes the supernatural and normalizes the paranormal, contributing to the development of a new cultural paradigm that can account for the kinds of experiences regularly dismissed by many other worldviews.

Deeply appreciative of the natural sciences, process thought uniquely integrates science, religion, ethics, and aesthetics. It portrays the cosmos as an organic whole analyzable into internally related processes. In this way, process thought offers a constructive postmodern alternative to the mechanistic model that still influences much scientific work and is presupposed in much humanistic literature. Articulating a relational worldview for the common good, process perspectives create positive social change toward an ecological civilization.

Books in this series combine academic rigor with broad appeal and readability. My hope is that this series will be particularly useful for students, scholars, and armchair philosophers and theologians. However, I also hope that those interested in process thought but intimidated by Whitehead's technical jargon will find value here. Some texts will be more technical than others, but together these volumes will reflect the depth and breadth of diverse perspectives in process studies.

Wm. Andrew Schwartz,

Series Editor, Executive Director, Center for Process Studies, Assistant Professor of Process Studies & Comparative Theology, Claremont School of Theology

May 23, 2022

Contributors

Andrew M. Davis is an American process philosopher, theologian, and scholar of cosmological wonder. He is program director for the Center for Process Studies where he researches, writes, teaches, and organizes conferences on various aspects of process-relational thought. An advocate of metaphysics and meaning in a hospitable universe, he approaches philosophy as the endeavor to systematically think through what reality must be like because we are a part of it. He is author, editor, or coeditor of several books, including *Mind, Value, and Cosmos: On the Relational Nature of Ultimacy* (2020, nominated for the International Society of Science and Religion's 2022 Book Prize); *Process Cosmology: New Integrations in Science and Philosophy* (2022); *Metaphysics of Exo-Life: Toward a Constructive Whiteheadian Cosmotheology* (2023); and *Astrophilospohy, Exotheology, and Cosmic Religion: Extraterrestrial Life in a Process Universe* (2024). Follow his work at andrewmdavis.info.

Daniel A. Dombrowski is professor emeritus of philosophy at Seattle University. He is the author of twenty-two books and over a hundred and ninety articles in scholarly journals in philosophy, theology, classics, and literature. Among his books are *Rethinking the Ontological Argument: A Neoclassical Theistic Response* (2006); *Contemporary Athletics and Ancient Greek Ideals* (2009); and *Process Philosophy and Political Liberalism: Rawls, Whitehead, Hartshorne* (2019). His most recent book is *Process Mysticism* (2023). His main areas of intellectual interest are metaphysics and philosophy of religion from a neoclassical or process perspective. He is the editor of the journal *Process Studies* and is past president of the Metaphysical Society of America. E-mail: ddombrow@seattleu.edu.

Anna Case-Winters is professor of theology at McCormick Theological Seminary, Chicago. She is author or editor of several books, including *God's Power: Traditional Understandings and Contemporary Challenges* (1990); *Reconstructing a Christian Theology of Nature* (2007); *Matthew: A Theological Commentary on the Bible* (2015); and most recently *God Will Be All in All: Theology through the Lens of Incarnation* (2021). She has published widely and lectured across the country on these topics. She is the recipient of three Templeton awards and is active in many professional organizations, including the American Academy of Religion, the American Theological Society (past president), the Center for Process Studies, and the Highlands Institute for American Religious and Philosophical Thought. She has served on the advisory board for the American Association for the Advancement of Science (in the Dialogue on Science, Ethics, and Religion) and is currently on the editorial board of *Zygon: Journal for Religion and Science*.

Thomas Jay Oord is a theologian, philosopher, and scholar of multidisciplinary studies. Oord directs the Center for Open and Relational Theology and doctoral students at Northwind Theological Seminary. He is an award-winning author and has written or edited more than thirty books. A gifted speaker, Oord lectures at universities, conferences, churches, and other institutions. He is known for his research on love, science and religion, open and relational theology, the problem of suffering, and the implications of freedom for transformational relationships. Follow his work at thomasjayoord.com

Wm. Curtis Holtzen is professor of philosophy and theology at Hope International University in Fullerton, California. He is the author of *The God Who Trusts: A Relational Theology of Divine Faith, Hope, and Love* (2019) as well as various essays related to open and relational theology.

Patrick J. Mahaffey is professor emeritus at Pacifica Graduate Institute, where he teaches Hindu traditions as a scholar-practitioner. He is the author of *Integrative Spirituality: Religious Pluralism, Individuation, and Awakening* (2019) and the editor of *Evolving God-Images: Essays on Religion, Individuation, and Postmodern Spirituality* (2014).

Sheri D. Kling is the director of Process & Faith with the Center for Process Studies and interim minister of Redeemer Lutheran Church in Bradenton, Florida. She is a theologian, songwriter, and spiritual companion, as well as a faculty member of the Haden Institute, adjunct faculty with Claremont School of Theology, and the author of *A Process Spirituality: Christian and Transreligious Resources for Transformation* (2020). She regularly delivers

CONTRIBUTORS

dynamic "Music & Message" presentations to groups and offers courses, concerts, and spiritual retreats. Follow her work at sherikling.com.

Matthew David Segall is a transdisciplinary researcher, writer, teacher, and philosopher applying process-relational thought across the natural and social sciences, as well as to the study of consciousness. He is associate professor in the Philosophy, Cosmology, and Consciousness Program at California Institute of Integral Studies and the chair of the Science Advisory Committee for the Cobb Institute. His recent books include *Physics of the World-Soul: Whitehead's Adventure in Cosmology* (2022) and *Crossing the Threshold: Etheric Imagination in the Post-Kantian Process Philosophy of Schelling and Whitehead* (2023). Follow his work at footnotes2plato.com.

Timothy C. Murphy currently serves as the senior pastor and teacher of Plymouth Congregational Church of Fort Wayne, Indiana. He has previously served in a variety of positions in the Southern California area, including as a pastor, as the executive director of Progressive Christians Uniting, and as a visiting assistant professor of religion and politics at Claremont School of Theology. His justice and service passions include dismantling racism, combating economic inequality, and addressing climate change, among several other areas. He is the author of three books, including an illustrated children's book titled *Jesus Learns to Glow* (2022) where over the course of one night, Jesus of Nazareth goes on a journey, making friends with a mushroom, a firefly, algae, and a jellyfish, before learning to glow like they do.

John J. Thatamanil is professor of theology and world religions at Union Theological Seminary in New York. He is the author of *Circling the Elephant: A Comparative Theology of Religious Diversity* (2020) and *The Immanent Divine: God, Creation, and the Human Predicament* (2006). He is currently working on a book titled, *Desiring Truth: The Quest for Interreligious Wisdom in a Post-Truth Era*. He is a past president of the North American Paul Tillich Society. He teaches a wide variety of courses, including Hindu Religious Thought and Practice, Paul Tillich as Public Theologian, Process Theology, and Double Belonging: On Multiple Religious Participation. Thatamanil is an Anglican/Episcopalian who also reads and practices in traditions of Hindu and Buddhist nondualism. He is also a priest in and the diocesan theologian for the Anglican Diocese of Islands and Inlets (colonial name: the Anglican Diocese of British Columbia).

Bruce G. Epperly has served as a seminary and university professor and administrator, a university chaplain, a congregational pastor, and a spiritual guide. He is the author of over eighty books, including recent publications,

Simplicity, Spirituality, and Service: The Timeless Wisdom of Francis, Clare, and Bonaventure (2023); *The Elephant Is Running: Process and Open and Relational Theology and Religious Pluralism* (2022); *Jesus: Mystic, Healer, and Prophet* (2023); and the three-volume collection, *Process Theology and Mysticism*; *Process Theology and Healing*; and *Process Theology and Prophetic Faith* (2023). In retirement, he remains on the faculty of Wesley Theological Seminary in Washington DC and is a walker, grandparent, and Reiki healing-touch teacher.

Catherine Keller is George T. Cobb Professor of Constructive Theology in the Graduate Division of Religion, Drew University. She works amid the tangles of ecosocial, pluralist, feminist philosophy of religion and theology. Her books include *Face of the Deep: A Theology of Becoming* (2003); *On the Mystery* (2007); *Cloud of the Impossible: Negative Theology and Planetary Entanglement* (2014); and *Political Theology of the Earth: Our Planetary Emergency and the Struggle for a New Public* (2018). She has coedited several volumes of the Drew Transdisciplinary Theological Colloquium, most recently *Political Theology on Edge: Ruptures of Justice and Belief in the Anthropocene* (2022). Her latest monograph is *Facing Apocalypse: Climate, Democracy, and Other Last Chances* (2021).

Bernard Loomer (1912–1985), was an American process philosopher and theologian. Loomer was former dean and professor at the University of Chicago Divinity School and the Graduate Theological Union in Berkeley, California. A leading proponent of empirical process theology, Loomer is known widely for his theodicy of "ambiguity" based upon a vision of divine "size" and "stature." For an introduction to his work and influence, see *The Size of God: The Theology of Bernard Loomer in Context*, edited by William Dean and Larry E. Axel (1987).

David Ray Griffin (1939–2022), was emeritus professor of philosophy and theology at the Claremont School of Theology, emeritus professor of religion at Claremont Graduate University, and cofounder with John B. Cobb Jr. of the Center for Process Studies in 1973. He was the author of numerous books in philosophy, religion, and politics and one of the most widely recognized and influential process philosophers of the twenty-first century.

Acknowledgments

This volume has emerged as a result of the Power and the God of Love conference held at CrossWalk Community Church in Napa, California, on November 4–5, 2022. Cosponsored by the Center for Process Studies and the Center for Open and Relational Theology, this event brought together a variety of philosophers, theologians, and ministers to consider the nature and implications of divine power and love as informed by process-relational conceptualities. A debt of gratitude is owed to pastor Pete Shaw and the community at CrossWalk for their diligent organizational efforts and aid in executing a successful conference. Thanks are also due to Tom Oord at the Center for Open and Relational Theology, who nurtured the original idea for the event.

Introduction

Returning to the Way of Persuasion

ANDREW M. DAVIS

One of the abiding themes of Alfred North Whitehead's late book *Adventures of Ideas* (1933) is the efficacy of persuasion in the rise of civilization. In a chapter titled "From Force to Persuasion," he discusses the emergence and operation of "persuasive agencies" at various levels of social evolution, development, and interaction. From base necessities like the need for food and shelter to economics, politics, and religion, he demonstrates how "the way of persuasion" functions as one of the chief means by which society progresses toward finer versions of itself.[1]

Yet Whitehead's convictions as to the way of persuasion also transcend these human domains, having both cosmological and theological significance. In this, he shows his indebtedness to Plato. "The creation of the world—said Plato—is the victory of persuasion over force."[2] Whitehead holds Plato in high regard with respect to this belief. "More than two thousand years ago, the wisest of men proclaimed that the divine persuasion is the foundation of the order of the world," he states, "but that it can only produce such a measure of harmony as amid brute forces it was possible to accomplish."[3]

According to Whitehead, Plato's conviction "that the divine element . . . is to be conceived as a persuasive agency and not as a coercive agency" should be seen as "one of the greatest intellectual discoveries in the history of religion." Moreover, after pointing to the "intellectual discovery" of divine persuasion in Plato, Whitehead then points to the *embodiment* of this persuasion in the

---

1. Whitehead, *Adventures of Ideas*, 69, 85.
2. Whitehead, *Adventures of Ideas*, 83.
3. Whitehead, *Adventures of Ideas*, 160.

life of Christ as "the supreme moment in religious history." He asks, "Can there be any doubt that the power of Christianity lies in its revelation in act of that which Plato divined in theory?"[4] Whithead had answered this question decisively in his earlier book *Religion in the Making* (1926): "The life of Christ is not an exhibition of over-ruling power. Its glory is for those who can discern it. Its power lies in its absence of force. It has the decisiveness of a supreme ideal, and that is why the history of the world divides at this point of time."[5]

Whitehead, however, laments that Christian theology did not hold fast to its founding revelation of divine persuasion in the formation of its doctrine of God. Instead, "the alternative doctrine" of coercive omnipotence prevailed. Where authentic divine power could have been upheld as persuasive love, as expressed in the life of Christ, the doctrine of God emerged as "the supreme agency of coercion" and was further "transformed into the one supreme reality, omnipotently disposing a wholly derivative world."[6] This, for Whitehead, is part and parcel of the "tragic history of Christianity."[7] The "brief Galilean vision" of persuasive love flickered uncertainly throughout history, and Plato's doctrine of divine persuasion became a relic of a distant and perhaps nobler past.[8]

Whitehead thus remains famous (for some, infamous) for advocating a rejection of divine omnipotence and a return to, or rediscovery of, divine persuasion as part of a "new reformation" in theology, religion, and society at large.[9] This advocacy continues today in the work of a variety of process-relational philosophers and theologians. Is it possible to *return* to Plato's conviction as to the efficacy of divine persuasion in the world? Can theology and religion *rediscover* their roots in divine persuasion as found in the life of Christ? If so, how might this transform our disciplines and interactions as a culture and society inundated with delusions of coercive omnipotence? What are the implications and/or justifications of this return? For decades, process thinkers have argued that divine persuasion is the operative power of the God of love. In what ways have they justified their claims, and what theoretical, practical, and personal implications are at stake?

This book features key contributions from advocates of process-relational theologies. It aims to further situate a shift *back* "from force to persuasion" and considers its implications across multiple thresholds of discourse, including philosophy and theology, spirituality and politics, and pluralism,

---

4. Whitehead, *Adventures of Ideas* 166–67.
5. Whitehead, *Religion in the Making*, 47.
6. Whitehead, *Adventures of Ideas*, 166.
7. Whitehead, *Adventures of Ideas*, 166; cf. Whitehead, *Process and Reality*, 342.
8. Whitehead, *Process and Reality*, 342.
9. See Whitehead, *Adventures of Ideas*, ch. 10.

axiology, and apocalypse. In doing so, it aims to reawaken attention to the operations of divine persuasion as ever-loving and inherently uncontrolling, but always at risk in an open and relational universe.

Rethinking Divine Power

This book is divided into three parts differently attending to key themes of power and love in process-relational perspective. Part 1 includes four chapters that rethink divine power from various philosophical, theological, and biblical perspectives.

In Chapter 1, "Omnipotence as a Philosophical Mistake," Daniel A. Dombrowski argues that where Charles Hartshorne famously called omnipotence a "theological mistake," it must also be made clear why omnipotence is a *philosophical mistake*. Philosophical and theological mistakes naturally implicate one another. According to Dombrowski, one of the main reasons "neoclassical" or process theism falls on deaf ears is because it is widely (but wrongly) assumed that God must be omnipotent to be "God." In challenging this widespread assumption, Dombrowski draws upon the insights of Plato, Anselm, David Hume, Hartshorne, Whitehead, Franklin Gamwell, and John Rawls in articulating key philosophical problems with omnipotence. In stressing divine power and knowledge as *ideal* rather than all-determining, Dombrowksi develops a new vision of the interplay of love and justice in both God and the world.

In Chapter 2, "Reconsidering Omnipotence," Anna Case-Winters probes different meanings of "omnipotence" and problematizes the concept in terms of coherence, religious viability, and moral adequacy. Her "constructive proposal" draws from both the Christian tradition and key process-relational voices to argue that divine power and love are by nature always generative, persuasive, and shared. For Case-Winters, the criticisms offered by process thought help clear away different theological overlays that obscure the deeper persuasive vision revealed in the life and ministry of Jesus. The "saving solidarity" and "redemptive resistance" found in the life of Christ, Case-Winters insists, is indeed the kind of power one might expect from a God of love.

In Chapter 3, "Omnipotence is Not Born of Scripture," Thomas Jay Oord addresses three biblical terms pertaining to divine power: *shaddai*, *sabaoth*, and *pantokrator*. Oord notes that biblical portrayals of divine power remain important for Christians who hold to the scriptures as authoritative. Trained theologians and everyday believers often appeal to the Bible in support their view that God is all-powerful, and Muslims, Jews, and other theists often assume that Christian scripture clearly affirms a God of unlimited power. Does it, however? In a wide-ranging discussion, Oord reveals that *shaddai*, *sabaoth*, and *pantokrator* have been wrongly translated as "almighty." Oord also confronts key biblical passages that prima facie support traditional interpretations of omnipotence. However, when considered more deeply, omnipotence is nowhere to be found. For Oord, the Bible in fact does not sanction the view that God exerts all power, can do absolutely anything, or is totally controlling at all. The Bible does not endorse omnipotence and the implications for Christian theology and practice are only beginning to come to light.

In Chapter 4, "Divine Love, Trust, and Vulnerability," Curtis Holtzen affirms a form of divine vulnerability or passibility that has rarely been examined by Christian theologians long beholden to divine impassiblity. Specifically, Holtzen argues that God is vulnerable, exposed, or open to various kinds of experiences that come solely from trusting a loved one. Trust comes with the risk of betrayal, a pain exclusive to having one's gift of faith abused or violated. However, trust for Holzten also leaves one open to feelings of thankfulness, appreciation, and gratitude for trustworthiness. Holzten thus demonstrates that if there is reason to believe that God has faith—that God seeks to trust us—then God, like us, is vulnerable to the pains of betrayal and the delights of gratitude. These convictions, moreover, are at home in various forms of relational theism.

From the Spirit to the Polis

Part 2 features four chapters that address different contours of spirituality and transformation as well as political theory and practice with the resources of process-relational philosophy and theology.

In Chapter 5, "Integrative Spirituality: God-Images, Individuation, and Awakening," Patrick J. Mahaffey draws from various Western and Eastern resources in reviewing his own encounter with process theology and its spiritual potential. In particular, he proposes that Jungian depth psychology and contemplative yoga provide forms of psychospiritual practice that align with process-relational theology and philosophy. "How can such practice enable persons to experience a God who may be found in everyone and everywhere?" Mahaffey asks. In describing his own version of integrative spirituality, he offers a rich approach to experiencing a God of love who continually incarnates in human experience through processes of individuation and spiritual awakening. For Mahaffey, a God of love lures us to cocreate a shared world of wholeness, creativity, and awakening on both individual and collective levels.

In Chapter 6, "The Whole-Making Numinous: Power and Love in Cosmos and Psyche," Sheri D. Kling argues for the fruitful integration of process thought, Jungian psychology, and a spiritual practice of dream work. These resources, Kling argues, can reveal the nature of all levels of reality—both cosmic and psychic—as integrated, value-soaked, relational, and transformative. For Kling, Whitehead and Jung can together address the fragmentation of American culture specifically, and Western culture more broadly. Both Jung and Whitehead also support the practice of dream work as a means of fostering embodied experiences of wholeness, belonging, and positive change. For Kling, theology must offer transformative change in the real world or it remains valueless. In calling the Divine Reality the "Whole-making Numinous," she affirms God as a reality of love and uncontrolling power. For each of us, Kling insists, God is present, internal, and in every moment of existence, and offers creative possibilities that transform the detriments of the past into new futures of wholeness and well-being. As a practice, dream work is a means by which we can raise the unconscious, imaginal aims of God to consciousness, allowing us to discern new possibilities, respond freely, and heal the fragmentation of both ourselves and society.

In Chapter 7, "Carl Schmitt's *Political Theology*: A Process Theological Intervention," Matthew David Segall endeavors a sustained discussion that critically engages Carl Schmitt's antiliberal political theology and offers key interventions from the related perspectives of Whitehead's cosmopolitical process theology, philosophical personalism, and Bruno Latour's Gaian political ecology. In doing so, Segall also tests Schmitt's criticisms of early twentieth-century liberalism against Daniel Dombrowski's recent defense of a process reading of Rawlsian political liberalism. Given Schmitt's nominal Catholicism, Segall also turns to the New Testament as a source of spiritual resistance to his fascist ideology. In addition to moving beyond both neoliberal capitalism and state communism, Segall stresses that "process liberalism" implies an expansion of the narrowly anthropocentric confines of modern political theories to embrace what Whitehead calls a "democracy of fellow creatures." What is more, Segall insists that process liberals can also decisively affirm that in the self-consciousness of our own freedom is the *parousia* of an all-loving God.

In Chapter 8, "Prehending Political Potentials: Reconstituting American Liberal Democracy," Timothy C. Murphy draws upon Whitehead's distinction between "pure possibilities" and "real potentials" and their positive or negative prehension (feeling) in offering an overview of some alternative political systems that might strengthen representative liberal democracy in the United States. These models come from around the world and suggest improvements to what Murphy stresses is a binary and dysfunctional US system. Murphy articulates how process theology supports an open-ended political vision that is inclusive of various potentialities relevant to ongoing political debates. Moreover, mirrored in its vision of a relational God that works with the world as it is, to bring it to where it can be, is an active political agenda holding that US citizens must work with what we have while also positively prehending real potentials for a still more perfect union.

To Pluralism, Axiology, and Apocalypse

Part 3 contains four chapters differently exploring the potential of process-relational categories for comparative religion and plurality, the nature and axiological basis of worship, and the meaning and implications of crucifixion and apocalypse for a precarious ecological future.

In Chapter 9, "The Buddha's Pedagogical Power: The Unlimited Capacity to Love and Liberate All Sentient Beings," John J. Thatamanil reveals how the question of the relationship between "love" and "power" presents intriguing and demanding challenges when considered from a Buddhist perspective. He also demonstrates some of the fruitful comparative possibilities between Buddhist and Christians with respect to these notions. Buddhist religious texts say much about love, or at least cognate concepts, but Buddhists in core religious texts do not speak of power as conventionally understood in theistic traditions because an "omnipotent" divine being is not a central Buddhist theme as found in western religions. Power, for Buddhist thinkers, has two core meanings according to Thatamanil. First, power is the capacity to awaken and see reality clearly. It is the capacity to awaken countless other living beings and to lead them out of their captivity to greed, hatred, and delusion and into liberation. Second, power is the vigor (*virya*) required to sustain the path toward such other-centered liberation and the resolve to maintain that quest over endless lifetimes. For Thatamanil, the Buddha's power is a pedagogical power which renounces political power. Understood as a comparative category, "pedagogical power" can also be recognized in Christ the rabbi who developed pedagogical communities and actively refused the power of Caesar. For Thatamanil, these resonant insights form the starting gestures of a comparative theology of pedagogical power.

In Chapter 10, "The Elephant Is Loving: Pluralism and Diversity as the Embodiment of God's Love," Bruce G. Epperly reframes a well-known parable describing a group of sight-impaired persons gathered around a large elephant. Each person feels a certain part of the elephant and assumes that the part they are touching is the totality of the creature. Each also believes that their experience of the elephant accurately describes the animal over and against their neighbors' experiences of it. Lyrically and autobiographically, Epperly re-expresses this parable as representing the dynamic and all-embracing love of God. According to Epperly, this parable's message is the same if we substitute blindfolded, culture-bound, or religiously committed persons for sight-impaired persons. We experience the Holy through the lenses, histories, experiences, and biases of our communities and faith traditions. Accordingly, we should not equate our spiritual path with the totality of God. In a processual universe, the elephant is not static, but *running*. For Epperly, we can celebrate the fact that there is always more to learn about the Holy, and our vocation is to be adventurous in our quest to experience a reality we can never fully catch.

In Chapter 11, "God, Value, and Ontological Gratitude: On the Axiological Foundations of Worship," Andrew M. Davis reconsiders a question that has been historically significant to the process-relational tradition: What kind of God is most worthy of worship?[10] In considering this question anew, Davis advocates a particular axiological approach in light of the deeper question of divine necessity: What is the nature of divine necessity? What reasons or explains God's existence? Why do God and a world exist at all? Different responses confront us: (1) reasonless brute fact, (2) unrelenting divine power, (3) logical necessity, and (4) utter mystery. Each of these responses, Davis argues, fails to ground a God worthy of worship. According to Davis, they also fail to illuminate what worship is. Through the resonant insights of John Leslie, Keith Ward, A. C. Ewing, Alfred North Whitehead, and Nicholas Rescher, Davis argues for a fifth response: (5) axiological necessity. For Davis, worthiness of worship is only to be assigned to that God whose reason for being is found in the creative supremacy of its own Value. Value thus also reasons the existence of the world, human beings, and human purpose as worshipful beings. For Davis, the axiological foundations of God and the world constitute worship as "ontological gratitude"—a gratefulness for existence—which manifests itself in a value-creative life.

In Chapter 12, "Power, Apocalypse, and the God of Love," Catherine Keller offers a theopolitical meditation on the last words of Christ (*Eloi, eloi, lema sabachthani*) in relation to the problem of evil, a precarious ecological future, and perennial Christian themes of forsakenness, crucifixion, resurrection, and apocalypse. In considering the relevance of godforsakenness to our own time, she interweaves the insights of Whitehead, David Ray Griffin, Jürgen Moltmann, John Cobb, and Tom Oord to rethink the nature of power in light of the gospel proclamation of suffering love. For Keller, the

10. This chapter originally appeared in the *Toronto Journal of Theology* 36/1 (2020) 33–43. It is republished in this volume with minor edits by the permission of University of Toronto Press.

alternative theo-logic of a process theodicy of persuasive love really does free us from the illusion of a controlling, monopolistic, divine power. Keller insists that this was not Jesus' God or God's *basileia* to start with. Apocalypse designates not the end of the world; *apokalypsis* does not close down but *discloses* the reality of God through voices of the prophetic tradition. Does advocating for the persuasive power of divine love, as process theologians do, give voice to something like a prophetic tradition in the contemporary world? In reaching back to the cross, Keller suggests affirmatively that the power of divine love is a *feeling-with* or *com-passion*, that folds the suffering of evil into the potential for good.

Prehending the Past

The appendices prehend the value of the past by republishing two important pieces by Bernard Loomer (1912–1985) and David Ray Griffin (1939–2022) that together amplify the various themes of power and love encountered in this volume.

In Appendix A, "Two Conceptions of Power," Bernard Loomer juxtaposes linear and relational power through a sustained consideration of various themes of human life and striving, including those of the theological tradition.[11] According to Loomer, linear power is the ability to produce an intended or desired effect in our relationships to nature or to those around us. More specifically, linear power is the capacity to adjust, manipulate, shape, control, or transform the human or natural environment to advance one's own interests. Relational power, by contrast, is the ability both to produce and undergo an effect without collapse—what Loomer calls "size." Relational power is the capacity to influence and be influenced through both giving and receiving and thus, has a constitutive role in relationships. It is the capacity to sustain a relationship and to be truly present to another with both stature and size. For Loomer, the God of unilateral power is an idol that is not large enough to merit our faith and devotion. Only a relational God of adequate size and goodness can engender our faith, hope, and trust.

In Appendix B, "Worship and Theodicy," David Ray Griffin considers the relationship between process theology and worship and, with signature clarity and rigor, defends process theodicy against key criticisms.[12] He not only demonstrates why the question of worship is crucial for process theodicy, but

---

11. This chapter originally appeared in *Process Studies* 6.1 (1976) 5–32. It is republished in this volume with minor edits by the permission of Daniel A. Dombrowski.

12. This chapter originally appeared under the same title in Griffin, *Evil Revisited*, 196–213. It is republished in this volume with minor edits by the permission of SUNY Press.

also considers whether worship presupposes perfect power and the nature of that power. In defending the God of process theism as perfectly good, Griffin stresses the importance of actively investing the insights of process theism in arenas other than those of the academy. Human life, psychology, and religious consciousness are all implicated in the shift from force to persuasion. Ours is a time of theological transition, of "living between Gods," according to Griffin. Whether process theodicy is found to be fully satisfactory, Griffin holds, is finally dependent upon us. It is dependent upon the kind of power we find divine, and therefore, upon the kind of persons we are or intend to become. If we academic philosophers and theologians find the God of persuasive love theologically satisfactory, it is up to us to *help God* bring about the kind of persons who will also find it religiously satisfying.

The chapters contained in this volume do not exhaust the contributions process-relational philosophers and theologians can make to contemporary discussions of power and the God of love. From the "intellectual discovery" of Plato to the lived embodiment of Christ, pivotal questions concerning the nature and efficacy of divine power reverberate throughout history and persist today. Whitehead merely echoes these seminal figures in advocating a return to the way of persuasion. Process theologians also echo Whitehead in holding that this *way* "dwells upon the tender elements in the world which slowly and in quietness operate by love."[13]

Bibliography

Davis, Andrew M. "God, Value, and Ontological Gratitude: On the Axiological Foundations of Worship." *Toronto Journal of Theology* 36.1 (2020) 33–43.
Griffin, David Ray. *Evil Revisited: Responses and Reconsiderations*. Albany: SUNY Press, 1991.
Loomer, Bernard. "Two Conceptions of Power." *Process Studies* 6.1 (1976) 5–32.
Whitehead, Alfred North. *Adventures of Ideas*. 1st Free Press paperback. ed New York: Free Press, 1967.
———. *Process and Reality*. Edited by David Ray Griffin and Donald W. Sherburne. Corrected ed. Gifford Lectures 1927–1928. New York: Free Press, 1978.
———. *Religion in the Making*. Lowell Lectures 1926. Cambridge: Cambridge University Press, 1926.

13. Whitehead, *Process and Reality*, 343.

Part One

Rethinking Divine Power

1

Omnipotence as a Philosophical Mistake

DANIEL A. DOMBROWSKI

Charles Hartshorne is famous (or infamous) for the provocative title to one of his later books, *Omnipotence and Other Theological Mistakes*.[1] The purpose of this opening chapter is to make the case in a concise way for omnipotence as a *philosophical* mistake. Because Hartshorne himself was a philosopher rather than a theologian, my efforts will be continuous with his. The topic of this chapter is important at the very least because perhaps the main reason it is difficult to get a fair hearing for neoclassical or process theism is that it is widely assumed (by theists and religious skeptics alike) that God *must* be omnipotent or the being in question would not be God, and that an alleged divine being who was not omnipotent would be too weak to be seen as God.

I would like to make it clear that I will not be giving up the concept of divine perfection. To the contrary, I will start with the well-known definition of "God" from Saint Anselm: that than which no greater can be conceived.[2] But I will call into question the historically pervasive *assumption* that God is omnipotent in the sense that God has *all* power. I will defend an alternative version of the logic of perfection (which involves dynamic perfection rather than the classical theistic static perfection) by claiming that God has *ideal* power, but not all of it. This view will be integrally connected to the distinction between *coercive* and *persuasive* power and the idea that we ought not jump too quickly to the position that assumes that ideal power is associated more with the former than with the latter.

As I see things, there are at least four major problems with the concept of omnipotence. First, belief in divine omnipotence creates the nastiest

---

1. Hartshorne, *Omnipotence and Other Theological Mistakes*.
2. See Dombrowski, *Rethinking the Ontological Argument*.

version of the theodicy problem. This is because on the basis of divine omnipotence all evil is either sent by God or is at least permitted by God. The disturbing examples are well known, as in an intensely painful disease experienced by a young child. It is no surprise that there are religious skeptics if it is assumed, as it has been historically, that theism requires belief in divine omnipotence. David Hume was correct to point out in his *Dialogues Concerning Natural Religion* that an omnipotent being *could* eliminate the suffering of the innocent; when conjoined with belief in divine omnibenevolence, which entails that God *would* eliminate such suffering, the presence of evil in the world becomes an insoluble mystery, in the pejorative sense of the term "mystery."[3]

That is, belief in divine omnipotence is at odds with belief in divine omnibenevolence. This is because both beliefs *together* entail the absence of evil and gratuitous suffering in the world. But there *is* evil and gratuitous suffering in the world, hence we need to modify what we say about at least one of these two concepts. In the remainder of this chapter, I will try to show the inferiority (indeed, the incoherence) of divine omnipotence in contrast to quite intelligible divine omnibenevolence. A further problem with belief in divine omnipotence, in addition to its leading to the nastiest version of the theodicy problem, is that it distracts our attention away from divine omnibenevolence. Instead of concentrating on divine love, which is the goal of a theocentric life in various theistic religions, one is always tempted on the basis of belief in divine omnipotence to be distracted or vexed by the question as to why intense suffering exists, especially suffering experienced by the innocent. In addition to Hume, neoclassical or process theists can also learn from Fyodor Dostoevsky's *The Brothers Karamazov* about the defects in classical theism.[4] As Hartshorne dramatically puts the point in an early essay, "if theism cannot be improved upon *profoundly*, then I for one have little desire to see it survive."[5]

It will be objected, of course, that by abandoning belief in divine omnipotence we would be open to the possibility that life would be tragic. I do not think that it is intellectually honest to sidestep this objection by trying to deny the possibility of tragedy. There is much to be learned from the ancient Greek conviction that life *is* tragic.[6] The sublime symbol for this conviction in Christianity is the cross. Rather than insist a priori that divine omnipotence

---

3. See Hume, *Dialogues Concerning Natural Religion*; and Griffin, *God, Power, and Evil*.

4. Dostoevsky, *Brothers Karamazov*.

5. Hartshorne, "Ethics and the New Theology," 92.

6. Arnison, "Tragic Vision for Christianity."

is a nonnegotiable concept in theism and then try (unsuccessfully) to find an explanation for why there is gratuitous suffering in the world, it makes more sense to *start* with the realization that life is tragic (the evidence for such realization is in abundance!) and then find the appropriate way to articulate the logic of perfection and the most defensible concept of God in such a logic. Once some tragic (or pathetic) suffering occurs, there is no evading that fact so long as there are those who remember the tragic suffering. In fact, such memory itself is a type of vicarious tragic suffering.

Second, divine omnipotence is at odds with Plato's claim that being *is* power.[7] This claim is a commonplace in Hartshorne's writings and in those of Alfred North Whitehead as well. In fact, it is a cornerstone of process metaphysics. The key idea here is that anything that exists exerts power (*dynamis*), however slight. In related terms, to be is to have the power not only to influence others, but also the power to be influenced by others, again in however slight a way. It must be admitted that Plato says "or" (*eite*) here, such that anything that exists either has the power to influence others or the power to be influenced by others. This leaves open the unfortunate possibility that there could be a being, say an unmoved mover, who could influence others but be altogether uninfluenced by them. Hartshorne and Whitehead offer an insightful and friendly amendment to Plato's view by suggesting that Plato should have said "and" (*kai*) rather than "or." Each actual occasion receives influence from the past and then exerts some influence on others in the future via momentary decisions or pulses of dynamic energy in the present. It is fortuitous in this regard that the Greek word for "power" (*dynamis*) is the etymological root for our word "dynamic."

The relationship between the definition of being as dynamic power and the critique of divine omnipotence is clear. If each existent has *some* power, however slight, to be influenced by others and to influence others, then no being (not even God) could have *all* power. Divine omnipotence in the sense of the possession of all power would render everything else powerless (i.e., nonexistent). (No doubt "omnipotence" may have other senses, in which case analysis of the concept would change accordingly.) But beings other than God obviously *do* exist, hence the indefensibility of divine omnipotence. If an actual entity is where it acts and is acted upon, and if being *is* power, then power is divided among many beings.

According to Whitehead, when Plato says in the *Sophist* (through the Eleatic Stranger) that it is the definition (*horon*) of being that it exert power, Plato reached the height of his genius as a metaphysician.[8] Hartshorne

---

7. Plato, *Sophist*, in Cairns and Hamilton, *Collected Dialogues*, 247e.
8. See, for example, Whitehead, *Adventures of Ideas*, 5–6, 25, 83, 118–22, 129,

agrees: power must be exercised upon something, at least if by power we mean active and passive influence. But the something that is "controlled" cannot be completely inert if being *is* dynamic power. There must be some resistance, however slight, to even ideal power and power that is resisted cannot be absolute. Contrary to what defenders of divine omnipotence might claim, the fact that God cannot "make us do" certain things does not really "limit" God's power because there is no such thing as power to make impossibilities true, as even classical theists would admit. Power over us would not really be power over *us* if we counted for nothing and had no being and hence no power. Power is the ability to influence and to be influenced; ideal power consists in the best possible ways to influence (not utterly dominate) *and to be influenced by* others.[9]

Whereas the first criticism (that belief in divine omnipotence leads to an intractable version of the theodicy problem) might lead some to nonetheless wistfully hope for an omnipotent God so as to eliminate all evil and suffering, the second criticism (that belief in divine omnipotence is at odds with the Platonic/process claim that being *is* power) calls into question the very coherence of the concept of divine omnipotence on the assumption that there are other beings (i.e., powers) in existence. In this regard we should remember the scholarship of Bernard Loomer, who best articulates both the two sorts of power—coercive and persuasive—and the superiority of the latter to the former in the logic of perfection.[10] Combined with Hartshorne's concept of dual transcendence, it can be said that the neoclassical, process, dipolar God is ironically *more* powerful than the classical, monopolar God in that the dipolar process God is the most powerful agent *and* patient, in contrast to the traditional view wherein God is altogether deficient in paciency powers.

Third, belief in divine omnipotence is closely connected to belief in creation ex nihilo, which is unintelligible. Here again Plato is helpful in distinguishing two different sorts of nonbeing or nothingness: relative and absolute.[11] Relative nonbeing is a rough synonym for otherness or difference, as when we say quite intelligibly that a corkscrew is not the same as a catcher's mitt (although both corkscrews and catchers' mitts exist). By contrast, to say that absolute nothingness *is* is to contradict oneself. Our awareness of absence depends on our awareness of presence, as Plato realized long ago when he committed parricide on "Father Parmenides" by showing the

---

166–69; See also, Dombrowski, *Platonic Philosophy of Religion*.

9. See Hartshorne, *Man's Vision of God*, xvi, 14, 89, 198–99, 205, 232, 244, 294.

10. See Loomer, "Two Conceptions of Power," Appendix A in this volume.

11. Plato, *Sophist*, in Cairns and Hamilton, *Collected Dialogues*, 241d.

necessity of *relative* nonbeing or otherness (*me on*), but nonetheless denying even the possibility of *absolute* nonbeing (*ouk on*). Neoclassical or process metaphysics explicates the semantic logic of existence, which requires "meontic" negativity, but not the "oukontic" sort.

A putative thought whose content is *completely* negative is, as I see things, meaningless. This is due to the fact that a putative thought whose content is self-contradictory is meaningless. One may utter the words "a colorless blue thing" or "the existence of absolutely nothing," but there is something contradictory and hence meaningless (due to a lack of content) in each case. Franklin Gamwell goes so far as to claim that "no decision in philosophical thought is more fundamental than whether or not 'something exists' is necessarily true."[12] The self-contradiction involved in belief in creation ex nihilo, built on belief in divine omnipotence, is both *semantic* (in that it exhibits self-contradiction within the *meaning* of a statement, as in a colorless blue object or the existence of absolutely nothing) and *pragmatic* (in that when one *says* that absolutely nothing exists one's own existence contradicts what one says).

Some in the Abrahamic traditions may worry that belief in creation ex nihilo or creation out of absolute nothingness is integral to biblical faith and hence that this sort of creation should not be rejected carelessly. Although this concern carries no weight philosophically, the fact that many philosophical theists are also Abrahamic believers makes it appropriate to notice that biblical creation is, according to many noted Hebrew scripture scholars, creation ex hyle (out of disorderly matter) and not ex nihilo.[13] When the spirit of God hovers above the waters in the beginning of Genesis, one gets the impression that both God and the aqueous muck have been around forever. That is, a critique of divine omnipotence and hence of creation ex nihilo need not be an impediment to biblical faith. In fact, biblical creation ex hyle is very close to Plato's similar view in the *Timaeus* of God's persuasive ordering of the chaotic material stuff of the world. Both are intelligible, in contrast to the unintelligible concept of absolute nothingness.

It is a commonplace in process theism that we should avoid paying metaphysical compliments to God that end up backfiring.[14] Divine omnipotence, I am claiming, is one of these "compliments." The source of the problem is that, at the time of the first centuries BCE and CE, coercive physical power was revered in political leaders, quintessentially in Caesar. This admiration was (in Feuerbachian fashion) transferred to God. I will return

---

12. Gamwell, *Existence and the Good*, 29.
13. Levenson, *Creation and the Persistence of Evil*; May, *Creatio Ex Nihilo*.
14. See, for example, Whitehead, *Science and the Modern World*, 179.

to this transfer momentarily. It should also be noted that one of the causal influences that has historically facilitated belief in divine omnipotence is male bias, as several feminist scholars have persuasively argued.[15]

And fourth, belief in divine omnipotence has historically had a negative effect on conceptions of political power. This effect reverberates in the way in which we live at present. The standard view in political philosophy is that *justice* is the first virtue of political institutions. This view was at least implied by most political philosophers from the time of Plato until John Rawls. It was also the view of Hartshorne and Whitehead, both of whom were political liberals; I defend it as well.[16] But there is an opposing view that was initiated in book 2 of Plato's *Republic* by the character Thrasymachus as conflicting theories of justice were being debated in that dialogue. Thrasymachus hurled himself into the debate by urging that politics is not primarily about justice but about *power*. On this view, which finds expression in contemporary political philosophy and culture on both the political right and the political left, theories of justice are ruses for the acquisition of power.

For theists, the standard view is that *love* is the first virtue of theological ethics. Therefore, a major conceptual problem for political theologians and political philosophers who are theists is to determine the best fit between justice and love. The issue is complex in that there is an understandable tendency to think that in a pervasively pluralistic society, although we have a duty to be just to everyone, love is *supererogatory*. The requirements of citizenship include the idea that we have to treat everyone fairly, but it seems to be asking too much of citizens in a pervasively pluralistic society that they love everyone in society, in that we cannot expect to have a pervasively pluralistic society where everyone is saintly. But we can require that everyone obeys the rules regarding basic fairness.

One persuasive way to deal with this problem is to find the best fit between justice and love via Rawlsian impartiality. In Rawls's famous thought experiment, we are asked to deliberate about what the general principles would be that would govern a truly just society. The needed decision-making procedure occurs in what Rawls calls a hypothetical *original position*. In order to counteract bias, the deliberations need to occur behind a *veil of ignorance* whereby we are not permitted to know our own religious beliefs (or lack thereof), our race or ethnicity, our economic class background, our gender, etc. Others in the original position will keep us honest, as it were, if background knowledge of our own characteristics inadvertently seeps into

---

15. Christ, *She Who Changes*.

16. See Morris, *Process Philosophy and Political Ideology*; Dombrowski, *Rawls and Religion*; Dombrowski, *Rawlsian Explorations in Religion and Applied Philosophy*; Dombrowski, *Process Philosophy and Political Liberalism*.

our deliberations. For example, it would not make sense to restrict freedom of religion in the original position if one did not know whether, when one left the original position, one would be a traditionalist or liberal Catholic, a Jew, a fundamentalist or progressive Protestant, a Muslim, a religious skeptic.

Some might wonder why we do not build up a political philosophy on a communal basis of love, in contrast to the allegedly cold procedure found in original-position rationalism. A response to this criticism points to the difficulty that arises when love of several persons leads to conflict if these distinct persons desire goods that are at odds with each other. In this situation love is at sea and requires principles of justice so as to fairly adjudicate the disputes that occur in a condition of conflicting loves. In this regard it is important to notice that love is a second-order notion in that it is concerned with one's own actions in relation to the (sometimes conflicting) actions of others whom we want to advance. There is nothing to be gained by attributing love to parties in the Rawlsian original position, in that such attribution could be seen as "cooking the books" in favor of Rawls's famous two principles of justice.

These are indeed principles of *justice* (very much compatible with Hartshorne's and Whitehead's political beliefs) and not mere power plays or ruses for economic class interests.[17] The first principle of justice, which Rawls alleges would be agreed to by all rational agents deliberating about justice in a fair decision-making procedure, is that all basic goods should be distributed equally in a just society. These basic goods would be both material (like food and access to health care) and formal (like freedom of speech and freedom of religion). The second principle of justice suggests both that any unequal distribution of goods beyond the basic ones be open to all (such that one cannot prevent some people from getting a larger slice of the pie, as it were, due to their race, gender, or other traits) and that any unequal distribution has to be to the advantage of everyone in society, especially to the least advantaged. This latter principle—the difference principle—reminds one of the preferential option for the poor found in many versions of contemporary religious ethics.

It should be noted that these principles might be instantiated either in some version of a market economy (but certainly not in a laissez-faire version of capitalism), or in some version of socialism (but certainly not in the command economies of communist states), or, more likely, in some hybrid version of these two. The wide gaps in wealth that have existed historically would be seen as unjust in light of these principles of justice; in fact, a Rawlsian state would be more egalitarian than any existing state, including those in the Scandinavian countries.

17. See Morris, *Process Philosophy and Political Ideology*.

It is remarkable that the combination of mutual disinterest in the Rawlsian original position and the well-known veil of ignorance (rather than the former alone) achieve the same purpose as love. This combination forces each person in the original position to take the good of others into account. The result is the same as would be achieved if the general contours of a just society were developed by a community of saints or a committee of loving agents. This is because in the original position the deliberating parties are forced to take the interests of others into account, which is, of course, the distinguishing feature of love. The fact that Rawls is able to achieve the goal of defensible principles of justice on such a parsimonious basis remains the greatest accomplishment in political philosophy of the past 150 years.[18]

However, the continued popularity of the Thrasymachean point of view implies for some political theologians and political philosophers who are theists that the key issue is the relationship between love and power. I will leave it to others to articulate what the proper relationship should be between these two concepts. At first glance is seems that there is something contradictory or at least oxymoronic in the effort to bring together agapic love and Thrasymachean power. Perhaps some theists have more imagination than I when trying to soften the edges of Thrasymachus's bellicosity. One concession that I am willing to make is that *some* efforts to defend certain actions as just *are* disguised power plays. But to hold that justice itself or that all theories of justice are mere veneers covering the hard core of power strikes me as hyperbolic, at best.

This foray into political theology and political philosophy is related to the topic of omnipotence in the following way. One can detect an authoritarian boomerang whereby Caesar's aforementioned power was transferred to the concept of God, a transference that facilitated defense of the concept of divine omnipotence, as Hartshorne and Whitehead have persuasively argued. Then after two thousand years this concept became entrenched such that it is now widely assumed that the greatest conceivable just *has to be* omnipotent. This assumption in turn has led to the legitimation of any number of human imitators of divine coercive power, from the divine right of kings to various political leaders with authoritarian tendencies, the latest of which is Donald Trump. The conceptual task, as I see things along with fellow political liberals like Hartshorne and Whitehead, is to break the circle by calling into question the idea that the logic of perfection requires omnipotence and the priority of coercive over persuasive power.

One final point is needed. Underlying the defenses of omnipotence offered by classical theists, it seems, is a deep-seated desire to *control* things.

---

18. See Dombrowski, "Community."

Such a desire is exhibited both by political rulers (obviously) and by classical theists (not so obviously) who wish to have everything make sense in the end on a cosmic scale. Two extremes can be detected. The aforementioned desire to control is expressive of the morbidly serious *homo gravis* conception of human nature, a conception devoid of any ironic distance regarding what used to be called the human predicament. Theists would do well to have this overly grim view balanced by the *homo ludens* stance wherein a lighthearted playfulness helps us to better understand and cope with the tragic dimension of our lives; such playfulness offers us an option other than giving in to the compulsion to imaginatively do away with tragic suffering by way of a supposed omnipotent deus ex machina.[19]

The point here is obviously not to eliminate seriousness, nor is it to give in to frivolity. Rather, the goal should be to hold seriousness in check with a ludic buoyancy. Shakespeare made a great deal of this in his tendency to introduce comic scenes at crisis points in his tragedies (e.g., the gravedigger scene when Hamlet learns of Ophelia's death or the drunken turnkey scene after Macbeth's regicide). His view was, and ours should be, I am arguing, *tragicomic*. In addition to the four problems with omnipotence mentioned above, there is also its positing of a Controller who can (or who at least will in the future) altogether eliminate tragedy. I am suggesting in this regard that it would be wise to manage our expectations.

Perhaps I am unfair in suggesting that the only motive behind belief in divine omnipotence is the desire to have hegemonic power triumph over evil. Fear is likely a motivating factor behind believing in divine omnipotence, in that especially when facing our own deaths or the deaths of those for whom we care, it is understandably easy to be overwhelmed by the indeterminacy of the future. Once again, however, I am encouraging us to manage our expectations of divine omniscience, which is often misunderstood for similar reasons that divine omnipotence is accepted and leads to problems. Just as a perfect being would exhibit ideal power, so also a perfect being would exhibit ideal knowledge.

But this does not mean that the greatest mind would know the outcome of future contingencies in any detail. The reason for this lies in the reality of temporal asymmetry. The best knower would comprehend past actualities as already actualized, present realities in their presentness (to the extent that this is possible in that there is a time lag between what is epistemically present and the reality perceived, as in a present sighting of a star that burned out light years ago), and future possibilities or probabilities

---

19. See Dombrowski, *Contemporary Athletics & Ancient Greek Ideals*; Huizinga, *Homo Ludens*.

as possibilities or probabilities. To claim to know a future possibility or probability as already actualized is not an example of omniscience, but rather of nescience. There simply are no future actualities to be known. If there were, they would not be future. As I noted before, divine power and divine knowledge do not consist in making impossibilities come true.

Nonetheless, God's power and knowledge are ideal, in contrast to our own relatively feeble abilities to receive influence from others and to exert positive influence on others, in contrast to our own fallible talents at knowing what has happened in the past and at realizing what is happening now, and in contrast to our extremely flawed ability to plot possibilities or probabilities regarding the future.

Bibliography

Anselm, Saint. *Basic Writings.* Translated by S. N. Deane. 2nd ed. LaSalle, IL: Open Court, 1962.

Arnison, Nancy Diane. "A Tragic Vision for Christianity: Aeschylus and Whitehead." PhD diss., University of Chicago, 2012.

Christ, Carol P. *She Who Changes: Re-Imagining the Divine in the World.* New York: Palgrave Macmillan, 2003.

Dombrowski, Daniel A. "Community." In *John Rawls and the Common Good*, edited by Roberto Luppi, 14–36. Routledge Studies in Contemporary Philosophy. New York: Routledge, 2021.

———. *Contemporary Athletics & Ancient Greek Ideals.* Chicago: University of Chicago Press, 2009.

———. *A Platonic Philosophy of Religion: A Process Perspective.* Albany: SUNY Press, 2005.

———. *Process Philosophy and Political Liberalism: Rawls, Whitehead, Hartshorne.* Edinburgh: Edinburgh University Press, 2019.

———. *Rawls and Religion: The Case for Political Liberalism.* New York: SUNY Press, 2001.

———. *Rawlsian Explorations in Religion and Applied Philosophy.* University Park: Pennsylvania State University Press, 2011.

———. *Rethinking the Ontological Argument: A Neoclassical Theistic Response.* Cambridge: Cambridge University Press, 2006.

Dostoevsky, Fyodor. *The Brothers Karamazov.* Translated by Constance Garnett. The Modern Library of the World's Best Books. New York: Modern Library, 1929.

Feuerbach, Ludwig. *The Essence of Christianity.* Translated by George Eliot. Harper Torchbooks. The Library of Religion and Culture. New York: Harper, 1957.

Gamwell, Franklin I. *Existence and the Good: Metaphysical Necessity in Morals and Politics.* Albany: SUNY Press, 2011.

Griffin, David Ray. *God, Power, and Evil: A Process Theodicy.* Philadelphia: Westminster, 1976.

Hartshorne, Charles. "Ethics and the New Theology." *International Journal of Ethics* 45.1 (1934) 90–101.

———. *Man's Vision of God, and the Logic of Theism*. New York: Harper, 1941.
———. *Omnipotence and Other Theological Mistakes*. Albany: SUNY Press, 1984.
Huizinga, Johan. *Homo Ludens: A Study of the Play Element in Culture*. Translated by R. F. C. Hull. Humanitas, Beacon Reprints in Humanities. Boston: Beacon, 1955.
Hume, David. *Dialogues Concerning Natural Religion*. Edited, with an introduction by Richard H. Popkin. Indianapolis: Hackett, 1980.
Levenson, Jon, D. *Creation and the Persistence of Evil: The Jewish Drama of Divine Omnipotence*. San Francisco: Harper & Row, 1988.
Loomer, Bernard. "The Size of the Everlasting God." *Process Studies Supplements* 18 (2013) 1–45.
———. "Two Conceptions of Power." *Process Studies* 6.1 (1976) 5–32.
May, Gerhard. *Creatio Ex Nihilo: The Doctrine of 'Creation out of Nothing' in Early Christian Thought*. Translated by A. S. Worrall. Edinburgh: T. & T. Clark, 1994.
Morris, Randall C. *Process Philosophy and Political Ideology*. Albany: SUNY Press, 1991.
Plato. *Collected Dialogues of Plato, Including the Letters*. Edited by Edith Hamilton and Huntington Cairns. Bollingen Series 71. Princeton: Princeton University Press, 1989.
———. *Platonis Opera*. Edited by John Burnet. 5 vols. Oxford Classical Texts / Scriptorum classicorum bibliotheca oxonie. Oxford: Clarendon, 1901–1976.
Rawls, John. *A Theory of Justice*. Cambridge: Harvard University Press, 1971.
Whitehead, Alfred North. *Adventures of Ideas*. 1st Free Press paperback ed. New York: Free Press, 1967.
———. *Science and the Modern World*. 1st Free Press paperback ed. New York: Free Press, 1967.

2

Reconsidering Omnipotence

Anna Case-Winters

People who affirm divine omnipotence have held a range of views as to what this entails. Most discussions on the topic focus on *how much* power God has. I like to shift the discourse to talk about *what kind* of power God has. What is the meaning carried by the *potens* (Latin) in "omnipotence"? This chapter will bring forward critiques, philosophical and theological, of an understanding of divine power that is prominent, popular, and problematic. Elements of that view include the assumption that God has all power, can do absolutely anything, and can control what happens in the world process. When we attach the qualifier *omni-* to such a meaning for power we run into problems of coherence, religious viability, and moral adequacy. The chapter will conclude with an affirmation of divine omnipotence rehabilitated with an alternative understanding of power.

Problems of Coherence

One common assumption regarding omnipotence is that for God to have "perfect" power, to be "all-powerful," God must have *all the power there is*—a monopoly on power. How does a monopoly on power make sense in a world where there are other beings, each with their own actuality and power? If, as Plato insists, actuality entails power, then as long as there are other actualities that are not God, there are other powers at work.

Another assumption seems to be that, being omnipotent, God can do absolutely anything. It would seem that any question that begins "Can God . . . ?" has to end with an answer in the affirmative. This assumption, however, leads to absurdities sometimes referred to as the "omnipotence paradox." Can God create a square circle? Can God create a rock so heavy that God cannot lift it? In the Middle Ages there was an extended debate about whether God can change the past. That question arises when this assumption is co-posited with divine eternity. It seems the past, present, and future would be equally open to divine intervention. Even the past becomes contingent.

A third assumption is that "omnipotence" must mean that God can control everything that happens in the world process, including what free beings will decide and do. This assumption embraces a fundamental contradiction. How are beings genuinely free if their actions and decisions are controlled by God? This seems to muddle the very meaning of freedom.

If the aim of affirming omnipotence is to ascribe "the greatest conceivable" power to God, this prominent and popular understanding does not finally succeed. It can be argued that the power it ascribes to God is not the "greatest" power, nor is it coherently "conceivable." When process-relational theology challenges the common understanding of divine power, critics charge that anything else is a "limitation" of divine power. Behind this charge there seem to be some implicit assumptions: (1) that power is quantifiable in such a way that granting power and genuine freedom to creatures reduces God's power, (2) that actuality as such does not necessarily entail power, (3) that power is limited to active modes only and does not allow for passive modes (the capacity to be affected, for example). These underlying assumptions are themselves contestable.

Charles Hartshorne makes a good point that the reconsideration proposed is not a "limitation" on divine power because, "to speak of *limiting* a concept seems to imply that the concept *without* its limitation makes sense."[1] Given the problems of coherence already enumerated above, we may question whether the common understanding "makes sense." God's power, Hartshorne affirms, "is absolutely maximal, the greatest possible, but even the greatest possible power is still one power among others . . . not the only power."[2] This kind of power is social-relational power, the kind of power befitting beings-in-relation.

Even *before* process-relational theology, there were thinkers who challenged the understanding of omnipotence problematized here. Thomas Aquinas, for example, saw the absurdities it created. While he maintained that God can do "anything," he went on to say that a logical contradiction (e.g., a square circle) is not properly a "thing." It is not that God cannot do it, but that it cannot be done.[3]

---

1. Hartshorne, *Divine Relativity*, 138.
2. Hartshorne, *Divine Relativity*, 138.
3. Aquinas, *Summa Theologica*, I, Q. 25, A. 3.

Anselm went even further. He pointed out that there are things *human beings* can do that God *cannot* do. God cannot lie or be corrupted, for example. To do so would contradict the divine nature. He insists, however, that this is not a *lack* of power on God's part. Rather it reveals a weakness on the part of human beings that we *can* lie and be corrupted. Here Anselm makes a decisive move, claiming that God's power is *more perfect* because of the things God *cannot* do. Anselm's proposal that God is "that, than which, nothing greater can be conceived" aids this discussion as well. Following this line of thought invites a questing to discern what is the "greatest power"?[4]

Problems of Religious Viability

Is the power ascribed in the popular understanding of omnipotence really the *greatest* power? Is it one that is worthy of being attributed to God? In addition to the problems of coherence outlined above, problems of religious viability arise. We might ask what image of God the popular understanding of omnipotence yields. Popular images of God often go awry in terms of their religious viability. One image in a cartoon from *The Far Side* may illustrate the point. In it, God is imaged as an old white man with a long white beard sitting at his computer. The world process is playing across the screen, and we see a man with a piano suspended above his head. Among the keys on the computer keyboard is a very large key marked "SMITE," and the divine finger is hovering there.[5] Theologians do well to maintain a critical distance from some of the popular images of God in our culture. As Jesuit priest, Father Greg Boyle quipped, "Obviously I do not believe it is preposterous to believe in God. I am just hopeful that people stop believing in a preposterous God."[6]

Talk of God has largely been eclipsed in our day. It may be that popular images and ideas are too preposterous to be taken seriously. Where public talk of God does occur, it is discredited by its invocation in connection with national and political interests, narrow-mindedness, various fanaticisms, and quests for personal blessing. Those who would continue to affirm and inquire into this "much-abused, yet holy name of God,"[7] need to give a more compelling account of what we mean by "God." A good beginning might be in articulating a concept of God that is more worthy of its subject. Toward that end, it helps to revisit a central affirmation of our faith tradition: God

---

4. Anselm, *Proslogion*, ch. 7.
5. Larson, "God at His Computer."
6. Boyle, *Whole Language*, 21.
7. Buber, *Eclipse of God*, 6.

is love. Congruence with this affirmation should be the criterion for any construction of God's attributes—including the attribute of power.

In his book *Omnipotence and Other Theological Mistakes*, Hartshorne suggests a way forward toward a more religiously viable accounting of divine attributes. He first critiques embedded assumptions in the classical delineation of divine attributes. He argues that these begin from philosophical concepts that set problematic parameters upon what perfection must require. Perfection from this particular starting point means being eternal, immutable (unchanging), and impassible (unable to suffer). The world is temporal, changing, and subject to suffering. It seems that in the interest of upholding divine transcendence, classical theism derived divine attributes in binary opposition to the attributes of the natural world. On the one hand, the way of negation reflects a fitting apophatic reserve. God is not the world and not anything in the world. On the other hand, it seems that what began as apophatic reserve has hardened into a binary opposition.

In effect, God has been structured out of the natural world. The world has been desacralized. God's presence and activity in the world become difficult to coherently conceive. How can an eternal God act in a temporal world? How can an unchanging God respond to what happens in an ever-changing world? What does it mean to pray to a God who cannot respond? If God does not suffer when God's beloved suffers, how do we make sense of the affirmation that "God is love"? The classical derivation of divine attributes seems to let go of the vision of God as a Being-in-relation. Process-relational theology, however, brings divine relationality back to the center.

In fairness, the classical tradition makes frequent reference to God's loving relation to creation, and it assumes freedom is real. From close reading, it is clear that the tradition does not intend to paint a picture of divine power as coercive force and absolute determination of all things. The problem is that loving relation to creation and genuine freedom do not easily map onto the classical delineation of divine attributes under a metaphysic of static perfection. Contradictions arise here, and theologians end up engaged in double-talk. It may be better to reconsider the metaphysical presuppositions at work.

Charles Hartshorne, one of the foremost interpreters of Whitehead, pointed out that classical theism was also working from assumptions about what "perfection" requires. Conclusions reached philosophically included that it is more "perfect" not to be subject to time or change or suffering. Hartshorne suggests an altogether alternative approach. Divine attributes should rather be derived in terms of their religious viability. What is most worshipful? What is most worthy of emulation? With Hartshorne's constructive innovation, we ask a different set of questions.

A different set of questions yields a different set of attributes. Attributes that attend creative-responsive love are the ones that come to the fore. They transcend the binaries classical theism envisioned. For example, God does not have to be thought of as either/or (changing or unchanging). God can be both/and—each in the way necessitated by creative-responsive love. The attributes would be derived with a view to their religious viability with "God is love" as an operative criterion. God may be both *unchanging* in faithfulness and *changing* in the sense of responding (faithfully) to us and our changing world. Following through with Whitehead's "dipolar theism,"[8] which Hartshorne later interpreted in terms of "dual transcendence,"[9] we might speak of God's transcendent-immanence, or an immanent-transcendence.

Problems of Moral Adequacy

In addition to problems of coherence and religious viability, there are also problems of moral adequacy that arise with the popular understanding of omnipotence. One problem is the way in which that understanding exacerbates the theodicy problem. If God has all the power, can do absolutely anything, and can control what happens in the world process, why is there so much suffering and evil in our world? It seems that such a God would be able to prevent suffering and overcome evil. Yet, God does not. The very goodness of God comes into question.

The tradition's recourse to a "free-will defense" as a response to the theodicy problem is blocked by assumption noted above that omnipotence means God is all controlling. To have a free-will defense there would need be a defensible account of free will. When it comes to free-will, problems of religious viability intersect with problems of moral adequacy. How are human beings free? How can we be responsible, accountable, moral agents? For there to be moral and ethical significance to our actions, God's power must be power of a kind that allows for genuine freedom.

Another problem of moral adequacy arises when we ask the question: What does this way of thinking about God image promote in the realm of human affairs? Hartshorne points out that the notion of God as holding all the power is an idealization of the tyrant-subject model. This is a negative image in the realm of human affairs, why project it onto God? According to Hartshorne, this analogy is "perhaps the most shockingly bad of all theological analogies, or at least the one open to the most abuses."[10] He under-

---

8. Whitehead, *Process and Reality*, 345.
9. Hartshorne, "Dipolar Conception of Deity."
10. Hartshorne, *Omnipotence and Other Theological Mistakes*, 11.

scores his point with Whitehead's famous comment, "the deeper idolatry, the fashioning of God in the image of the Egyptian, Persian and Roman imperial rulers was retained. The church gave unto God the attributes that belonged exclusively to Caesar."[11]

The tyrant-subject model is a vision of God that is not particularly worshipful, nor is it worthy of emulation. Furthermore, the regular association of the divine with this kind of power has the unwanted side effect of elevating and blessing the use of this kind of power in the realm of human affairs. With the examples of autocratic, megalomaniacal political leaders in recent history, we may want to beware of theologies that seem to lend a sanction to this kind of power.

An important dynamic of "two-way traffic" between our theological constructions and our social-political world is at work here. When, for example, an image from our political world like "king" is used as an image for God, kingship gains ascendency by association. It is not a far leap from there to "divine right of kings." The dynamic of two-way traffic was put succinctly in Mary Daly's famous observation, "If God is male, then male is God."[12] These associations caution attentiveness to our theological constructions and their social-political consequences.

A Constructive Proposal

Surely the attribute of power is central to the Christian tradition's concept of God. We affirm that God is all-powerful—omnipotent. Our intent is to attribute to God the highest perfection of power. The question is not *how much* power to attribute to God, but rather w*hat kind* of power.

Here we return to the central conviction that "God is love." Whatever God's power may be, it is the power of love and nothing less than that. The power of love is decidedly different from, and arguably greater than, the power to dominate and control. It is a more perfect power. Process-relational thinkers have offered an alternative vision of power that is generative in its nature, persuasive (rather than coercive) in its exercise, and shared—embracing mutuality and solidarity. These may be further elaborated.

God's power is generative in its nature. Traditional approaches have sometimes treated power as if it were a substance or a commodity that is quantifiable. Further they assume scarcity, as if power were a pie being divided. There is only so much to go around. More power for you means less power for me. Yet what if power is not like that? What if it really is more

11. Whitehead, *Process and* Reality, 342.
12. Daly, *Beyond God the Father*, 19.

like love? Love is generative in nature. It does not diminish in the giving, but grows. What if power is like that too? Giving power to others does not necessarily mean losing one's own power. In fact, it may generate new synergies that expand the range of what is possible for all involved.

Here we might also underscore God's world-generating and life-giving power displayed in the vast cosmos. We see divine creativity, *concursus*, and a calling in all that is. Divine generative power is, always and everywhere, loving things into being, letting things be (accompanying and upholding creatures in their integrity and freedom), and continually calling and luring toward the good in all things.

God's power is persuasive, not coercive, in its exercise. In the realm of human affairs most of us appreciate persuasion more than coercion. In delineating divine perfection is it not reasonable to attribute to God the kind of power that we deem most admirable and most worthy emulation? Furthermore, if *God is love*, it is not in love's nature to coerce or seek to control the beloved. Love would respect the freedom of the beloved and seek to preserve it.

If God's power is empowering and persuasive, not overpowering and coercive, then we have a more religiously viable response to the theodicy problem. Evil remains a problem, a mystery, and an absurdity, but it does not have to be thought of as something that is done or willed or controlled by God. The world has its own authentic existence where creaturely freedom and self-determination are genuine. There is always risk that free beings will not always choose wisely or well.

God's power is shared power—embracing mutuality and solidarity. In a social-relational world, sharing power commends itself as a model more admirable and more worthy of emulation than monopolizing power. It is a better fit with the criterion of love. It is the model we hope for in our social-political relations.

Process-relational approaches affirm that God's relation to the world is internal to God (affecting God) rather than external to God (not affecting God) as classical theism assumed. The external relation to God and divine impassibility solidified the view that God cannot suffer in relation to what happens in world process. Theology in the twentieth century saw a seismic shift in thinking on this question. In addition to process theologians, there were number of contemporary theologians who accepted divine suffering. The view was compellingly presented in Jürgen Moltmann's book, *The*

Crucified God.[13] Joseph Sittler put the matter starkly, "Unless you have a crucified God, you don't have a big enough God."[14]

The mutuality and solidarity affirmed here assumes that God is with us in our situation of suffering. Whitehead put it well. In relation to our suffering, God is "the great companion—the fellow sufferer who understands."[15] When it comes to the suffering associated with transitoriness, our situation of "perpetual perishing," our every moment is received into the divine life, and God exercises a "tender care that nothing of value be lost."[16] We might characterize God's way of being with us in our suffering and perpetual perishing as a "saving solidarity."

When it comes to the suffering associated with evil, God is working persuasively and powerfully to redeem and transform. It can really be said that in all things God is working for good. Whatever happens in world process—and that is largely up to us—God experiences it. God grieves when we make a wreckage of our possibilities, but judges the wreckage with compassion. Working to redeem and transform, God offers back to the world new and better possibilities, ever luring toward the good. God's way of being with us in the face of evil might be thought of as a "redemptive resistance."

Conclusion

The philosophical and theological critiques brought to the prominent and popular view of omnipotence give good reason to reconsider what we mean by omnipotence. What kind of power do we mean to be attributing to God? The intent of the chapter has been to set forth an alternative understanding of God's power that is more coherent, religiously viable, and morally adequate. God's power is envisioned here as generative, persuasive, shared power that is manifest in saving solidarity and redemptive resistance. This is the kind of power we might expect to see if God is love.

I commend this new vision to us as a "still more perfect way." At the same time, I acknowledge that we should in fitting humility before Holy Mystery, acknowledge the limitations of even our best insights on this topic. It is easier to affirm the power of God than to develop a satisfactory understanding of it. This is the endeavor of many and the achievement of none.

---

13. Moltmann, *Crucified God*.
14. Sittler, *Grace Notes*, 228.
15. Whitehead, *Process and Reality*, 357.
16. Whitehead, *Process and Reality*, 346.

PART ONE: RETHINKING DIVINE POWER

Personal Note

I write as a philosophically interested theologian and one who has a deep appreciation of process philosophy in particular. Process thought has offered a lifeline in an ongoing quest to find a more "adequate" concept of God—one more promising than prevalent classical and popular alternatives. Of course, God is and remains a Holy Mystery incomparably greater than all our best visions and concepts of God. Nevertheless, it is important to articulate concepts that at least gesture in good directions. Whitehead spoke of the "brief Galilean vision" that has "flickered uncertainly through the ages."[17] It is my belief that this vision is more credible, more religiously viable, and more morally adequate than what many popular and traditional presentations of it have offered. Process thought critiques and clears away some of the theological overlay that obscures the deeper vision available to us from the life and ministry of Jesus of Nazareth. As a theological conversation partner, process thought has been a welcome source of correction and new illumination—a breath of fresh air for me as a theologian. The dynamism in process approaches and the centrality of relationality have much to offer to the discussion at hand. Engagement with process philosophy in the work of theology is a bit of an "adventure of ideas."[18] I believe such adventures are warranted and even essential to progress in theology. As Victor Lowe has pointed out, "Theology, like metaphysics, is dead when it ceases to be a continuing business."[19]

Bibliography

Boyle, Gregory. *The Whole Language: The Power of Extravagant Tenderness*. First Avid Reader Press paperback ed. New York: Avid Reader, 2021.
Buber, Martin. *Eclipse of God: Studies in the Relation between Religion and Philosophy*. New York: Harper, 1952.
Daly, Mary. *Beyond God the Father: Toward a Philosophy of Women's Liberation*. Boston: Beacon, 1973.
Hartshorne, Charles. "The Dipolar Conception of Deity." *Review of Metaphysics* 21 (1967) 273–89.
———. *The Divine Relativity: A Social Conception of God*. The Terry Lectures. New Haven: Yale University Press, 1948.
———. *Omnipotence and Other Theological Mistakes*. Albany: SUNY Press, 1984.
Larson, Gary. "God at His Computer." *The Far Side*, September 17, 1991.

---

17. Whitehead, *Process and Reality*, 342.
18. Whitehead, *Adventures of Ideas*.
19. Lowe, *Understanding Whitehead*, 92.

Lowe, Victor. *Understanding Whitehead*. Baltimore: Johns Hopkins University Press, 1962.
Moltmann, Jürgen. *The Crucified God: The Cross of Christ as the Foundation and Criticism of Christian Theology*. Translated by R. A. Wilson and John Bowden. New York: Harper & Row, 1974.
Sittler, Joseph. *Grace Notes and Other Fragments*. Selected and edited by Robert Herhold and Linda Marie Delloff. Philadelphia: Fortress, 1981.
Whitehead, Alfred North. *Adventures of Ideas*. New York: Macmillan, 1933.
———. *Process and Reality*. Edited by David Ray Griffin and Donald W. Sherburne. Corrected ed. New York: Free Press, 1978.

3

Omnipotence Is Not Born of Scripture

Thomas Jay Oord

The words "omnipotent" and "omnipotence" are not in the Bible. But English translators render some Hebrew and Greek words as "almighty," and many readers consider almighty a synonym for omnipotent. Other biblical passages seem to support the meaning of omnipotence, in the sense that God can do absolutely anything or control creation.

These issues are obviously important to Christians who think of the Christian scriptures as authoritative in some way. In fact, many Christians—both trained theologians and everyday believers—appeal to the Bible to support their view that God is all-powerful. But Muslims, Jews, and other theists often assume Christian scripture affirms a God of unlimited power.

In this chapter, I address three biblical words and phrases pertaining to divine power: *shaddai*, *sabaoth*, and *pantokrator*.[1] I reveal that each has been wrongly translated "almighty." I also address biblical passages some believe point to the meaning of omnipotence. My conclusion: the Bible does not sanction the view God exerts all power, can do absolutely anything, or controls. The Bible does not endorse omnipotence.

El Shaddai

"Almighty" first appears in scripture as a translation of the Hebrew word *shaddai* (אֵל שַׁדַּי; *'el shaddai / šadday*). We find it in Genesis 17, when God appears to Abraham and says, "I am *el shaddai*." Many Bibles translate this

---

1. The Christian Bible has many forms, versions, and translations. I will focus primarily on the sixty-six books Protestants consider the canon, recognizing that the ancient manuscripts from which these books derive are pluriform and therefore somewhat fluid. In fact, there is no definitive canon. On this diversity, see Felushko, "Linguistic Dating of Biblical Texts."

phrase, "I am God Almighty." Upon self-introducing, God promises to make a covenant with Abraham and to "make you exceedingly numerous," provided he walks faithfully and is blameless (17:1–2).

"God Almighty" is a mistranslation of *el shaddai*.[2]

The oldest and most likely meaning of *shaddai* is "breasts."[3] The Genesis passage and others in which God is linked with *shaddai* are better translated, "I am God of breasts" or "I am the breasted God." This makes good sense given the Priestly writer's reference to Abraham's descendants; they will be born, and their mother's breast will nourish them, metaphorically speaking, so they "greatly increase."[4]

Nearly every occurrence of *shaddai* in Genesis is associated with nourishing breasts and fertility.[5] We read, for instance, that *el shaddai* "will bless you with blessings of heaven above, blessings of the deep that lies beneath, blessings of the breasts and of the womb" (Gen 49:25). Isaac blesses Jacob saying, *el shaddai* "bless you and make you fruitful and numerous, that you may become a company of peoples" (28:3). And *el shaddai* "appeared to me at Luz in the land of Canaan, and he blessed me, and said to me, 'I am going to make you fruitful and increase your numbers'" (Gen 48:3–4).[6] When self-introducing to Jacob, God says, "I am *el shaddai*, be fruitful and multiply" (Gen 35:11). These examples lead David Biale to conclude that "the conception of the Hebrew God as a fertility god in general and as represented by breasts in specific has support in both biblical and extrabiblical sources."[7]

Based on its appearance early in scripture and in poetic contexts, biblical scholars consider *shaddai* one of the oldest names for deity.[8] In Exodus,

---

2. See Albright, "Names Shaddai and Abram"; Abel, "Nature of the Patriarchal God"; Bailey, "Israelite 'El Šadday."; Cross, "Yahweh and the God of the Patriarchs"; Cross, *Canaanite Myth and Hebrew Epic*, 52–60; Dever, *Did God Have a Wife?*; Ouellette, "More on 'El Šadday."

3. Most scholarly assessments of the meaning of *shaddai* note a diversity of meanings but suggest "breast" and "mountain" as the most likely. In addition to the sources cited in the footnotes below, see Biblical Studies Press, *NET Bible*.

4. See Zoller, "Il nome divino Šadday." For why it makes sense to think of God in feminine ways, see Mollenkott, *Divine Feminine*.

5. Koch, "Saddaj," 323.

6. See Janzen's extensive analysis of *el shaddai* in relation to a personal God in *At the Scent of Water*.

7. Biale, "God with Breasts," 252. The connection between God and breasts apparently derives from Amorite and Canaanite cultures. See also Cross, *Canaanite Myth and Hebrew Epic*, 52–60.

8. Nahum M. Sarna argues that "the overwhelming appearance [of *el Shaddai*] in poetic contexts points a priori to a venerable tradition, for Hebrew poetry tends to preserve or consciously to employ early forms of speech." Sarna, *Exodus*, 269. See Alter, *Hebrew Bible*; and Steins, "Šadday."

the Lord says, "I appeared to Abraham, Isaac, and Jacob as *el shaddai*" (6:3), a passage that predates the Mosaic age.[9] The earliest biblical passages portray God as one with breasts who nourishes.

Shaddai can also refer to God as "the one of the mountain," because the Hebrew word *shadu* (mountain) is similar to *shaddai*.[10] And mountains are often compared to breasts.[11] The Grand Teton mountains of Wyoming, for instance, received their names from French explorers who thought they looked like breasts: *tétons*.[12]

Comparing breasts to mountains is more than visual. The connotation is that mountains provide refuge, in the way mothers protect children.[13] The psalmist draws upon this protective theme: "You who live in the shelter of the Most High, who abide in the shadow of [*shaddai*], will say to the Lord, 'My refuge and my fortress; my God, in whom I trust'" (91:1–2). If Abraham's descendants are to be numerous, they will also need protection, and mountains represent refuge.

El shaddai is not only mistranslated "God Almighty," but nourishment and protection do not require omnipotence. God can do these activities without possessing all power, being able to do absolutely anything, or controlling others. After all, human mothers nourish and protect without being omnipotent. *El shaddai* as "God Almighty" misleads readers into thinking God is omnipotent rather than a nourishing breast or protective mountain.

In later books of the Bible, *shaddai* takes another meaning: it is destructive or warring.[14] For instance, "Wail, for the day of the Lord is near;

---

9. On this, see Sarna, *Exodus*, 269. *Shaddai* is used in the blessings promised Jacob as well (Gen 28:1–4; 35:9) and figures into the Joseph story as blessing (Gen 49: 22–26).

10. Cross prioritizes "breast" over "mountain" as a translation of *shaddai*. "The primitive meaning [is] . . . breast . . . However, the secondary meaning 'mountain' developed for transparent reasons, and early in Semitic, in view of its occurrence in both East and West Semitic." See Cross, *Canaanite Myth and Hebrew Epic*, 55.

11. Perhaps the first to see the connection between mountains and *el shaddai* is Deilitzsch, *Assyrisches Handwarterbuch*. For an argument for how "breast" became "mountain," see Albright, "Names Shaddai and Abram." Manfred Weippert argues for a minority view, which says the word refers to the plains rather than mountains, "Erwagungen zur Etymologie." See also Friedman, *Commentary on the Torah*, 60; Hamilton, "Almighty," 907.

12. I thank Tripp Fuller for pointing out this connection.

13. See Nöldeke's review of Delitzsch, *Prolegomena eines neuen hebr.—aram. Wörterbuches zum AT* (1886); and Lang, *Monotheism and the Prophetic Minority*, 50–51. William Albright doubts this connection, however, citing "fatal phonetic obstacles," and saying, "words for 'breast' often develop the meaning 'elevation, mound, hill, mountain;' mountains shaped somewhat like breasts are frequently called 'breast, two breasts' in Arabic." Albright, "Names Shaddai and Abram," 183, 184.

14. *Shaddai* appears in the earlier written books but reappears in books written

it will come like destruction from [*shaddai*]! (Isa 13:6; cf. Joel 1:15). The psalmist sometimes depicts God as a powerful warrior: *shaddai* "scattered the kings there" (68:14).[15] In these instances, *shaddai* can appear "as a remote, mysterious and even destructive," says Biale.[16]

The destruction motif is especially evident in Job, because *shaddai* is sometimes portrayed as causing or allowing pain, death, and destruction.[17] Job says, for instance, "the arrows of [*shaddai*] are in me" (6:4).[18] But *shaddai* can also mean nourishment and protection in this narrative, for instance when Job recalls good days when [*shaddai*] "was still with me" (29:5).

Job's dialogue partners—Eliphaz, Bildad, and Zophar—associate *shaddai* with destruction and pain.[19] Eliphaz says, for instance, "How happy is the one whom God reproves, therefore do not despise the discipline of [*shaddai*]" (5:17). Given that Job's friends misunderstand God, however, we have reason to question the connecting of *shaddai* with God causing destruction. According to the story, after all, these friends do not know who God is or how God acts.

Job's fourth friend, Elihu, rightly speaks for God. But he does *not* associate *shaddai* with destruction. He uses the word as the Genesis writers might: "The spirit of God has made me, and the breath of [*shaddai*] gives me life" (33:4). The Jewish Publication Society Tanakh translates Elihu's final reference to *shaddai* this way: Shaddai "is great in power and justice / And abundant in righteousness; He does not torment" (37:23 JPS).

In the book of Job, the Hebrew words for God, Lord, etc., never precede *shaddai*. We find *shaddai*, but we do not find *el shaddai*. And words for God—*el, yahweh, elohim,* and *Adonai*—do not immediately precede *shaddai*

---

during or after the exile. The later occurrences point to God as destructive and warlike. See Steins, "Šadday," 445. Sarna argues that "The great antiquity of the name and its obsolescence in Israel in the Mosaic period explain why there are no consistent traditions as to its meaning and why the ancient versions have no uniform rendering." Sarna, *Exodus*, 269.

15. Gregory A. Boyd addresses Hebrew Bible portrayals of God as a violent warrior in *Crucifixion of the Warrior God*.

16. Biale, "God with Breasts," 245–46.

17. William Dever notes that the association of *el shaddai* with mountains was "probably conceived in pre-Israelite religion as the old Amorite-Canaanite storm god, associated with the awesome (and procreative) powers of nature." See Dever, *Did God Have a Wife?*, 259.

18. *Shaddai* also occurs in Ruth 1:20–21 as a reference to God turning against Ruth, and scholars consider this reference as entirely poetic. On this, see Alter, *Hebrew Bible*, 3:628.

19. Steins, "Šadday," 438.

in any passage that describes pain and destruction.[20] Some speculate that Old Testament writers use *shaddai* to refer to vital forces, sheer powers, or natural factors that destroy rather than to God.[21] The point is important, so I will repeat it: biblical references to *shaddai* as destructive are not directly connected with God.

These divergent meanings of *shaddai* lead us to wonder why later biblical writers use the word differently than earlier ones. Why connect God's nourishing breasts and protection with violence and destruction?

One answer says some biblical writers wanted to portray deity as both good and evil. Despite not directly connecting God with destructive *shaddai*, they wanted to say God both nourishes *and* destroys. This approach fits Isaiah's quote from the Lord: ""I form light and create darkness; I make weal and create woe; I the Lord do all these things" (45:7). It also fits stories that describe God as violent, wanting or causing destruction in various ways.

Another possibility is that biblical writers intentionally exchanged the God of feminine breasts for a God of masculine aggression. "The transformation of *el shaddai* from a fertility god with feminine characteristics to a seemingly male god of war makes great theological and even psychological sense," argues Biale. "What better way to suppress one interpretation of a god than by substituting its opposite?"[22] This wish for God to sanction violence persists among readers today.

There is obvious tension if not outright contradiction between God as a nourisher/protector and God as a destroyer/killer. For millennia, readers of the Bible have wrestled with this tension in the text. Some try to hold the opposing visions together, incoherent though the result may be. A good God, this view says, sometimes nourishes and sometimes kills.

Others choose one image and reject the other. J. Gerald Janzen opts for God as loving nourisher, for instance, based upon its frequent recurrence in the Hebrew Bible. "In a paradigm in which God is giver of conception, birth, nurture, guidance and protection and the divine source and sanction for the kin virtues of *ḥesed* and *rahàmim*, God is first a God of compassion."[23]

---

20. Only in Genesis and Ezekiel is *Shaddai* immediately preceded by words for God. In all of these cases, *shaddai* is positive rather than destructive.

21. See Jacobsen, *Treasures of Darkness*, 163. Jacobsen reads the conflict in Job as a conflict between visions of God: either God is personal and concerned with individuals or God is a cosmic force. Robert Di Vito plays with a similar theory about the conflict between a parental God and an impersonal royal God in *Studies in Third Millennium Sumerian and Akkadian Personal Names*.

22. Biale, "God with Breasts," 256.

23. Janzen, *At the Scent of Water*, 36–37. For similar arguments, see the arguments in Fretheim, *What Kind of God?*; Seibert, *Disturbing Divine Behavior*; and Seibert, *Violence of Scripture*.

However one addresses this tension among *shaddai* meanings, my fundamental point transcends that decision: *shaddai* in scripture does not mean omnipotent and is mistranslated "almighty." Even when biblical writers portray God as destructive, *shaddai* does not mean all-powerful. Just as breasts do not require omnipotence to nourish, warriors do not require omnipotence to destroy. A God of *shaddai* does not have all power, cannot do absolutely anything, and does not control others.

We are wise, therefore, to separate two questions. The first asks whether God, in addition to nourishing and protecting, also destroys and kills. The other asks whether *shaddai* means "omnipotent." The second question has been my focus here, and the answer is straightforward:

El shaddai does not mean "God Almighty."

Sabaoth

The second Hebrew word sometimes translated "almighty" is *sabaoth* (צְבָאוֹת; *ṣĕbāʾôt*). This is also a mistranslation.[24]

Rather than "almighty," *sabaoth* means "forces," "armies," "hosts," "ranks," "congregation,"[25] or "council."[26] When *yahweh* or *elohim* precedes it, the phrase is better translated "lord of hosts," "leader of armies," or "head of a council."[27] When *sabaoth* is not preceded by a Hebrew word for God, biblical scholars *never* translate it "almighty."[28] Never. In such cases, *sabaoth* is simply translated "hosts" or something similar.

24. The term is translated "Almighty" in the NIV in many instances. As examples, see 1 Sam 1:3, 11; 4:4; 15:2; 17:45; 2 Sam 5:10; 6:2, 18; 7:8, 26, 27; 1 Kgs 18:15; 19:10, 14; 2 Kgs 3:14; 17:7, 24; 19:31; Pss 24:10; 46:7, 11; 48:8; 59:5; 69:6; 80:4, 7, 14, 19; 84:1, 3, 8, 12; 89:8.

25. For the various ways *sabaoth* does not imply a military, see Quine, "Host of Heaven and the Divine Army." For an example in which *sabaoth* refers to a council leader, see Psalm 82.

26. See Eichrodt, *Theology of the Old Testament*; Eissfeldt, "Jahwe Zebaoth"; Hartley, "Hosts,"; McClellan, "Dominus Deus Sabaoth"; Miller, *Divine Warrior in Early Israel*; and Ross, "Jahweh Sebaʾot in Samuel and Psalms."

27. *Sabaoth* can be preceded by many words for deity, including *Yahweh*, *Elohim*, and *Adonai*. The Septuagint occasionally uses "Lord of powers" (*kyrios (ho) theoʾs tōn dynaʾmeōn*) for what in Hebrew would be "Lord of hosts."

28. I'm grateful to Brian Felushko for research on this important anecdote. Felushko found that Yahweh Sabaoth (יהוה צבאות) occurs 237 times and is translated in the NRSV as "the Lord of hosts" or "O Lord of hosts." Yahweh Elohai Sabaoth (יהוה אלהי צבאות) occurs 35 times and is translated in the NRSV as "O Lord, God of hosts" or "the Lord, the God of hosts" or "Lord, God of hosts." Elohim Sabaoth (אלהים צבאות) occurs twice and is translated in the NRSV as "O God of hosts." Ha-adon Yahweh Sabaoth (האדון יהוה צבאות) occurs five times, only in Isaiah, and is translated in the NRSV as

Sabaoth is absent in the first five books of the Bible, but it becomes a common reference to the Lord's leadership during and after Israel's exile. The hosts led are sometimes warriors of Israel. Other times, they are cosmic councils—other deities, planets and suns, or angels (Deut 4:19, 17:3; 2 Kgs 22:19; Ps 103:20–21). Sometimes the Lord of *sabaoth* even battles Israel.

In the religions of Israel's neighbors, cosmic conflict occurred often. Warrior gods and their assemblies fought among themselves and in relation to creatures and creation. Biblical writers worked out their views in response to these nearby communities, sometimes integrating what they encountered, other times assimilating it, and sometimes rejecting the views. "In many respects the Israelite notion of a divine assembly was quite similar to that of the surrounding cultures, particularly Canaan and Mesopotamia," says Patrick Miller, "and assuredly adapted from them."[29] Biblical scholars today explore how ancient mythologies influenced Israel's theology.

Sabaoth never means "omnipotence" in the Bible. To lead hosts, a lord does not need to have all power, to be able to do absolutely anything, or to control. That Yahweh leads others, in fact, indicates God *doesn't* have all power. Those being led have power to cooperate or impede the Lord's plans. The fact that lords are not always followed—whether creaturely lords or the divine Lord—suggests they have neither all power nor the ability to control others.

In his summary of how *sabaoth* is used in the Bible, Patrick Miller puts the divine-creaturely interaction this way: "At the center of Israel's warfare was the unyielding conviction that victory was the result of a fusion of divine and human activity . . . it was yet possible for the people to see themselves as going to the aid of Yahweh in battle (Judg. 5:23). Yahweh fought for Israel even as Israel fought for Yahweh (Josh. 10:14; Judg.7:20–22; and so on)."[30]

Not only does the Lord of *sabaoth* lead others with power, this warrior battles foes—divine or creaturely—with power. God cannot have *all* power if engaged in combat with opposing forces. This Lord does not control those he fights. While Israel often says their Lord is stronger than rivals, the God of *sabaoth* leads some but not all.

In sum, *sabaoth* does not mean "almighty." The God whom biblical writers say leads hosts, armies, or councils acts alongside or against others with power. In fact, there is no Hebrew equivalent for the English words

---

"the Sovereign, the Lord of hosts." But when Sabaoth (צבאות) is not preceded by a word for deity, which occurs five times, it is translated in the NRSV as "companies," "troops," or "armies."

29. Miller, *Divine Warrior in Early Israel*, 59–66.
30. Miller, *Divine Warrior in Early Israel*, 156.

"God Almighty."[31] All of this leads Abraham Joshua Heschel to conclude, "the idea of divine omnipotence . . . is a non-Jewish idea."[32]

Neither Elohim sabaoth nor Yahweh sabaoth is omnipotent.

Pantokrator in the Septuagint

Biblical writers believe God acts in powerful ways. But *shaddai* and *sabaoth* do not mean "omnipotent" and are mistranslated "almighty."

What led to these mistranslations?

The answer comes from the Septuagint (LXX). This ancient collection is a Greek translation of Hebrew scriptures. The Septuagint's first five books—the Pentateuch—were likely translated in the third century BCE and the remaining books in the second century. This Greek version of the Old Testament was read during Jesus' lifetime and influenced the apostle Paul. In fact, New Testament writers quote the Septuagint more than Hebrew-language texts, and early church fathers used it more than Hebrew-language scriptures.

The authors of the Septuagint translate *shaddai* and *sabaoth* with the Greek word *pantokrator* (παντοκράτωρ). The prefix *panto-* means "all"; the root *krater* or *krateō* has various meanings, including "hold," "seize," and "attain." For instance, God holds (*krateō*) the stars in divine hands, according to John's Revelation in the New Testament (1:16). *Pantokrator* might best be translated "all-holding" or "all-sustaining."[33]

In her explanation of how *pantokrator* emerged, biblical scholar Judith Krawelitzki says, "there is strong evidence that the [verb of] *pantokrator* has been created and established by the translators of the Septuagint." And "it seems [translators] coined a new word," she continues, "to avoid conceptualizing Yhwh's power with an already known word utilized to express the power of other deities, especially Zeus's power in Greek philosophy."[34]

---

31. For an especially insightful article on this, see Krawelitzki, "God the Almighty?" "God is neither explicitly characterized nor named as 'almighty' at any place in the Hebrew or Greek Psalters" (442).

32. Heschel, "Teaching Jewish Theology in the Solomon Schecter Day School," 12.

33. Ian Robert Richardson notes that "when considering God's power as providentially sustaining the universe, *kratein* was followed by the accusative case because that was used to express 'holding' rather than 'reigning.'" See Richardson, "Meister Eckhart's Parisian Question" 17. The second-century bishop Theophilus, for instance, says God "is called *Pantokrator* because He Himself holds (*kratei*) and embraces (*emperiechei*) all things (*ta panta*). *Ad Autolycum* 1, 4.

34. Krawelitzki, "God the Almighty?" 442–43. Krawelitzki says that "according to the Thesaurus Linguae Graecae, less than 1% of the approximately 1400 references for

Septuagint translators, says Krawelitzki, did not want to portray Israel's God as omnipotent. "It cannot be accidental that even in the Septuagint Psalter God's power is not conceptualized by the notion of omnipotence," she says. "The reluctance to name God... 'the Almighty' seems to be rooted in the texts themselves, which prescind from any kind of theoretical reflection about the extent of God's power."[35]

An all-holding God is not all-controlling.

The decision to represent *shaddai* and *sabaoth* as *pantokrator*, says Georg Steins, "had considerable theological repercussions."[36] It not only affected the Septuagint, but it also affected the New Testament and later translations of both Hebrew and Greek scriptures.

And then, six centuries later (in the fourth century AD), Jerome translated *pantokrator* as the Latin word *omnipotens* when writing the Vulgate version of the Bible. His decision to say God is *omnipotens* depends upon the Septuagint *pantokrator* and not Hebrew-language scriptures.[37] Had Jerome followed the original texts, he probably would not have used *omnipotens*, and Christians thereafter would not call God "omnipotent."

Scholars often complain that Christian theology has been unduly influenced by Greek metaphysics and Roman views of sovereignty.[38] In this case, Greek thought likely influenced translators who chose *pantokrator*, and Roman ideas about kingly sovereignty influenced Jerome as he translated it as "omnipotent." The mistranslation, in turn, affected the writers of the creeds who called God "almighty" (*pantokrator/omnipotens*). The mistranslation even passed to Islam.[39] Jerome's mistaken translation from a mistaken Greek translation of Hebrew led the world's two largest religions to adopt a bogus view of divine power!

Mistaken translations of *shaddai* and *sabaoth* as *pantokrator* misrepresent God as omnipotent.

[verb form of] *pantokrator* can be found in pagan literature"(cf. Kruse, "*Pantokrator*," 829–30). Although the adjective (form of) *pantokrator* "all-powerful" is found only in 2 Macc 3:22, it can be found often in Greek literature (cf. Montevecchi, "Pantokrator," 402). On the use of *pantokrator* in Greek philosophy, see Hommel, "Pantokrator," 142–43; Feldmeier, "Nicht Übermacht noch Impotenz," 25, 30–31; Bachmann, *Göttliche Aumacht und theologische Vorsicht Zu Rezeption, Funktion und Konnotation*, 147–60.

35. Krawelitzki, "God the Almighty?," 443.

36. Steins, "Šadday," 447. On this matter, see Michaelis, "Κράτος (θεοκρατία), Κρατέω, Κραταιός, Κραταιόω, Κοσμοκράτωρ, Παντοκράτωρ," 914–15.

37. Weippert, "Šadday," 1621.

38. Among the many, see Pannenberg, "Appropriation of the Philosophical Concept of God." Harnack is often the cited as one of the first to make this charge. See his *History of Dogma*. See also Koester, *History, Culture, and Religion of the Hellenistic Age*.

39. Lidzbarski, *Ephemeris für semitische Epigraphik*, 1:258.

Pantokrator in the New Testament

"Almighty" appears ten times as a translation of *pantokrator* in English versions of the New Testament. Nine of those instances come in the book of Revelation, and one in Paul's Second Letter to the Church in Corinth. In this section, I look at the influence of previous mistranslations.

Let me restate that *pantokrator* appears just ten times in the New Testament. This scarcity is remarkable, given that many Christians think God is omnipotent, and major creeds describe God as "almighty." There are about 138,000 Greek words in the New Testament, depending on differences among early manuscripts. This means *pantokrator* occurs 0.00726 percent of the time. That qualifies as rare! To put it another way, New Testament writers rarely refer to God as *pantokrator*, a word often translated "almighty" in English, and mistranslated from the Hebrew, as I've pointed out here.

Outside Revelation, the only reference to *pantokrator* is in Paul's Second Letter to the Church in Corinth. Paul writes, "As God has said: 'I will live with them and walk among them, and I will be their God, and they will be my people. Therefore, come out from them and separate from them,' says the Lord, and touch nothing unclean; then I will welcome you, and I will be your father, and you shall be my sons and daughters, says the Lord Almighty (*pantokrator*)'" (2 Cor 6:16b–18).

In this passage, Paul is quoting Septuagint translations of 2 Samuel 7:8, 14.[40] These verses draw from the Hebrew *yahweh sabaoth*. We earlier saw that this phrase is rightly translated "Lord of hosts" or something similar, not "the Lord Almighty."[41] The only time the apostle Paul—who wrote more New Testament books than anyone—refers to *pantokrator* is when he cites the Septuagint.[42]

This leads to the nine instances *pantokrator* appears in Revelation. English Bibles often render the word "almighty," as in the phrase "the Lord almighty." In most instances, *pantokrator* is a phrase of worship, with little context to discern what it means (see 1:8; 4:8; 11:17; 15:3; 16:7; 19:6; 21:22).[43]

---

40. A minority of scholars believe Paul is quoting Jeremiah 31:35 here. *Yahweh sabaoth* is also used in Jeremiah. My point stands in either case.

41. The New International Version is unique among translations when it uses "almighty" to render two New Testament words. In Romans 9:29 (Paul is citing Isaiah 1:9) and James 5:4, the NIV translates "hosts" in the Greek as "almighty." These are additional mistranslations of *sabaoth*.

42. In his analysis of Paul's reference to *pantokrator*, Wilhelm Michaelis says "it has only a loose connection with the dogmatic concept of the divine omnipotence, which is usually linked with the omnicausality of God." Michaelis, παντοχράτωρ, 914–15.

43. Michaelis notes *pantokratosr* is a title found in early Jewish prayers and its liturgical use influenced the writer of Revelation. Michaelis, παντοχράτωρ, 914–15.

In these cases, *pantokrator* serves a liturgical function, but the precise connotation of the word is not identified.

John twice uses *pantokrator* to compare God to creaturely kings and emperors (16:14; 19:15). His point seems to be that God is or will be more powerful than earthly leaders. In these cases, notes Eugene Boring, "'almighty' is bound to the title 'Lord' (*kurios*), a title which properly belongs only to God but has been usurped by the emperors and used of Domitian and the other Caesars in the emperor cult."[44]

While Alexander the Great and other Hellenistic and Roman rulers *claim* to exert universal power, only God's influence is truly universal.[45] The point is *not* that God controls, can do absolutely anything, or has all power. The point is that only a universal leader—God—exercises universal influence.

We earlier saw that *pantokrator* is a compound word, with the prefix meaning "all." In the New Testament, the verb form of the word—which refers to active power—is translated "hold," "seize," "cling," "attain," or something similar. In other words, the verb form of *krat* does not mean controlling, doing absolutely anything, or having all power.[46]

Dunamis is the Greek word in the New Testament translated "power." It occurs ten times as often as *pantokrator* and means "ability," "strength," or "influence." Biblical writers use *dunamis* to refer to the power expressed by God, Jesus and others. The verb form of the word—*dunamai*—occurs about twenty times more than *pantokrator* in the New Testament. It also refers to the ability to do something.

Neither the verb nor noun forms of *dunamis* have a prefix meaning "all" in the New Testament. If terms like *pantodunamis* or *pandunamai* were present in the Bible, we would have scriptural words that straightforwardly mean "all-powerful," "almighty," or "omnipotent." Such words are not present in scripture.

No New Testament passages record Jesus calling God "almighty." Nor does he call God "omnipotent." Jesus doesn't use *pantokrator* or some version of *dunamis* to describe God as all-powerful. He says God is greater than himself (John 14:28), and he praises God in various ways. The word Jesus uses most often for God is "Father" or *abba*, a term of loving endearment not of overriding control.

---

44. Boring, "Theology of Revelation," 259.

45. See also "Almighty," in *The New Interpreter's Dictionary of the Bible*, 1:105.

46. For instance, see verb forms of *krateō* in Matt 9:25; 12:11; 18:28; 21:46; 22:6; 26:4; 26:48; 26:50; 26:55; 26:57; 28:9; Mark 1:31; 3:21; 5:41; 6:17; 7:3, 4, 8; 9:10, 27; 12:12; 14:1, 44, 46, 49; 14:5; Luke 8:54; Acts 2:24; 3:11; Col 2:19; 2 Thess 2:15; Heb 4:14; 6:18; Rev 2:1, 13, 14, 15, 25; 3:11; 7:1; 20:2.

In sum, while New Testament writers describe God as having immense power, they do not use words that mean "omnipotent," "almighty," or "all-powerful." They do not use words that mean God has all power, is able to do absolutely anything, or controls. And if we think Jesus knows God best, that he does not call God omnipotent should influence how we think about divine power.

Omnipotence isn't in the New Testament.

Is the *Meaning* of Omnipotence in Scripture?

No biblical words literally mean "omnipotent," "almighty," or "all-powerful." If portraying God as omnipotent were as important as many argue, one would expect writers of sacred writ to use words that straightforwardly mean omnipotent. They don't. However, a person might claim the *meaning* of these words is present in the Bible. Perhaps biblical authors believe God is omnipotent but don't use words that explicitly say so. We need to explore this possibility.

Exerts All Power?

The claim that God literally exerts all power is the least defensible with scripture. It's obviously false, given the biblical witness to creaturely actions of various kinds, especially actions God does not want. Sinful actions come to mind. In addition, *sabaoth* passages identify God working alongside or against others with power, as do numerous other Old Testament passages.

New Testament writers speak of creaturely *dunamis* alongside God's. Creatures engage, negotiate, disobey, and act variously using their powers. We are God's fellow-workers (*synergoi*), says Paul. The overwhelming biblical evidence says God is not the only one who exerts power. Creatures also exert power.

In theological circles, the idea God literally exerts all power is today typically linked to John Calvin. This view can be called "theological determinism" or "monergism." Whether Calvin is a full-blown theological determinist or not, other theologians are.[47] According to them, God determines all, because God is the only power.

In his essay, "God Causes All Things," the contemporary Calvinist theologian Paul Kjoss Helseth offers a word to capture theological

---

47. Anna Case-Winters explores Calvin's view of omnipotence in *God's Power*.

determinism: omnicausality.⁴⁸ As the omnicause, God causes all things, because God exerts all power. Consequently, even sin, which is contrary to God's will, is caused by God. "In a wonderful and ineffable way," says John Calvin, "nothing happens contrary to [God's] will, even that which is contrary to his will!"⁴⁹

Some who claim God exerts all power also say creatures exert power. In philosophical circles, this confusing view is called "compatibilism." It says that in some inexplicable way, an omnipotent God exercises all power, but creatures exercise some.

Hermann Bavinck puts compatibilism this way, "There is no division of labor between God and his creature, but the same effect is totally the effect of the primary cause [God] as well as totally the effect of the proximate cause [creatures]."⁵⁰ Notice the words "totally" in this quote.⁵¹ Those who adopt compatibilism assume a truly sovereign God is the total cause of all events, but creatures are also causes.

Compatibilism makes no sense to me and to most people I know. It's nonsense, like saying "the sandwich was made totally by Jim, but Carol also made it." If something is done totally by one person, another person can't contribute. Compatibilism is the attempt to join one's prior assumption that God exerts all power to empirical observation that we and other creatures exert power. No wonder those who adopt this position call it inexplicable. It's better to say . . .

Compatibilism is a conceptual mistake.

I consider the popular phrase "God is in control" a form of "God exerts all power." To be in control, God must be the omnicause. But "When God is seen so totally in control," says Anna Case-Winters, "any credible concept of freedom and autonomy for human beings is relinquished and human actions lose their significance."⁵² I agree.

Many say, "God is in control," but also think creatures exercise agency. They endorse compatibilism, even if many don't know the word. But this makes no sense. God can't be in control if creatures have self-control; God can't cause all if creatures exercise self-causation; God can't will all if creatures have free will.

---

48. Helseth, "God Causes All Things," 52.
49. Calvin, *Secret Providence of God*, 81.
50. Bavinck, *Reformed Dogmatics*, 605.
51. Some versions of Thomas Aquinas's primary-secondary causal scheme amount to compatibilism. For an example of a Thomist who embraces compatibilism using the primary-secondary scheme, see Dodd, *Unlocking Divine Action*.
52. Case-Winters, *God's Power*, 9.

Believing God exerts all power fails to fit life as we know it. It does not align with our sense of making free choices nor with our assumption that others choose freely. It makes God the cause of sin and evil, thereby negating our moral responsibility and undermining God's perfect love. Believing God exerts all power opposes scripture, because biblical writers portray humans and other creatures as exercising power.

The Bible doesn't say God exerts all power, and we should not say, "God is in control."

Able to Do Absolutely Anything?

While I find no biblical support for thinking God causes all things, some scripture passages seem to say God can do absolutely anything. These texts are rare, but this is what they say:

"Ah Lord God! ... Nothing is too hard for you" (Jer 32:17).[53]

"I know [God] can do all things, and that no purpose of [his] can be thwarted" (Job 42:2).

"For mortals it is impossible, but for God all things are possible" (Matt 19:26; cf. Mark 14:36; Luke 1:37).

Although phrasings differ, these passages suggest God can do absolutely anything. There are philosophical problems with this claim. Because of such problems, most scholars do not say, "with God all things are possible," without making numerous qualifications.

The biblical argument *against* believing God can do absolutely anything draws from other passages. These scriptures say or imply God *cannot* do some activities. Some things *are* impossible for God; God's purposes *can* be thwarted; some things *are* too hard for God. Let me cite some:

"It is impossible for God to lie" (Heb 6:18, my translation; cf. Titus 1:2).

"If we are faithless, [God] remains faithful—for he cannot deny himself." (2 Tim 2:13).

"God cannot be tempted by evil and he himself tempts no one" (Jas 1:13b).

"The Lord is the everlasting God, the Creator of the ends of the earth. He does not faint or grow weary" (Isa 40:28).

---

53. Some translations of Genesis 18:14 have the Lord asking, "Is anything too difficult for the Lord?" This is a response to the announcement of Sarah's upcoming pregnancy. Other translations say, "Is anything too wonderful for the Lord?" Both are questions not declarations.

God cannot revoke the gifts and call (Rom 11:29).

"For I am the Lord, *I cannot change*" (Mal 3:6, my translation; cf. Jas 1:17).[54]

"I cannot break my covenant nor alter the thing that is gone out of my lips" (Ps 89:34, my translation; cf. Lev 26:44).

"Israel, I cannot let you go. I cannot give you up" (Hos 11:8a, my translation).

"The Lord was with Judah, and he took possession of the hill country, but could not drive out the inhabitants of the plain, because they had chariots of iron" (Judg 1:19).

"The power of the Lord came on [Elisha]. And he said, 'Thus says the Lord, "I will make this wadi full of pools." For thus says the Lord, "You shall seee neither wind nor rain, but the wadi shall be filled with water, so that you shall drink, you, your cattle, and your animals." This is only a trifle in the sight of the Lord, for he will also hand Moab over to you. You shall conquer every fortified city and every choice city; every good tree you shall fell, all springs of water you shall stop up, and every good piece of land you shall ruin with stones.' . . . And great wrath came upon Israel, so they withdrew from him and returned to their own land." (2 Kgs 3:16–19, 27).

Some biblical passages identify impossible activities given who God is. It's impossible for God to lie, for instance, because this would mean denying God's necessary characteristic of being truthful. Other biblical passages point to the limits logic places on God. The final stories point to inabilities given creaturely factors and actors. Each example undermines the claim God is omnipotent in the sense of being able to do absolutely anything.

Scholars of scripture are not surprised by the examples I've listed. And they could add more. Consequently, most interpret passages that say "nothing is impossible for God" or "God can do all things" as not actually true without numerous exceptions. These statements are made in the context of specific actions God does in relation to creation; they are not broad statements about God's unlimited abilities.[55] God's abilities are not infinite.

My point: according to the Bible, God cannot do some activities.

---

54. I argue that God's inability to change pertains to God's unchanging nature. Many biblical passages say or imply, however, that God's experience changes and that God repents. For my arguments, see Oord, *Open and Relational Theology*, ch. 2.

55. On this issue, Gijsbert van den Brink notes a difference between "abstract philosophical reasons" and "the living communication between God and man." See *Almighty God*, 64–65.

Controls Creatures and Creation?

The final question asks whether biblical writers portray God as omnipotent, understood as controlling creatures or creation. To control another person, creature, or situation, a controller must entirely determine the other or outcome. To use philosophical language, to control is to act as the sole and sufficient cause. In more common language, to control is to bring about a result singlehandedly. A controlling person produces outcomes without influence from other actors or factors.

Biblical examples of God controlling would include at least two elements. First, such examples would explicitly say God acts. Second, such examples would explicitly say *no* creaturely actors, factors, or forces exert power alongside or in addition to God. Biblical passages that explicitly describe divine omnipotence as control, therefore, portray God as causing an outcome singlehandedly and indicate that creaturely forces, factors, or actors did not exert causal influence.

Given these criteria, I know of no examples of omnipotent control in the *entire* Bible.

To put it more directly, I know of no scripture passages that say God controlled creatures or creation in the sense of being the only cause. Biblical writers do not describe God controlling when God created the world,[56] when God hardened Pharaoh's heart, or when God acted in other Old Testament stories;[57] neither was God controlling when Mary became pregnant or when God became incarnate in Jesus, or when Jesus performed miracles, or when raising Jesus from the dead;[58] and God will not be controlling in the eschaton.[59] No biblical passage explicitly says God alone caused or will cause an outcome such that no creaturely factors, actors, or forces play a role.

---

56. For those who affirm creatio ex nihilo, there was nothing for God to control when initially creating. Those who reject creation ex nihilo usually say God worked with creaturely elements God previously created. I explain this view in various books, but see Oord, *Pluriform Love*, ch. 8.

57. Biblical writers say God hardened Pharaoh's heart *and* Pharaoh hardened his own heart (Exod 7:13; 8:11, 15, 32; 9:34). I agree with Terence Fretheim that "an act of hardening does not make one totally or permanently impervious to outside influence; it does not turn the heart off and on like a faucet." And "divine hardening did not override Pharaoh's decision-making powers." Fretheim, *Exodus*, 99. Those who interpret "hardening" as "control" impose a view of omnipotence not required by the text.

58. On Mary's cooperation with the Spirit, Jesus' miracles, and God raising Jesus from the dead—all of which do not require control—see Oord, "Essential Kenosis Christology." Many come to these stories assuming God controls and wrongly read them as examples of omnipotence. The texts do not require this.

59. I address in various writings God's relentless love that does not control now or at the eschaton. See, for example, Oord, *Questions and Answers for God Can't*, ch. 7.

The Bible does not say God controls.

Readers of scripture often *assume* God controls, however. Many come to the Bible supposing God is omnipotent and then, through eisegesis, read controlling power into the text. Even when biblical texts explicitly mention creaturely factors, many readers overlook the causal roles creatures and creation play.

The most common instances in which readers assume God is the only cause occur when biblical passages mention only God as acting and do not mention creaturely factors. A biblical passage might say, "God did x." In this case, many readers jump to the conclusion God acted alone and controlled creatures or creation. Because the text does not mention creaturely causes, many *assume* God omnipotently brought about an outcome singlehandedly.

Compare "God did x" with how we talk about everyday events. We might say, for instance, "LeBron James won the basketball game." This can be true and yet also true that other actors and factors—his teammates, the coach who drew up the plays, opposing players, his own physical health, the fans, and the referees—played causal roles in the victory. Although we say, "LeBron won the game," it wasn't LeBron acting alone.

Or we might say, "Graysen rode her bike to the store." This may sound as though *only* Graysen brought about the result. The truth is that many forces, factors, and actors were necessary, including a functioning bicycle; cooperative humans, and perhaps dogs, who could have impeded her; the force of gravity; healthy legs capable of responding to Graysen's desires; decent weather; and much more. "Graysen rode her bike to the store" does not mean Graysen alone produced the outcome.

"But LeBron and Graysen aren't the omnipotent God of the universe," someone might respond. This is true. But notice that God's omnipotence is an assumption one brings to God. While we all have assumptions, the Bible doesn't explicitly support the assumption God is omnipotent in the sense of singlehandedly bringing about results.

Every situation or event in life involves multiple forces, factors, and actors. No one brings about outcomes singlehandedly. Unfortunately, many readers of scripture set aside what they know from experience and assume God acts as a solitary cause. But I know of no biblical passage that says God alone brought about an outcome *and* no creaturely actors or factors were involved.

Several biblical texts say, for instance, "God brought Israel out of Egypt." Readers might assume the texts mean God did this delivering acting alone. This assumption ignores the creaturely factors, actors, and forces that played essential roles in Israel's release from captivity, even though the biblical accounts explicitly identify such creaturely causes.

Take as another example the first verses of Genesis (1:1–2). The NIV interprets them this way: "In the beginning God created the heavens and the earth. Now the earth was formless and empty, darkness was over the surface of the deep, and the Spirit of God was hovering over the waters." The updated version of the NRSV renders the same passage this way: "When God began to create the heavens and the earth, the earth was complete chaos, and darkness covered the face of the deep, while a wind from God swept over the face of the waters."

Both versions say God created. But neither says God created *all alone*. The text does *not* say "An omnipotent God singlehandedly created everything, and no creaturely factors or actors contributed." In fact, the Genesis writers identify creaturely forces and factors present (e.g., earth, deep, waters, chaos).[60]

Terence Fretheim notes the significance of multiple actors and factors in the biblical texts. "The creation accounts demonstrate that God chooses not to act alone in bringing the creation into being," he says. "While God is certainly the initiator and primary actor in creation, God certainly involves both the human and the nonhuman in the continuing process of creation."[61] God's creating is not solitary: "God works creatively with already existing realities to bring about newness."[62] Fretheim offers this hermeneutical principle: "God and creation must be considered together, because again and again the texts keep them together."[63]

Does Mighty Deeds?

I've mentioned God's creating the world and delivering Israel alongside creaturely actors, factors, and forces. Biblical scholars identify other events they call the "mighty deeds" of God. Many readers assume those mighty acts could only occur if an omnipotent God singlehandedly accomplished them. Mighty deeds require control, this argument says.

---

60. This list of biblical scholars who reject creation from nothing is long. See, for instance, Fretheim, *God and World in the Old Testament*, 5; Knierim, *Task of Old Testament Theology*, 210; Levenson, *Creation and the Persistence of Evil*; Paul, "Creation and Cosmogony in the Bible;" Smith, *Priestly Vision of Genesis 1*, 50; Waltke, *Creation and Chaos*; Walton, *Lost World of Genesis One*, 42; Westermann, *Genesis 1–11*, 110; Young, "Creatio Ex Nihilo."

61. Fretheim, *God and the World in the Old Testament*, 48.

62. Fretheim, *God and the World in the Old Testament*, 5.

63. Fretheim, *God and the World in the Old Testament*, xvi.

Gijsbert van den Brink appeals to this logic: "God's omnipotence appears from His *actions*."⁶⁴ Assuming God has "unlimited power or ability to bring things about by acting in the world," van den Brink says the Bible supports omnipotence. "From their experience of God's mighty acts, people [in scripture] came to the conclusion that nothing could be impossible for this God."⁶⁵ In short, "the best reason to believe that God is omnipotent is because He has revealed Himself as such, and that the way in which His omnipotence should be interpreted is determined by this revelation."⁶⁶

I disagree. I affirm the mighty deeds of God in scripture, but they don't require omnipotence. I believe I can offer a theology of God's power that accounts for the mighty deeds but denies God is all-powerful. Although there is not space here, I offer instead five responses to the idea God must control creatures or creation—in the sense of singlehandedly bringing about results—to do mighty deeds.

First, biblical writers do not explicitly say God acted alone to bring about the mighty deeds in salvation history. The text doesn't plainly say God is omnipotent in the sense of controlling others. This is an assumption many bring to the Bible not a conclusion it requires.

Second, it is possible that God did these mighty deeds—including miracles—alongside and with the cooperation of creation rather than by omnipotent control. Perhaps God *requires* creaturely cooperation or the conducive conditions of creation. In other words, God can do mighty deeds *alongside* cooperating creatures and conducive conditions of creation, so the "mighty acts of God" don't require singlehandedly determining outcomes.

Judith Krawelitzki joins Fretheim and other biblical scholars who note that Old Testament writers repeatedly describe God working *with* creatures to bring about outcomes. "Yhwh is my strength," says Krawelitzki, "because he enables my rescue by letting me participate in his power." God's "mighty deeds are not demonstrations of [God's] power for his own sake," she continues. "Rather, they are salvific and rescuing deeds. God bestows his power in creation and history in order that his people can participate in his power by his deeds."⁶⁷

---

64. Van den Brink, *Almighty God*, 166. The emphasis on actions is the author's.
65. Van den Brink, *Almighty God*, 176, 177.
66. Van den Brink, *Almighty God*, 5.
67. See Krawelitzki, "God the Almighty?" 441–42. Walter Brueggeman argues similarly: "the theological substance of Hebrew Scripture is essentially a theological process of vexed, open-ended interaction and dialogue between the Holy One and all those other than the Holy One." Brueggeman, *Jews, Christians, and the Theology of the Hebrew Scriptures*, 100.

Third, although many scholars deny God controls humans, they assume God must have absolute control when it comes to less complex creatures and inanimate matter. Scripture does not require a hard distinction, however, between God's activity alongside complex humans and less complex creatures. In fact, this hard distinction is based on metaphysical assumptions about creation as "dead," "vacuous," or "mindless." By contrast, biblical writers often describe creation—animals, plants, elements—as alive, enchanted, or spirited. Perhaps God works alongside and with even the simplest of entities and basic elements.

Fourth, and especially important, biblical writers describe many times God does *not* perform mighty deeds. God sometimes fails to rescue Israel, for instance, or deliver people from suffering and death. While in exile, in captivity, or ruled by foreigners, the people called for divine help. God did not always rescue. Some wondered if God had abandoned them; others wondered if God was punishing. The writers of scripture often lament when God *fails* to liberate, and this failure is not rare.

A robust description of divine power must account for what a loving God does and doesn't do. It must explain the mighty acts of salvation history *and* the history of suffering and evil. It must explain why sometimes God can rescue and sometimes can't.

Finally, most Christians consider Jesus Christ the clearest revelation of God. In the witness of Jesus, we find a God who does not dominate (*astheneias*). God is made known to us in the one whose crucifixion, according to the apostle Paul, demonstrates divine weakness (1 Cor 1; 2 Cor 13:4). Jesus' servant-like life reveals God as self-giving (*kenosis*) rather than controlling (Phil 2). The life, death, and resurrection of Jesus display strength and weakness but not control.[68] That witness ought to influence our view of divine power.

In sum, the Bible fails to support omnipotence understood as control. And given widespread biblical references to God working alongside creatures and creation, we have grounds to speculate that God does mighty acts without coercing. Accounting for God's might and weakness—the mixed witness in scripture and mixed witness today—is required to account for God's power.

---

68. John D. Caputo explores this theme in *The Weakness of God*. We find it also in Martin Luther's theology of the cross. See McGrath, *Luther's Theology of the Cross*; and Fiddes, *Creative Suffering of God*.

Conclusion

The Bible does not support omnipotence.

The Hebrew words *shaddai* and *sabaoth* are mistranslated as *omnipotens* in Latin and as "almighty" in English. The words actually mean "breasts," "mountains," "hosts," "armies," or something similar. Further, Greek writers of the Septuagint (LXX) mistranslated these words as *pantokrator*, and this led to immense confusion and error. *Pantokrator* does not mean almighty or omnipotent, in the sense of God exerting all power, controlling others, or being able to do absolutely anything. It is better translated as "all-holding."

New Testament writers do not consider God omnipotent. They rarely use the word pantokrator and never employ dunamis, the Greek word for "power," in ways that mean God is all-powerful. The apostle Paul uses *pantokrator* only once, and that's when he's quoting the Septuagint. Jesus never says God is almighty. The New Testament does not portray God as omnipotent.

The meaning of omnipotence is not in scripture. If it means "exerts all power," the Bible repeatedly describes creatures exerting power, often in opposition to what God wants. If omnipotence means "able to do anything," numerous biblical passages and stories describe activities God cannot do. If omnipotence means "controlling creatures or creation," no biblical passage claims God controls. No passage says God brings about results singlehandedly such that no creaturely actors, factors, or forces are involved. As described in the Bible, God is strong and weak; God sometimes does mighty acts and other times God fails.

Omnipotence is *not* born of scripture.

Bibliography

Abel, E. L. "The Nature of the Patriarchal God "El Sadday."" *Numen* 20.1/3 (1973) 49–59.

Albright, William. "The Names Shaddai and Abram." *Journal of Biblical Literature* 54.4 (1935) 173–204.

"Almighty." In *The New Interpreter's Dictionary of the Bible*, A–C, Vol. 1. Nashville: Abingdon, 2006. Alter, Robert. *The Hebrew Bible: A Translation with Commentary*. 3 vols. New York:. Norton, 2019.

Bachmann, Michael. *Göttliche Allmacht und theologische Vorsicht Zu Rezeption, Funktion und Konnotation des biblisch-frühchristlichen Gottesepithetons pantokrator*. Stuttgarter Bibelstudien 188. Stuttgart: Katholisches Bibelwerk, 2002.

Bailey, Lloyd R. "Israelite 'El Šadday and Amorite Bêl Šadê." *Journal of Biblical Literature* 87 (1968) 434–38.

Bavinck, Herman. *Reformed Dogmatics*. Vol. 2. Edited by John Bolt. Translated by John Vriend. Grand Rapids: Eerdmans, 1989.

Biale, David. "The God with Breasts: El Shaddai in the Bible." *History of Religions* 21.3 (1982) 240–56.
Biblical Studies Press. *NET Bible: A New Approach to Translation, Thoroughly Documented with 60,932 Notes by the Translators and Editors.* Spokane, WA: Biblical Studies, 2005.
Boring, M. Eugene. "The Theology of Revelation: 'The Lord Our God the Almighty Reigns.'" *Interpretation* 40.3 (1986) 257–69.
Boyd, Gregory A. *Crucifixion of the Warrior God: Interpreting the Old Testament's Violent Portrait of God in Light of the Cross.* 2 vols. Minneapolis: Fortress, 2017.
Brink, Gijsbert van den. *Almighty God: A Study of the Doctrine of Divine Omnipotence.* Kampen: Kok Pharos, 1993.
Brueggemann, Walter. *Jews, Christians, and the Theology of the Hebrew Scriptures.* Edited by Alice Ogden Bellis and Joel S. Kaminsky. Society of Biblical Literature Symposium Series 8. Atlanta: Society of Biblical Literature, 2000.
Calvin, John. *The Secret Providence of God.* Edited by Paul Helm. Translated by Keith Goad. Wheaton, IL: Crossway, 2010.
Caputo, John D. *The Weakness of God: A Theology of the Event.* Indiana Series in the Philosophy of Religion. Siphrut 14. Bloomington: Indiana University Press, 2006.
Case-Winters, Anna. *God's Power: Traditional Understandings and Contemporary Challenges.* Louisville: Westminster John Knox, 1990.
Cross, Frank Moore. *Canaanite Myth and Hebrew Epic.* Cambridge: Harvard University, 1973.
———. "Yahweh and the God of the Patriarchs." *Harvard Theological Review* 55.4 (1962) 225–59.
Deilitzsch, Friedrich. *Assyrisches Handworterbuch.* ATLA Monograph Preservation Program. ATLA Historical Monographs Collection Series 2. Leipzig: Hinrichs, 1896.
Dever, William G. *Did God Have a Wife? Archaeology and Folk Religion in Ancient Israel.* Grand Rapids: Eerdmans, 2005.
Di Vito, Robert A. *Studies in Third Millennium Sumerian and Akkadian Personal Names: The Designation and Conception of the Personal God.* Studia Pohl. Series maior 16. Rome: Pontifical Biblical Istitute Press, 1993.
Dodd, Michael J. *Unlocking Divine Action: Contemporary Science & Thomas Aquinas.* Washington, DC: Catholic University of America Press, 2017.
Eichrodt, Walther. *Theology of the Old Testament.* Vol. 1. Translated by J. A. Baker. Old Testament Library. Philadelphia: Westminster, 1961.
Eissfeldt, Otto. "Jahwe Zebaoth." In *Kleine Schriften*, edited by Rudolf Sellheim and Fritz Maass, 3:103–23. Tubingen: Mohr Siebeck, 1966.
Feldmeier, Reinhard. "Nicht Übermacht noch Impotenz. Zum biblischen Ursprung des Allmachtsbekenntnisses." In *Der Allmächtige: Annäherungen an ein umstrittenes Gottesprädikat*, edited by W. H. Ritter et al., 13–42. Biblisch-theologische Schwerpunkte 13. Göttingen: Vandenhoeck & Ruprecht, 1997.
Felushko, Brian G. "Linguistic Dating of Biblical Texts: Proponents, Challengers and Judges 5." PhD diss., University of British Columbia, 2018.
Fiddes, Paul S. *The Creative Suffering of God.* Oxford: Clarendon, 1992.
Fretheim, Terence E. *Exodus:* Interpretation. Louisville: Westminster John Knox, 2004.
———. *God and World in the Old Testament: A Relational Theology of Creation.* Nashville: Abingdon, 2005.

———. *What Kind of God? Collected Essays of Terence E. Fretheim*. Edited by Michael J. Chan and Brent A. Strawn. Winona Lake, IN: Eisenbrauns, 2015.

Friedman, Richard Elliott. *Commentary on the Torah: With a New English Translation and the Hebrew Text*. New York: HarperOne, 2003.

Hamilton, Victor P. "Almighty." In *Theological Wordbook of the Old Testament*, edited by R. Laird Harris et al., 907. Chicago: Moody, 1999.

Harnack, Adolf. *History of Dogma*. Translated by Neil Buchanan. London: Williams & Norgate, 1897.

Hartley, John E. "Hosts." In *Theological Wordbook of the Old Testament*, edited by R. Laird Harris et al., 750–51. Chicago: Moody, 1999.

Helseth, Paul Kjoss. "God Causes All Things." In *Four Views on Divine Providence*, edited by Dennis W. Jowers, 25–52. Counterpoints: Bible and Theology. Grand Rapids: Zondervan, 2011.

Heschel, Abraham Joshua. "Teaching Jewish Theology in the Solomon Schechter Day School." *The Synagogue School* 28 (Fall 1969) 4–33.

Hommel, Hildebrecht. "Pantokrator." In *Sebasmata: Studien zur antiken Religionsgeschichte und zum frühen Christentum*, 1:131–77. 2 vols. Wissenschaftliche Untersuchungen zum Neuen Testament 31–32. Tübingen: Mohr Siebeck, 1983.

Jacobsen, Thorkild. *The Treasures of Darkness: A History of Mesopotamian Religion*. New Haven: Yale University Press, 1976.

Janzen, J. Gerald. *At the Scent of Water: The Ground of Hope in the Book of Job*. Grand Rapids: Eerdmans, 2009.

Knierim, Rolf P. *The Task of Old Testament Theology*. Grand Rapids: Eerdmans, 1995.

Koch, Klaus. "Saddaj: zum Verhältnis zwischen israelitischer Monolatrie und nordwestsemitischem Polytheismus." *Vetus Testamentum* 26 (1976) 299–332.

Koester, Helmut. *Introduction to the New Testament*. Vol. 1, *History, Culture, and Religion of the Hellenistic Age*. 2 vols. 2nd ed. Berlin: de Gruyter, 1995.

Krawelitzki, Judith. "God the Almighty? Observations in the Psalms." *Vetus Testamentum* 64.3 (2014) 434–44.

Kruse, G. "Pantokrateo." In *Pauly-Wissowa* 18.3 (1949) 829–30.

Lang, Bernhard. *Monotheism and the Prophetic Minority*. The Social World of Biblical Antiquity Series 1. Sheffield, UK: Almond 1983.

Lidzbarski, Mark. *Ephemeris für semitische epigraphik*. Vol. 1, *1900–1902*. Giessen: Ricker, 1902.

McClellan, W. H. "Dominus Deus Sabaoth." *Catholic Biblical Quarterly* 2.4 (1940) 300–307

McGrath, Alister. *Luther's Theology of the Cross: Martin Luther's Theological Breakthrough*. Oxford: Blackwell, 1990.

Michaelis, Wilhelm. "Κράτος (θεοκρατία), Κρατέω, Κραταιός, Κραταιόω, Κοσμοκράτωρ, Παντοκράτωρ." *Theological Dictionary of the New Testament*, edited by Gerhard Kittel, 3:905–15. 10 vols. Translated by Geoffrey W. Bromiley. Grand Rapids: Eerdmans, 1964.

Miller, Patrick D., Jr. *The Divine Warrior in Early Israel*. Harvard Semitic Monographs 5. Cambridge: Harvard University Press, 1973.

Mollenkott, Virginia Ramey. *The Divine Feminine: The Biblical Imagery of God as Female*. New York: Crossroad, 1988.

Montevecchi, Orsolina. "Pantokrator." In *Studi in onore di Aristide Calderini e Roberto Paribeni*, edited by Edoardo Arslan 2:401–32. 3 vols. Milan: Ceschina, 1957.

Nöldeke, T. Review of Delitzsch, *Prolegomena eines neuen hebr.—aram. Wörterbuches. zum AT* (1886). *Zeitschrift der deutschen morgenländischen Gesellschaft* 40 (1886) 735–36.

Oord, Thomas Jay. "Essential Kenosis Christology." In *Methodist Christology: From the Wesleys to the Twenty-First Century*. Edited by Jason Vicker and Jerome Van Kuiken. Nashville: Wesley's Foundery, 2020.

———. *Open and Relational Theology: An Introduction to Life-Changing Ideas*. Grasmere, ID: SacraSage, 2021.

———. *Pluriform Love: An Open and Relational Theology of Well-Being*. Grasmere, ID: SacraSage, 2022.

———. *Questions and Answers for God Can't*. Grasmere, ID: SacraSage, 2020.

Ouellette, Jean. "More on 'El Shadday and Bêl Shadê." *Journal of Biblical Literature* 88 (1969) 470–71.

Pannenberg, Wolfhart. "The Appropriation of the Philosophical Concept of God as a Dogmatic Problem of Early Christian Theology." In *Basic Questions in Theology*, 2:119–83. Translated by George H. Kehm. 2 vols. Philadelphia: Fortress, 1971.

Paul, Shalom M. "Creation and Cosmogony in the Bible." In *Encyclopedia Judaica*, edited by Cecil Roth, 5:1059–63. 17 vols. Jerusalem: Keter, 1972.

Quine, Cat. "The Host of Heaven and the Divine Army: A Reassessment." *Journal of Biblical Literature* 138 (2019) 741–55.

Richardson, Ian Robert. "Meister Eckhart's Parisian Question of 'Whether the omnipotence of God should be considered as *potentia ordinata* or *potentia absoluta*?" PhD diss., King's College London, 2002.

Ritter, W. H., et al., eds. *Der Allmächtige: Annäherung an ein umstrittenes Gottesprädikat*. Biblisch-theologische Schwerpunkte 13. Göttingen: Vandenhoeck & Ruprecht, 1997.

Ross, J. P. "Jahweh Seba'ot in Samuel and Psalms." *Vetus Testamentum* 17 (1967) 76–92.

Sarna, Nahum M. *Exodus: The Traditional Hebrew Text with the New JPS Translation*. JPS Torah Commentary. Philadelphia: Jewish Publication Society, 1991.

Seibert, Eric A. *Disturbing Divine Behavior: Troubling Old Testament Images of God*. Minneapolis: Fortress, 2009.

———. *The Violence of Scripture: Overcoming the Old Testament's Troubling Legacy*. Minneapolis: Fortress, 2012.

Smith, Mark S. *The Priestly Vision of Genesis 1*. Minneapolis: Fortress, 2010.

Steins, Georg. "adday." In *Theological Dictionary of the Old Testament*, edited by G. Johannes Botterweck and Helmer Ringgren, 14:418–46. Translated by John T. Willis. 16 vols. Grand Rapids: Eerdmans, 2004.

Waltke, Bruce K. *Creation and Chaos: An Exegetical and Theological Study of Biblical Cosmogony*. Portland, OR: Western Conservative Baptist Seminary, 1974.

Walton, John H. *The Lost World of Genesis One: Ancient Cosmology and the Origins Debate*. Downers Grove, IL: IVP Academic, 2009.

Weippert, Manfred. "Erwagungen zur Etymologie des Gottesnamens 'El Shaddaj.'" *Zeitschrift der Deutschen Morgenlandischen Gesellschaft* 111, n.s. 36 (1961) 42–62.

———. "Šadday." In *Theological Lexicon of the Old Testament*, edited by Ernst Jenni and Claus Westermann, 3:1621. Translated by Mark E. Biddle. 3 vols. Peabody, Ma: Hendrickson, 1997.

Westermann, Claus. *Genesis 1–11*. Translated by John J. Scullion. Continental Commentaries. Minneapolis: Augsburg, 1984.

Young, Frances M. "'Creatio Ex Nihilo': A Context for the Emergence of the Christian Doctrine of Creation." *Scottish Journal of Theology* 44 (1991) 139–51.

Zoller, Israele. "Il nome divino Šadday." *Rivista degli studi orientali* 13 (1931) 73–75.

4

Love, Trust, and Divine Vulnerability

WM. CURTIS HOLTZEN

For most of the Christian era God was understood as impassible power. Early on this served to distinguish the Christian God from the lustful and petty Greco-Roman gods. Over time impassibility made its way into the great church councils, became a staple of classical Christianity, and was declared orthodoxy. But, as Paul Helm said, "The doctrine of God's impassibility has fallen on hard times."[1] By the mid-1980s a passible, suffering God had, for many, become the "new orthodoxy."[2]

While it is quite common for both theologian and philosopher to affirm God's passibility, there seems to be no universal definition.[3] I like Roberto Sirvent's simple and succinct description of divine passibility as "emotional vulnerability."[4] This vulnerability means God is open to a variety of experiences, both pleasurable and painful. God is open to joy, happiness, compassion, sympathy, empathy, frustration, anger, and so on.

I believe the changes in thinking concerning God's relation to the creation are positive and I affirm divine passibility. In this chapter I discuss a kind of divine vulnerability that is rarely examined, specifically that God is vulnerable, exposed, or open to the unique kinds of experiences that come solely from trusting a loved one. Trust comes with the risk of betrayal, a pain exclusive to having one's gift of faith abused or violated. Trust, however, also leaves one open to feelings of thankfulness, appreciation, and gratitude that

---

1. Helm, "Divine Impassibility."
2. Goetz, "Suffering of God," 385.
3. Passibility can be affirmed in either a weaker or stronger form. The former suggests that God freely wills to be affected by this world while the latter argues that God's nature necessitates God's passibility. For more on these two approaches see Peckham, "Qualified Passibility"; and Oord, "Strong Passibility."
4. Sirvent, *Embracing Vulnerability*, 38.

the one trusted proved trustworthy. This chapter therefore will endeavor to demonstrate that if there is reason to believe that God has faith—that God seeks to trust us—then God is vulnerable to the pains of betrayal but also open to the delights of gratitude.

What Is Faithfulness?

To begin this discussion of divine faith let's do a thought experiment. Think to yourself what it means for someone to be faithful. That is, if someone was described as "a faithful x" (x meaning some kind of person in a relationship such as spouse, parent, friend, coworker, etc.) what sort of characteristics would that description necessitate? For example, think of what it would mean for a spouse to be faithful. I can image the first things that come to mind are that the spouse does not engage in any sexual activities with anyone other than their own husband or wife. Others might add that a faithful spouse is one who works hard to provide material goods for the family (shelter, food, clothes, entertainment). In this case we could think of the spouse as a "faithful provider." Perhaps we would think of a faithful spouse as one who does not suffer addictions to drugs, alcohol, gambling, or whatever might demand their energies.[5] Lastly, we might think of a faithful spouse as one who is not abusive and genuinely cares for their partner. In all these cases we could plausibly suggest that the spouse was in some manner or fashion faithful. Let's even add that the spouse is helpful around the house, spends time with their partner, even brings home gifts now and again. This is not a complete list, but I think most would have real trouble thinking of this person as unfaithful.

But what if we think about this a bit further? What if the spouse, who met the standards above (did not stray sexually, was a good provider, suffered no additions, and was not abusive physically or emotionally, etc.) refused to trust his wife? Perhaps he demands his wife account for every dollar spent, minute of screen time, or calorie eaten. Maybe even hires a private detective to follow her so he knows everywhere she has been. What if he reads her diary or regularly questions her friends? For most, this husband would be considered controlling, manipulative, maybe even emotionally abusive. "Unfaithful," however, would be an unusual descriptor. My question though is, shouldn't we include that a necessary aspect of being faithful is being full of faith? That is, to be thought of as faithful is more than being

---

5. A faithful spouse does not adulterate the marriage by bringing in what does not belong. We might suggest that a "workaholic" spouse is less than faithful. Some spouses must share their husband or wife with sports, hence the term "golf widow."

trust*worthy*; it should also include being trust-*willing*. I suspect this is what most people think it means to be a faithful Christian, to have faith *in* God. Well, if that is true, should we not at least consider that part of what it means for God to be faithful is that God is willing to have faith *in* us? A trustworthy God is a God who trusts.

Most of us are intuitively less willing to trust those who are unwilling to trust us. A parent must show they are willing to trust their child if they expect the child to trust them in return. Certainly, spouses and friends will be very stingy with their trust if the other in the relationship rarely offers their own gift of trust. It is hard to think of a person in a relationship—based on love, such as a marriage, a parent-child relationship, or even a friendship—in which one claims to love the other but has no want or need to trust the other. Thus, to be a faithful spouse, parent, friend, or even God requires that all parties in the relationship be more than worthy of trust. Faithfulness in its fullness includes the willingness and longing to trust. The next question however is key—is there reason to think God is a being of faith?[6]

The Bible and Divine Trust

The word "faith" can be difficult to pin down. First, in English, faith is always a noun, never a verb. We think about faith as a commodity in that people may have a lot of faith, a little faith, or none at all. We speak of people finding faith, losing faith, building faith, sharing faith, and even having a dead faith. But when it comes to *doing* faith, English fails. We would never say "I faith the Apostles' Creed" or "I faith Jesus with all my heart." "Faith" just does not work as a verb, so we use other words such as "believe," "trust," "affirm," "commit," or "devote." While the English word "faith" has its various, apparent, synonyms, the Greek has basically one word, *pistis*. But, unlike the English word "faith," the Greek word can be used as a noun or verb. When we read the Bible and see words like "faith," "belief," and "trust" we need to remember these are all variations of one word, *pistis*. The challenge for biblical scholars and exegetes is to assess what is the best English word to capture the fullest meaning because "believe," "trust," "commit," and "affirm" can have some rather important differences.

Avery Dulles claims that "In many Pauline texts *pistis* and its cognates can be translated as 'trust' no less accurately than as 'faith.'"[7] I agree, and in fact I think *pistis* is, by and large, best captured by the English word "trust."[8]

6. Holtzen, *God Who Trusts*.
7. Dulles, *Assurance of Things Hoped For*, 13.
8. Paul McReynolds in his translation always uses the word "trust" for *pistis* and its

Even though *pistis* might mean more than "trust," I can think of no occasions in which it would mean less than "trust." It should also be noted that the Greek word *paradidomi* is on occasion translated as "entrust." While it is most often translated as "betrayed" or "handed over," the clear implication is of giving something or someone over to the power of another. The giving over can have positive connotations in the cases when it is translated "entrust,"[9] negative connotations when it is translated as "betrayed,"[10] or no specific connotations when it merely means "to give" or "to pass down."[11]

Many readers may have missed it, but the Bible makes several references to God's faith, that is, trust—sometimes explicit and others implicit. For example, Numbers 12:7–8 says that God spoke "face to face" with Moses because "he is entrusted with all my house." Paul says that "the Jews were entrusted with the oracles of God" (Rom 3:2) and that he "had been entrusted with the gospel for the uncircumcised, just as Peter has been entrusted with the gospel for the circumcised" (Gal 2:7).[12] In these cases it is clear, God trusted these servants and so entrusted them with what was valuable to God.

Other passages may not use the word "trust" explicitly, but the context reveals that God is trusting another. God regretting putting some in positions of authority reveal they have failed to prove worthy of God's trust.[13] Regarding the opening pages of the Hebrew Bible, John Caputo found it interesting that in the creation epic we supposedly get a picture of God as one who has "little taste for the risk of creation, for the risk of parenting."[14] I disagree; the creation epic in Genesis 2 need not be read as the story of a couple freshly created, tested, and found sinful. It is a story of space given for development and growth, which itself demands faith. The early chapters of Genesis are better read as "a story of trust given, trust tested, trust betrayed, and trust continued."[15] The Job tale too probes us to consider God's faith in one servant. There is much to wrestle with in this story, but one thing should be remembered: God believed in Job, trusted Job would be faithful.

---

variations. McReynolds, *Word Study Greek-English New Testament*.

9. E.g., Matt 25:14; Rom 6:17; 1 Pet 2:23; Jude 1:3.

10. E.g., Mark 3:19 and John 18:2.

11. E.g., Acts 6:14 and 1 Cor 11:12.

12. See also 1 Thess 2:4; 1 Cor 9:17; 1 Tim 1:11; Titus 1:3 which all speak of Paul being entrusted with the gospel.

13. E.g., Saul in 1 Sam 15.

14. Caputo, *Weakness of God*, 68.

15. Holtzen, *God Who Trusts*, 157.

The parable of the talents is also easily read as a divine trust story.[16] Talents are distributed to various servants, a clear sign of trust. The parable shows that the servants were expected to use the talents, not merely hold them, an even greater sign of trust.[17] Additionally, the various calls for followers of God in Christ to be faithful, (that is, trustworthy) disciples, suggest that it is God's trust they are proving worthy of. One can only be trustworthy if they are worthy of someone's trust, and context suggests that calls for faithfulness are calls for being worthy of God's trust.[18] It must be remembered that when God is called faithful, we mean worthy of our trust; so likewise, calls for human faithfulness are calls to be trustworthy. Finally, the entire motif of covenant only works if each of the parties enters into the agreement intending to trust the covenant partner. If it is true that, as Clark Pinnock writes, we have "a God who loves being in covenant partnership," then we have a God who loves to trust.[19]

Certainly, more could be said about the Bible and divine trust, but I will end here with an idea that will transition us into the next section.[20] Paul writes in his well-known "love chapter" (1 Cor 13) that love has several characteristics and qualities, including that love "believes all things" or better, that "there is no limit to [love's] faith."[21] Add to this the radical claim from 1 John 4:8 that God is love. I am not claiming either author was aware of the other or his claims, but as Christians who are tying to make sense of the entire canon, we must at least consider each idea in the shadow of the other: If God is love and that these are the true qualities of love, then we should not hesitate to say that God, who is love, trusts without limit. Trust, it seems, is an essential character of love, and it is this idea I address next.

Love and Trust

It is not difficult to see trust functioning as a crucial element in relationships that are not defined as "loving relationships." In the realms of business,

---

16. It is understood that there are alternative readings of this text which might yield a different rendering.

17. For more of the parable of the talents as a story of divine trust see Holtzen, *God Who Trusts*, 150–53.

18. E.g., Luke 16:10–13; Rom 3:3; Gal 5:22; Eph 6:21; Col 1:7, 4:7; 1 Tim 1:12; Heb 3:2; Rev 2:10.

19. Pinnock, *Most Moved Mover*, 5.

20. For more on the New Testament and divine faith see Morgan, *Roman Faith and Christian Faith*; and Morgan, *New Testament and the Theology of Trust*.

21. 1 Cor 13:7. The NRSV is a bit clunky in its rendering of *panta pisteuei*, and the better translation is given by Anthony Thiselton, *First Epistle to the Corinthians*, 1056.

politics, education, and many of our day-to-day encounters trust in the other is needed for life to continue as normal. I do not have to love a congressperson, repair person, or student to trust them to do what they have been entrusted to do. But, as in the example of faithfulness above, love necessarily employs trust; at least in relationships of love such as between lovers, friends, and parents and children. These kinds of relationships rightly function only when there is mutual trust. Feelings of love and the desire to do good for the other may remain when trust is betrayed, but intimacy will be damaged or lost. A parent can love their drug-addicted child even if that child cannot be trusted to be alone with the drug or money. A spouse can still love their partner while they attend counseling to repair the trust lost due to adultery. Even a friend can love a friend after promises have been broken, but the confidence of the friendship will be fragile until the trust is restored. So, while trust does not actively seek out those to love, love will actively seek out ways to trust, build trust, or repair trust.

There is a reason why love is deemed a "passion"; it is because love is willing to suffer, or more accurately, willing to be vulnerable to suffering. William Placher writes, "Love means a willingness to take risks, to care for the other in a way that causes the other's fate to affect one's own, to give to the other at real cost to oneself, to chance rejection."[22] This means that for the one who loves (i.e., the lover), love is more, but not less, than compassionate acts of kindness toward another without regard to the lover's attitudes about the other. Authentic or relational love desires the other. It longs for the love given to be returned, but love is more, without being less, than a desire for the other's love. Love then is not reducible either to beneficial acts for the other's welfare or to desire for the other and their love. Either beneficial acts or desires may be fully loving, but neither alone is the fullness of love. While each is an aspect of love, deep intimate relational love includes but exceeds kind acts and desires for the other. It is not merely *because* God loves us that God risks, but it is the ways God loves that constitute a risk, namely by sharing power and entrusting us with the very things God loves. God's entrusting love is risky.

What is unique about God is that God's desire, that we be in a loving relationship with God, is at the same time God seeking after our well-being. God's love, by my lights, is desirous of a partnership (fellowship, communion) in which each partner cares for the other and for what the other values.[23] God is unsatisfied loving from afar. God wants intimacy, and the

---

22. Placher, *Narratives of a Vulnerable God*, 16.

23. I understand the call for Christians to have the "mind of Christ" (Phil 2:4–5) to mean, roughly, to value what God values.

provocative language of our living in God and God living in us is a testimony to God's desire that faith be mutual.[24]

Part of what it means to love is to be an encouragement to the beloved. This can happen in many ways, but a significant form of encouragement is to trust the other and express confidence in them. "Someone can be heartened by our trust, both moved and encouraged by it. Similarly, others can be disheartened by our failure to trust them."[25] Love seeks to build up the other, to give them confidence and self-trust. God's love tells us that we are truly lovable, and God's trust tells us we are ultimately worthy of trust.

God and the Nature of Trust

I have quickly labored to demonstrate that the biblical witness testifies that God is a being of faith understood chiefly as trust. Furthermore, that trust is a natural and logical expression of a God who is love. So now it is pertinent to describe trust and how certain depictions of God not only allow for divine trust but may demand it. Annette Baier has, what I think is, the best description of trust: "For to trust is to give discretionary powers to the trusted, to let the trusted decide how, on a given matter, one's welfare is best advanced, to delay the accounting for a while, to be willing to wait to see how the trusted has advanced one's welfare."[26] Trust, in its thickest sense, is giving another power over something you care about, and/or being pleased that they have such power, in the hope that some good will be attained or preserved which may otherwise not be possible. From these ideas let's unpack what are arguably necessary elements of trust.

Trust is a form or brand of reliance. We rely on many things, and when we are aware of such reliance our plans must include such things or persons. I am reliant on my car to get me to school, so the plans I make assume this reliance. However, reliance does not necessitate trust. I can be reliant on those I do not trust. Sometimes this means actively distrusting someone, such as when I am reliant upon them to deliver my packages when there is a history of the company delivering them to the wrong address.[27] Other instances of reliance involve neither trust nor distrust. For example, I am reliant upon drivers to yield to the stop sign, but I may not even be aware of their existence and so cannot be said to trust or distrust them. Trust, as

---

24. E.g., 1 John 4:13–20.
25. Darwal, "Trust as a Second-Personal Attitude," 48.
26. Baier, "Trust."
27. I will not mention the company, but they delivered several items to wrong addresses. However, I had no say in what delivery company the sender used.

a brand of reliance, means we knowingly rely on another for some desired good, be that a healthy marriage, robust friendship, or safe and timely trip to the airport.

Trust differs from reliance in that one who trusts generally has positive feelings about relying on the one being trusted. We cannot trust another while simultaneously thinking they are unreliable because of their lack of skill or faulty character.[28] When entrusting another with what we value, we think or assess that it is more likely the other will meet our expectations rather than not. We may still have worries or trepidations, but trust means we feel more positive than negative about acting in trust.

Trust necessarily involves risk, and therefore uncertainties or trepidations are natural. There is the risk that the entrusted person does not have the skill set you hope they have or the character you believe they have displayed. The more intimate the relationship of trust, the greater the risk of betrayal or exploitation. Now, this risk is mitigated by how well you know the skill set or character of the one trusted, but risk is never eliminated. Adriaan Peperzak states it well: trusting implies that "I leave it to you whether and how precisely you are and do what I trust you to be and do. Risk is therefore inherent in all trust."[29]

Trust is most often a voluntary action. We may not always have control over who we rely on, but we generally choose who we trust. Because trust has an inherent risk element, there is a cognitive element, a mindfulness, and so a decision is made whether to trust or not trust. Even if I am unable to believe that a person is trustworthy, I can still take a chance and entrust this person with something I value. Or I may offer what is called "therapeutic trust" in that I desire a person to develop a sense of trustworthiness, and so I willfully chose to trust them. It may also be that some situations require us to rely on another; there is no choice in the matter. However, if one has positive feelings about trusting a person, if one is pleased to rely on this person and not on a different person, we can rightly say one trusts the person one is relying on. On such occasions trust is a matter of attitude more than free action.

Volition, in part, is what makes trust a moral event. As I suggested in the thought experiment above, in circumstances when it is right to trust another, it is morally wrong to not act on that trust. Spouses are morally obligated to trust spouses, friends to trust friends, parents to trust children, etc.[30] To not trust another who is by all accounts trustworthy is to misjudge

---

28. I will give a unique exception to this rule in the form of "therapeutic trust."
29. Peperzak, *Trust*, 19.
30. Of course, trusting children depends on the right conditions of age and maturity.

their character, to deem them unworthy of faith, and treat them unjustly. On the other hand, to entrust another is to proclaim and promote their integrity and virtue. This does not mean trust ceases to be a risk; people will fail to live up to our, and their own, expectations. But to choose not to trust has its own risks. The one who fails to trust "risks committing serious wrongs herself: mistreating the people whose decency, or capacity for decency, she fails to recognize. And she risks missing opportunities both to prevent people from acting poorly and to enter into meaningful relationships with them."[31] Rational trust does not take careless or unreasonable risks, but it will seek opportunities to trust because of the benefits intimate relationship or character development. One can offer trust in the hope that the entrusted will rise to the occasion. Trust in this sense may become a self-fulfilling prophecy.[32]

Here is one final thought on the nature of trust: it cannot be demanded; it can only be invited. You can, through force or fear, cause another to do your bidding, to obey you, but trust is more volitional, more vulnerable, and far more precious than obedience. Obedience requires no positive feelings about the one being obeyed. The obedience may be due to coercion or promise of compensation. Those who obey us need not respect us, but the same is not true for trust. Trust opens avenues of mutuality; trust begets more trust and mutual faith. Obedience, while good and necessary in many circumstances, does not naturally promote intimacy or mutuality. God will never gain our trust through demands of obedience but only through invitations to trust and by demonstrations of trust.

Readers at this point certainly understand that a classical conception of the divine could not be a God of faith. Only if God faces an open future and seeks authentic relationship could God actively trust or be a God of faith. To make this point clear I see four conditions necessary for divine faith, which include a purpose for creation, human freedom, an open future, and divine concern. If God has faith in, or seeks to trust, humanity, as I have argued above, then it is necessary to conceive of God's nature in the following terms.

If God is a God of trust, this suggests that God trusts for a reason. As I noted above, some good or goods can be obtained only by trusting another. Some good states cannot be attained by God alone and so it is necessary that God partner with others. These good states would include intimate love, fellowship, and community. As Keith Ward writes, "the basic reason for creation is that it brings about forms of goodness and value which otherwise

---

31. Preston-Roedder, "Faith in Humanity," 11.
32. Preston-Roedder, "Faith in Humanity," 21–22.

would not exist... It makes it possible for God to be God of love, possessing the properties of creativity, appreciative knowledge, and sharing communion, which are the highest perfections of personal being."[33] There seem to be goods that God desires this world produce, and yet God is dependent upon others to bring these goods into reality.

Another good that God alone cannot produce by divine fiat is human maturity or virtue. Much to the chagrin of parents, children cannot be coerced into maturity. Friends, lovers, and citizens cannot be compelled to have virtuous characters. Character, maturity, trustworthiness cannot, as Linda Zagzebski argues, be "acquired at the flip of a switch," even if God does the flipping.[34] Trust and trustworthiness each require their own struggles to be authentic. Trust comes only by trusting another, taking the risk they will fulfill their obligations. And trustworthiness emerges only by demonstrating character amid opportunities to fail. But people can be helped into maturity and virtue by being presented with opportunities to develop virtues and maturity. One way to help another develop character is by offering therapeutic trust, a trust which is "undertaken with the intended aim of bringing about (or increasing) trustworthiness."[35] And if God desires humans to be trustworthy, God will find opportunities to entrust them. Perhaps it will be five talents, two talents, or only one, but God will seek opportunities to trust because trust is what produces trustworthiness, and trustworthiness is a good end.

Secondly, if God is a God who trusts, this says something significant about humanity, that we are significantly free. It means God has given us power of agency, the power to partner with God in the attainment of the good mentioned above. But it also means God's desire for these good ends is risky. Trust, understood as the giving of discretionary power, means God's power depends, at least in part, upon our power to work with God or to thwart God's plans.

Many Christians affirm some kind of compatibilism, that God is the remote cause of every event ever, but that humans are nonetheless "free" to choose. The mechanics of how God can predeterminately cause all events while human freedom remains intact are quite perplexing but also unnecessary for this chapter. What is important is that if any sort of theological determinism is true, then divine faith is unnecessary since God ultimately is the cause of every choice we make. God would not be trusting; God would be controlling. What if there is a way to suggest that God is not the cause, but is

---

33. Ward, *Rational Theology*, 85.
34. Zagzebski, *Virtues of the Mind*, 120.
35. Carter, "Therapeutic Trust," 38.

omnisciently aware of our future free choices? That is, what if God infallibly knows the future without being its cause? This leads to our third condition.

Once again, if it is the case that God is a being of faith, that God depends upon us to be faithful to what God has entrusted to us to do or be, then the future must be open to real novelty, otherwise God's trust would be impossible. God then, as a being of faith, faces an open future, unknowable because much of the future is ontological potential without being actual. We have the real potential to be trustworthy or not. If God were able to know our future free choices, as if they were actual, it would mean God had no need for trust since God would know every choice made, faithful and unfaithful. But, as open and process thinkers alike agree, God can only know our future free choices as potential, not actual. Faith and trust are risky because the trustor cannot know for certain if the trustee will be faithful. That is what makes trust unique, even for God. Trust, in its very essence, requires that we cannot know the outcome of trusting. This is what makes it an act of faith.

Is it enough that God works with others to accomplish good ends, that we are free to partner with God or not, and that God cannot know the outcome of our partnering in order for God to have faith? Not quite, it is also necessary that God authentically care whether these goods are accomplished. This world cannot just be an epistemological experiment for God, a mere question of divine curiosity. For God to genuinely trust, God must have some skin in the game. Trust can result in disappointment or frustration but trust means that God is vulnerable to what may be the hardest emotional blow one can face: betrayal.

Trust and Vulnerability

William Placher reminds us that "To read the biblical narratives is to encounter a God who is, first of all love (1 John 4:8). Love involves a willingness to put oneself at risk, and God is in fact vulnerable in love, vulnerable even to great suffering."[36] The kind of suffering that theologians most often speak of falls under some kind of identification. God understands and identifies with our sufferings; God experiences them with us. As Thomas Jay Oord writes, "God feels compassion *in response to* suffering, for instance, as creatures cause God to experience pity, sympathy, or empathy."[37] There is no doubt God is the "fellow-sufferer who understands,"[38] but does God

36. Placher, *Narratives of a Vulnerable God*, xiii.
37. Oord, "Strong Passibility," 130 (italics added).
38. Whitehead, *Process and Reality*, 351.

chance other vulnerabilities because of love? Placher states that because of God's love God risks rejection.[39] This is a different kind of suffering; it is not a suffering *with the other* but suffering *at the hands of another*. But even this kind of vulnerability does not quite capture the risks God is willing to take. Rejection of love spurned is difficult, but love betrayed is dreadful.[40]

There is no doubt that trust involves "the willingness to make oneself vulnerable to another person's actions, based on beliefs about that person's trustworthiness."[41] This is true whether you're trusting a stranger in the coffee shop to watch your laptop as you refill your coffee, or whether you decide to trust an enemy waving the white flag, who swears they will surrender without incident. Love brings its own vulnerabilities while trust has its own. In my assessment, the vulnerability risked when trust is given out of love cannot be matched. Solomon and Flores rightly state, "There is no greater trauma than trust betrayed except, perhaps, love betrayed, for love, typically, perhaps necessarily, involves the most profound trust and so gives rise to the most violent reactions when betrayed."[42] Love from a distance risks rejection; love in relationship risks betrayal.

We can be betrayed by people we do not necessarily love or are not necessarily in love with, but the pain of betrayal by a loved one is multiplied exponentially. A bit of self-reflection will surely support this claim. If this is true for us, it seems likely true for God. God loves, and if it is true that God trusts, then God experiences the grief only a spouse can know when their lover and partner is sexually unfaithful.[43] Because God gives trust out of love, God can know the kind of pain felt when a friend divulges information given in confidence. As a God whose trust is motivated by love, God knows the burden of trusting a child only to have that trust exploited when the one entrusted uses God's trust for their own gain. The reality is, the more intimate the relationship, the more vulnerable one is to betrayal. This does not mean betrayal is necessary or imminent. Nor does it mean all acts of betrayal bring about the same intensity of pain. Trust, nonetheless, exposes one to risks otherwise not possible.

---

39. Placher, *Narratives of a Vulnerable God*, 16.

40. I am not suggesting or assuming that God suffers in the exact same ways humans suffer, and therefore God likely does not experience betrayal in the exact way we feel betrayal. However, scripture, in depicting God's passions, is attempting to communicate something true about God even if in metaphoric language. But while there may be some asymmetry between human experiences and divine experiences of betrayal, I am suggesting God truly experiences betrayal.

41. Bohnet, "Trust in Experiments," 253.

42. Solomon and Flores, *Building Trust*, 103.

43. The Hebrew Bible uses this kind of imagery.

While God can become angry with, or frustrated by, the world at large, it is the church with which God has a unique relationship. As the "body of Christ" the church is the primary, though not the exclusive, means by which God facilitates the ministry of reconciliation. Therefore, when the church, as the representative of Christ, perverts the gospel, acts violently, or ignores injustice, the church betrays God's faith. Betrayal can also happen at the personal level when individuals who have died to themselves in order to live for Christ later chose to live for the self at the expense of others.

Trust makes one vulnerable to the pains of betrayal, but the risk seems to be worth it since there is no intimacy without trust. Love will, ultimately, be left unfulfilled without mutual trust between lovers. Along with the reward of intimacy, trust opens one to feelings of gratitude and appreciation. When we trust another with our thoughts, beliefs, desires, our very selves in the hope of gaining some good we otherwise could not obtain, it is only natural to feel a sense of appreciation and gratitude when the trust is met. I am thankful for those who help me achieve my goals, and I see is no reason to not think God is thankful for us when we are faithful coworkers.

It may seem odd for some to think of God being grateful or expressing appreciation, and to be fair the Bible does not seem to have an obvious example of this. But if God genuinely relies on us as covenant partners, working to bring greater good into existence by inviting us to cooperate with God, then it seems natural that God would be appreciative and thankful when we meet our obligations. Paul writes that the church has been entrusted with message of reconciliation, that we have been entrusted to be ambassadors for Christ, and that "God is making his appeal through us" (1 Cor 5:19–20). When the church meets its obligations, serves faithfully as ambassadors of reconciliation, God must surely feel a sense of gratitude. If not, then can we truly lift God up as the exemplar of love? Perhaps since God is love and love always rejoices in truth (1 Cor 13:6), God thankfully rejoices in our being true to the relationship as true friends.

Finally, it makes sense to say that as a being of pure love God is thankful when we prove trustworthy with what we have been entrusted. Parents are naturally thankful when their children show themselves trustworthy. Lovers are rightfully appreciative that they can open themselves to their partner without suspicion that their trust is being abused. Friends should express gratefulness to one another for one another. This sense of thankfulness is born out of love for the other, out of feeling safe in their company and care. Is it too much to think that God is thankful for and appreciates our faithfulness? That God has a sense of gratefulness that can only come by first taking the risk to entrust us with "talents"? I believe God can experience a particular kind of appreciation that only comes when faith given is met with faithfulness.

Conclusion

In this chapter I have sought to demonstrate that God is vulnerable to both the joys and woes that come only with having faith in another. God first trusts that each human will return to God the love God has given, not only in the forms of praise, worship, and appreciation, but also in our endeavors to be thoroughly human. God has entrusted the church with the unique mission of reconciliation, with announcing and embodying the gospel of Christ, with proclaiming peace and striving for justice. In our own experience, and so (as I have suggested) also in God's, such vulnerability born out of love can result in the pains and frustrations of betrayal or in the pleasures of a loved one's rising to the occasion. Trust then opens opportunities for God that would otherwise not be possible.

Those who fancy themselves "relational theists" need to consider that an essential part of a relationship, especially one born out of love, is mutual, reciprocal faith. Relationships, even loving ones, lack intimacy without shared faith. God may not always trust us, but God always longs to trust us and labors to help us prove ourselves trustworthy. William Lad Sessions, speaking of human faith, argues that the chief features of trust are acceptance, loyalty, and love.[44] Those who trust accept, are loyal to, and love the object of their trust. Certainly if God loves us, accepts us and is loyal to us, it is but a short leap to think this means God has faith in us.

Bibliography

Baier, Annette C. "Trust." Lecture presented as part of the Tanner Lectures on Human Values, Salt Lake City, 1991. https://tannerlectures.utah.edu/_resources/documents/a-to-z/b/baier92.pdf/.

Bohnet, Iris. "Trust in Experiments." In *Behavioural and Experimental Economics*, edited by Steven N. Durlauf and Lawrence E. Blume, 253–57. The New Palgrave Economics Collection. London: Palgrave Macmillan, 2010.

Caputo, John D. *The Weakness of God: A Theology of the Event*. Indiana Series in the Philosophy of Religion. Bloomington: Indiana University Press, 2006.

Carter, J. Adam. "Therapeutic Trust." *Philosophical Psychology* 37.1 (2024) 38–61. https://www.tandfonline.com/doi/full/10.1080/09515089.2022.2058925/.

Darwal, Stephen. "Trust as a Second-Personal Attitude (of the Heart)." In *The Philosophy of Trust*, edited by Paul Faulkner and Thomas Simpson, 35–50. Oxford: Oxford University Press, 2017.

Dulles, Avery. *The Assurance of Things Hoped For: A Theology of Christian Faith*. New York: Oxford University Press, 1994.

---

44. Sessions, *Concept of Faith*, 30–34. Sessions writes that these features are important for both the subject and object of faith, but his focus is on the former.

Goetz, Ronald. "The Suffering of God: The Rise of a New Orthodoxy." *Christian Century* 103.13 (1986) 385–89.

Helm, Paul. "Divine Impassibility: Why Is It Suffering?" Reposted on *Triablogue* (blog), as part of "What does God feel?" by Steve Hays on October 28, 2005. https://triablogue.blogspot.com/2005/10/what-does-god-feel.html/.

Holtzen, Wm. Curtis. *The God Who Trusts: A Relational Theology of Divine Faith, Hope, and Love*. Downers Grove, IL: IVP Academic, 2019.

Matz, Robert J., and A. Chadwick Thornhill, eds. *Divine Impassibility: Four Views of God's Emotions and Suffering*. Downers Grove, IL: IVP Academic, 2019.

McReynolds, Paul R. *Word Study Greek–English New Testament: A Literal Interlinear Word Study of the Greek New Testament United Bible Societies' Third Corrected Edition with New Revised Standard Version New Testament and Word Study Concordance*. Wheaton, IL: Tyndale House, 1999.

Morgan, Teresa. *The New Testament and the Theology of Trust*. Oxford: Oxford University Press, 2022.

———. *Roman Faith and Christian Faith: Pistis and Fides in the Early Roman Empire and Early Churches*. Oxford: Oxford University Press, 2015.

Oord, Thomas Jay. "Strong Possibility." In *Divine Impassibiity: Four Views of God's Emotions and Sufferings*, edited by Robert J. Matz and A. Chadwick Thornhill, 129–51. Downers Grove, IL: IVP Academic, 2019.

Peckham, John, C. "Qualified Possibility." In *Divine Impassibility: Four Views of God's Emotions and Sufferings*, edited by Robert J. Matz and A. Chadwick Thornhill, 87–113. Downers Grove, IL: IVP Academic, 2019.

Peperzak, Adriaan T. *Trust: Who or What Might Support Us?* New York: Fordham University Press, 2013.

Pinnock, Clark H. *Most Moved Mover: A Theology of God's Openness*. Didsbury Lectures 2000. Grand Rapids: Baker Book House, 2001.

Placher, William C. *Narratives of a Vulnerable God: Christ, Theology, and Scripture*. Louisville: Westminster John Knox, 1994.

Preston-Roedder, Ryan. "Faith in Humanity." 1–36 PhilPapers.org (website), https://philpapers.org/archive/PREFIH-2.pdf/.

Sessions, William Lad. *The Concept of Faith: A Philosophical Investigation*. Cornell Studies in the Philosophy of Religion. Ithaca: Cornell University Press, 1994.

Sirvent, Roberto. *Embracing Vulnerability: Human and Divine*. Eugene, OR: Pickwick Publications, 2014.

Solomon, Robert C., and Fernando Flores. *Building Trust: In Business, Politics, Relationships, and Life*. Oxford: Oxford University Press, 2001.

Thiselton, Anthony C. *The First Epistle to the Corinthians*. The New International Greek Testament Commentary. Grand Rapids: Eerdmans, 2000.

Ward, Keith. *Rational Theology and the Creativity of God*. New York: Pilgrim, 1982.

Whitehead, Alfred North. *Process and Reality*. Edited by David Ray Griffin and Donald W. Sherburne. Corrected ed. New York: Free Press, 1978.

Zagzebski, Linda Trinkaus. *Virtues of the Mind: An Inquiry into the Nature of Virtue and the Ethical Foundations of Knowledge*. Cambridge: Cambridge University Press, 1996.

Part Two

From the Spirit to the Polis

5

Integrative Spirituality

God-Images, Individuation, and Awakening

PATRICK J. MAHAFFEY

Process theology has continued to shape my God-image since my first encounter as a graduate student with the philosophy of Alfred North Whitehead. In my view, his conception of the primordial and consequent nature of God is among the most compelling ways of understanding divinity one can find in Western and Eastern traditions of philosophical or religious thought. Philosophy and theology are theoretical and offer us coherent ways of conceptualizing the divine and its relationship to the world. Spirituality, by contrast, consists of modes of practice by which we cultivate an experiential relationship to the divine. For the past thirty years, I have taught courses on Hindu traditions and C. G. Jung's writings on God-images at a graduate school devoted to the study of depth psychology. I also engage the psychological and spiritual practices associated with these visions of human life. This chapter proposes that Jungian depth psychology and contemplative yoga provide forms of psychospiritual practice that align with the philosophical worldview of process-relational theology. How can such practice enable persons to experience a God who may be found in everyone and everywhere?[1] A description of my version of integrative spirituality is included to exemplify an approach to experiencing a God of love who continues to incarnate in human experience through the process of individuation and spiritual awakening.

---

1. See Davis and Clayton, *How I Found God in Everyone and Everywhere*, for essays that align with my own endeavor to experience the panentheistic God conceptualized in process theology.

PART TWO: FROM THE SPIRIT TO THE POLIS
Two Modes of Human Development

Two forms of human development are important for integrative spirituality. One is the psychological process of integrating the contents of the psyche into greater wholeness; it is exemplified by Jungian psychology. The other form of development is spiritual awakening, and it is exemplified by contemplative traditions that seek to discover one's unconditioned nature, what Zen Buddhists refer to as your Original Face before your parents were born. Each of these modes of inner work is a profound endeavor. However, the pursuit of one without the other is often unbalanced or incomplete. For instance, a person can diligently engage in psychological work for decades without discovering a place of deep stillness within that confers an almost unimaginable degree of freedom and peace or contentment. Conversely, a person who meditates diligently for years—and who may, on occasion, experience ecstatic or profoundly insightful states of consciousness—may find that they are still besieged by emotional complexes and/or relationship problems. Thus, one should not expect meditation to be an end-run around one's psychological issues; doing so has aptly been described as spiritual bypassing.

Spiritual experiences of expanded *states* of consciousness typically do not enable a person to develop the *structures* of consciousness and forms of intelligence that are necessary for psychological well-being and integrity. States are transitory; structures are enduring. Thus, to be a fully actualized human being altered or expanded states must become altered traits.[2]

Western developmental theories study and delineate *stages* of human development. Contemplative traditions, by contrast, have emphasized the cultivation of states of consciousness.

Ken Wilber's integral theory refers to the stages of psychological development as *growing up*, an evolution aligned with the individuation process delineated by Jungians. He calls the process of spiritual development *waking up*. Only recently have pioneers, including Wilber himself, theorized the qualities of each mode of development and sought to integrate them in a manner that allows both forms of development to unfold synergistically. He adds that mature spirituality also entails *cleaning up*, a phrase that refers to what Jungians call integrating the shadow aspects of the psyche, and *showing up*, the capacity to engage others and the world in a manner that is caring and compassionate.[3] With the distinction between psychological and spiritual development in mind, I turn now to some comments on how

---

2. See Goleman and Davidson, *Altered Traits*, for a discussion of empirical research that aligns with views I present in this chapter.

3. Wilber distinguishes these modes of human development in many of his works. For the most detailed exposition, see Wilber, *Religion of Tomorrow*.

Jungian psychology and contemplative yoga are important sources for what I refer to as integrative spirituality—a spirituality that engenders wholeness and awakening.

Jungian Psychology

Jung's depth psychology can be engaged as a form of spirituality, one that emerged from his own intense process of inner work documented in his memoir and in *The Red Book*. His inner work led him to discover the Self, a term that describes the totality of the psyche, which encompasses ego consciousness and the larger matrix of the unconscious that contains it. The Self, for Jung, is also what he referred to as a God-image. The God-image is a unifying and transcendent symbol that integrates fragments and polarized opposites in the psyche. It functions as a "church within" and represents a person's highest value whether expressed consciously or unconsciously.[4] Jung describes the developmental process of discovering the Self as individuation, a ceaseless endeavor that requires a vigilant engagement with one's interiority. It is the primary purpose of a well-lived human life; it is the opus of a lifetime.

Many aspects of the Jungian approach to our inner life are important for integrative spirituality. First, his psychology provides an effective response to the death of God in the modern West. The death of God, for Jung, means the death of a God-image that is no longer viable for persons who cannot embrace traditional theistic conceptions of the divine. Like Jung, many of us in the twenty-first century resist the contemporary *spirit of the times* and seek a way to respond to *the spirit of the depths* that calls to us. Secularism and scientific materialism are an insufficient basis for a fulfilling life. Jung's psychology offers an alternative approach to spirituality, neither premodern/traditional nor modern/secular, based on the idea of integrating the divine into the human.[5] The Self, in effect, is the God within, something we must discover in the depths of the psyche.

Additionally, Jung's dialogue with Christianity, his inherited tradition, addresses many issues with which Christians and others struggle in the contemporary world. Most significant is the tendency to split the psyche into irreconcilable opposites—good against evil, masculine against feminine, spirit against body. Jung counters this in his *Answer to Job*, a creative narrative concerning the biblical God-image's individuation. The God-image in the biblical book of Job is shown to be deficient. For Jung, the

---

4. Samuels et al., *Critical Dictionary of Jungian Analysis*, 61–62.
5. Stein, *Minding the Self*, 6.

incarnation—the integration of the divine into the human figure of Jesus—symbolizes the archetypal Self's entrance into the domain of ego consciousness. It represents a dramatic change in the God-image: from an arbitrary power to a being conscious of and assuming responsibility for his own shadow. Through this shift, human beings become individually responsible for redemption, atonement, and the reconciliation of opposites. Instead of viewing the incarnation as a unique event in which God becomes human in the person of Jesus Christ, we can also understand it in a psychological way as the process by which the unconscious becomes assimilated during the course of an individual's lifetime. This process may be rendered not only as individuation, but also as *continuing incarnation, incarnation for all*, or the *christification of the many*.[6]

Third, Jungian psychology further revises the prevailing God-image of the West by recovering the divine feminine that has been eclipsed by the Abrahamic traditions. This recovery is best exemplified in the writings of Jungians such as Marion Woodman and Anne Baring.

Woodman focuses on Sophia and the Black Madonna, images she associates with the wisdom of the body and the presence of the divine in matter.[7] Baring sees the Shekinah as restoring the missing connective cosmology of the soul that had been lost. In her view, soul is not limited to the psychic life of individuals; it is also the *anima mundi* or the Soul of the World, the immense web of relationships that connects us to each other and to the earth.[8]

Finally, Jungian psychology provides several forms of inner work that can be done with an analyst or on one's own, including dream work, active imagination, and integrating shadow material.

Contemplative Yoga

There are many versions of contemplative yoga that include the teachings of the Upanishads, the classical teachings of the *Yoga Sutras*, and forms that extend through the centuries to Tantric traditions and modern iterations. Here I focus on three forms: the Bhagavad Gita, the tantric tradition of Kashmir Shaivism, which I refer to as Nondual Shaiva Tantra, and the Integral Yoga of Sri Aurobindo. All are householder rather than monastic forms of spirituality. All are integrated approaches to spiritual life that engage the

---

6. Stein, *Minding the Self*, 17–19.

7. Woodman et al., *Leaving My Father's House*, 1–2. See also Woodman and Dickson, *Dancing in the Flames*.

8. Baring, *Dream of the Cosmos*, 26–27.

body, emotions, intellect, and imagination as synergistic instruments for embodying Self-realization in the world.

The Bhagavad Gita may be read as a progressive teaching that moves from partial views of yoga to a comprehensive text that integrates the paths of knowledge (*jñana*), action (*karma*), and devotional love (*bhakti*). Each path is integrally related to and supports the others.[9] In this way, the Gita validates all the strands of yoga that precede it while offering innovative paths involving action and love. Contemplative knowledge is conjoined with action, renunciation is reconceived as service, while love unifies and motivates *sadhana*, or spiritual practice.

A Jungian interpretation of the Gita is, I believe, compatible with theistic or bhakti-oriented Hindu perspectives. In this text, the divine appears in a personal form and depicts a relationship between the soul and the divinity. The divinity, Krishna, is called Bhagavan, the beloved one; and his devotees are *bhaktas*, those who adore and love the beloved one. In Jungian psychology, a vital relationship between the ego and the Self, called the ego-Self axis, is of paramount importance.

A Jungian reading of the Gita suggests affinities between Krishna as a God-image and the archetypal Self in Jungian psychology. The discourse or dialogue in the text between Krishna and Arjuna can be likened to a dialogue between the ego or ego attitude and the Self. Krishna, or the archetypal Self, lovingly guides Arjuna, or the ego-attitude, through his despair or depression toward Self-realization. The uncertain and ambivalent ego steps back from action and social expectations to engage in a dialogue with the Self. The dialogue is informed by detachment from outer and material concerns, by introverted attention, and by deep listening to the guidance that unfolds from this relational process. As the process intensifies, the ego experiences a numinous encounter with the transpersonal Self—depicted as a theophany in chapter 11 of the text. For a moment, Arjuna beholds the grandeur and vastness of the divine. However, the ego does not dissolve into the Self; it persists in a deeper, stronger relationship with the Self. Expressed in the language of Hindu tradition, Krishna, the God-image, is not only the impersonal Brahman or ground of Being but also a God of love who befriends his devotees. Arjuna's egocentric doubts and one-sided perspective are overcome. He finds the courage to be himself and act as the situation requires. Action informed in this way may be described as nonattached or, as I prefer to put it, non-egocentric action—action that is aligned with the

---

9. Many commentators on the Gita take this view. See, for instance, Easwaran, *Essence of the Bhagavad Gita*; and Sri Aurobindo, *Essays on the Gita*. Aurobindo offers, perhaps, the strongest articulation of the view that the Gita is a comprehensive teaching that synthesizes knowledge, action, and devotion.

restoration of harmony in the world, or *dharma*. In developmental terms, such action is worldcentric rather than egocentric or ethnocentric.

Nondual Shaiva Tantra offers several forms of yoga called *upayas*. One *upaya* can be termed "the way of the body" (*anavopaya*). Illustrative practices are hatha yoga postures, breathing exercises, ritual worship, and karma yoga or the active yoga of service. Another *upaya*, "the way of the mind" (*shaktopaya*), comprises practices such as the use of mantra, self-inquiry, and contemplations that uplift the mind. A third *upaya* is "the way of pure consciousness" (*shambhavopaya*). The object of meditation is the thought-free consciousness out of which thoughts arise; it is the witnessing awareness underlying thought.[10] Thus, the *upayas* provide an integrated approach to yoga spirituality, methods that can be combined as needed to help practitioners holistically engage their physical, emotional, cognitive, and imaginative capacities.

This form of contemplative yoga teaches that it is not enough to go inside and experience bliss or expanded meditative states during meditation. This is a necessary but insufficient form of spirituality. To discover the Self within is the first stage of spirituality called *atma-vyatpi*, merging in the Self. The ultimate aim of spiritual practice is *Shiva-vyapti*, merging with the world. The perception that we are different from the world and need to be emancipated from it is a distorted and limited vision of life. To the contrary, God or the divine is immanent in everyone and everything. Thus, it offers us a God-image that is at once the transcendent ground of Being, the immanent Self abiding in the cave of the heart, and radiantly present in the great web of phenomenal, relational life. The *upayas* or yogas expand one's vision of life and engender the experience of wonder that emerges from seeing the grandeur and splendor of the Self in its myriad expressions in the world. First one sees the divinity within, then one beholds it everywhere.

In *Religion in the Making*, Alfred North Whitehead describes God-images that have arisen in evolution of religion. The worship of glory arising from power, he says, is dangerous and arises from a barbaric conception of God.[11] With a refinement of the image of divinity, the goodness of God replaces the will of God. You study his goodness, he writes, to be like him; God becomes the companion you emulate.[12] Whitehead's notion of God the companion resonates with the Bhagavad Gita and the integral yoga of Sri Aurobindo. In *The Synthesis of Yoga*, Aurobindo says that religion begins

---

10. Swami Shankarananda, *Consciousness Is Everything*, ch. 10. See also Wallis, *Tantra Illuminated*, 345–420.

11. Whitehead, *Religion in the Making*, 54.

12. Whitehead, *Religion in the Making*, 40.

with some conception of Power that creates a gulf between Power and the worshiper. Yoga, which is union, abolishes the gulf.[13] He observes that yoga places little emphasis on the fear of God. Instead, the focus is on the love, beneficence, fearlessness, and harmlessness of the saint and God-love. To grow into the divine nature is, he writes, the consummation of our ethical being.[14] The divine does not punish anyone; nor does he threaten or force obedience. It is the human soul that must freely come to the divine in a relationship that uplifts it. Love, he says, is the key to this relation. To serve God is, in Indian yoga, "the happy service of the divine Friend or the passionate service to the divine Beloved."[15] This image of the divine, exemplified in the Bhagavad Gita, is the friend, guide, and higher Self who describes himself as the friend of all creatures. As Aurobindo further elaborates, "It is not the fatherhood of God as the creator who demands obedience because he is the maker of our being, but the fatherhood of love which leads us towards the closer soul-union of Yoga."[16]

Aurobindo's integral yoga articulates a panentheistic God-image, the triple Brahman, that is at once transcendent, cosmic, and individual. The transcendent aspect of God is impersonal and the source of all forms. The cosmic aspect, immanent in all of nature and incarnate in human figures such as Christ and Krishna, is a God of love we can relate to as the Friend or Beloved. The individual aspect of God may be realized in our deep interiority, described in yoga texts as the cave of the heart. Therein, as Jungian psychology affirms, continuing incarnation may continue to occur in each of us. Such a vision of the divine, I suggest, also aligns well with the process-relational worldview. We are lured, by a God of love, to co-create a world that engenders wholeness, creativity, and awakening in our individual lives and communities.

My Form of Integrative Spirituality

My version of integrative spirituality has developed over the past thirty years. It engages the somatic, contemplative, devotional, and relational aspects of my being.[17]

---

13. Aurobindo, *Synthesis of Yoga*, 528.
14. Aurobindo, *Synthesis of Yoga*, 537.
15. Aurobindo, *Synthesis of Yoga*, 541.
16. Aurobindo, *Synthesis of Yoga*, 541.
17. For a more detailed discussion, see Mahaffey, *Integrative Spirituality*.

PART TWO: FROM THE SPIRIT TO THE POLIS

Somatic Practice and Contemplative Reading

My somatic practices include morning stretches and some hatha yoga postures, walks, and one or two Yin Yoga classes per week. After my morning stretches and poses, I engage in contemplative reading for half an hour while drinking tea.

Prayer and Worship

When I first started meditating in my early twenties, I had little interest in ritual or prayer. After joining the faculty at Pacifica Graduate Institute, I felt a desire to pray, but was unsure how to begin or whether it was even a possibility for me. I engaged in an experiment. I put aside the question of whether there was a being or beings who could hear me; instead, I assumed a creative attitude, believing that prayer could be viewed as an imaginal activity that evoked energies and qualities in my unconscious. Within a few weeks I not only felt comfortable doing this, but also began with relative ease to create a personal liturgy that has evolved and changed over time. For the past decade or so, invoking the divine feminine through prayer and mantra has been at the heart of my devotional practice.

Chanting

I have also cultivated the affective aspect of spiritual practice through *kirtan*, the devotional group chanting of the names of the divine in a call and response manner, a practice common among Hindus, especially in bhakti traditions. This practice kindles my love for the divine and helps me feel the love of God for me.

Meditation

Daily meditation on my heart-seed mantra is the heart of my sadhana, or spiritual practice.[18] I am among those who feel that meditation is the royal road to spiritual awakening. However, I came to feel that it is necessary but insufficient for integrative spirituality. Meditation gives one access to the stillness at the core of one's being and the witness that observes sensations,

---

18. A heart-seed mantra refers to a *bija* mantra. A *bija* is a "seed" sound used by a meditator to attune one's consciousness with the divine. *Sadhana* is the term used in yogic traditions that refers to spiritual discipline or spiritual practice.

feelings, and thoughts. This is the unconditioned part of ourselves, what I referred to earlier in this chapter as our Original Face. Experiencing the Self is a profound experience with salutary effects but it is not enough. We continue to live as embodied, relational beings with plenty of psychological content to deal with as we live our lives as skillfully as possible. To deal with that content we need other practices.

Self-Inquiry and Psychotherapy

An encompassing term for these practices is self-inquiry, or simply inquiry, and it can take multiple forms. For instance, I use a form called the Shiva Process that I learned from Swami Shankarananda while on retreat at his ashram in Australia. The basic practice is to become aware of what you are feeling through A-Statements: accurate statements of present feeling. A practice of this kind brings awareness to unconscious material that blocks awareness of the Self and that complicates our relationships with others.[19] Another closely related form of inquiry is journaling. My journal is also where I record and reflect upon dreams, engage shadow material, and practice active imagination. Psychotherapy is another practice I engage in periodically. It is a relational form of self-inquiry and has been important for navigating transitional moments in my life and relationship issues.

Service

Service, in my view, is another essential ingredient of integrative spirituality. As a Bob Dylan song puts it, "You gotta serve somebody." Hindu spirituality extols service and refers to it as seva and karma yoga. Service, by definition, is a relational spirituality providing us with an opportunity to benefit others; and it also can be worship when we offer our work to the divine.

Retreat and Pilgrimage

Retreat and pilgrimage are two other practices that nourish my spirituality. I engage in three retreats a year and am grateful for having had the opportunity to make seven pilgrimages to India.

---

19. See Shankarananda, *Self-Inquiry*. The book includes a compact disc of guided self-inquiry practices.

PART TWO: FROM THE SPIRIT TO THE POLIS
Dedication of Practice

Many spiritual traditions hold that spiritual practice is not done only for the practitioner, but also for others and for the environment that supports our lives. Mahayana Buddhists, for instance, refer to this as dedication of practice, the heartfelt wish that it may benefit all sentient beings. I also embrace this practice. I conclude this chapter with the prayer I offer after meditating each day.

> May all beings be safe.
> May all beings be free from suffering.
> May all beings discover the freedom and bliss of their true nature.
> May all beings enjoy material well-being: clean water, nourishing food, adequate shelter, and quality healthcare.
> May all beings dwell in peace.
> Om shantih, shantih, shantih

Bibliography

Aurobindo, Sri. *Essays on the Gita*. Sri Aurobindo Birth Centenary Library 13. Pondicherry, India: Sri Aurobindo Ashram, 1970.

———. *The Synthesis of Yoga*, Sri Aurobindo Birth Centenary Library 21. Pondicherry, India: Sri Aurobindo Ashram, 1971.

Baring, Anne. *The Dream of the Cosmos: A Quest for the Soul*. Dorset, UK: Archive, 2013.

Davis, Andrew M., and Philip Clayton, eds. *How I Found God in Everyone and Everywhere: An Anthology of Spiritual Memoirs*. Rhinebeck, NY: Monkfish, 2018.

Easwaran, Eknath. *Essence of the Bhagavad Gita: A Contemporary Guide to Yoga, Meditation, and Indian Philosophy*. Wisdom of India 2. Tomales, CA: Nilgiri, 2011.

Goleman, Daniel, and Richard J. Davidson. *Altered Traits: Science Reveals How Meditation Changes Your Mind, Brain, and Body*. New York: Avery, 2017.

Mahaffey, Patrick J. *Integrative Spirituality: Religious Pluralism, Individuation, and Awakening*. London: Routledge, 2019.

Samuels, Andrew, et al., eds. *A Critical Dictionary of Jungian Analysis*. London: Routledge & Kegan Paul, 1986.

Shankarananda, Swami. *Consciousness Is Everything: The Yoga of Kashmir Shaivism*. Mount Eliza, Australia: Shaktipat, 2003.

———. *Self-Inquiry: Using Your Awareness to Unblock Your Life*. Mount Eliza, Australia: Shaktipat, 2008.

Stein, Murray. *Minding the Self: Jungian Meditations on Contemporary Spirituality*. New York: Routledge, 2014.

Wallis, Christopher D. *Tantra Illuminated: The Philosophy, History, and Practice of a Timeless Tradition*. 2nd ed. Petaluma, CA: Mattamayūra, 2012.

Wilber, Ken. *The Religion of Tomorrow: A Vision for the Future of the Great Traditions—More Inclusive, More Comprehensive, More Complete*. Boulder, CO: Shambhala, 2017.

Woodman, Marion, and Elinor Dickson. *Dancing in the Flames: The Dark Goddess and the Transformation of Consciousness*. Boston: Shambhala, 1996.

Woodman, Marion, et al. *Leaving My Father's House: A Journey to Conscious Femininity*. Boston: Shambhala, 1993.

Whitehead, Alfred North. *Religion in the Making: Lowell Lectures, 1926*. New York: Meridian, 1926.

6

The Whole-Making Numinous

Power and Love in Cosmos and Psyche

SHERI D. KLING

As a constructive theologian focused on psychospiritual wholeness and transformation, in my research I aim to show how integrating process thought and Jungian psychology combined with a spiritual practice of dream work reveals the nature of all levels of reality—cosmic and psychic—to be integrated, value-soaked, relational, and transformative. To that end, I offer the integrative resources of Alfred North Whitehead and Carl Gustav Jung to address the fragmentation that I see in American culture specifically, and Western culture more broadly. Thinking with Whitehead and Jung and practicing dream work fosters embodied experiences of wholeness, and through such experiences we come to know for ourselves that we matter, we belong, and we can experience positive change. I deeply developed these foundational ideas in a previous text.[1]

In this contribution to the discussion around power and the God of love, I open with the conviction that if theology does not do *real work* in the world—if it does not *transform* human lives—then it is of no value. What work do I expect theology to do today? I expect it to heal our fragmentation, to help us integrate all aspects of our lives into a unified whole. Theology must show us that there is a unity to reality that can then facilitate our own integration. I call this aspect of Divine Reality the *Whole-making Numinous* and propose that this is a reality of Love and uncontrolling power.

---

1. Kling, *Process Spirituality*.

Wholeness, Love, and the Power of the Numinous

Wholeness

If it is indeed fragmentation that plagues us, what is the wholeness that we seek? John B. Cobb Jr. describes whole people as

> 'at-home' in their bodies, in their conscious and unconscious feelings and senses, in their human relationships, and in their total natural environment. They are 'at-home' with who they are, and therefore they are comfortable being just that. Because they are 'at-home' in themselves, they are free from defensiveness toward others. Others experience their warmth—that is their openness, their concern, and their affection. One is not the object of good deeds or just treatment from the whole person. One is the recipient of acceptance and understanding.[2]

A limited wholeness that is merely personal or subjective cannot address our fragmentation because it is not interwoven with the ever-nested circles within which we live, including the cosmos itself. Personal or psychic wholeness without cosmic wholeness leaves us atomistically fragmented, without transpersonal belonging or connection. The kind of wholeness that can make a difference, then, must be characterized as (1) understanding all aspects of our lives and human experience as *one coherent whole*, (2) feeling *undivided* or having a sense of "at homeness"[3] or "at-onement," (3) seeing ourselves and *life itself* as meaningful, (4) seeing ourselves *in relation to* the transpersonal whole, and (5) understanding transpersonal Reality as whole and *able to facilitate our own wholeness*.[4]

Love

In an exploration of power and Divine Love, we might ask what the connection is between Love and wholeness. While the Greeks personified Love as the god Eros, Carl Jung uses the term *eros* to describe the principle in the human psyche that drives our urge to "psychic relatedness"; it is "everywhere present" and the "great binder or loosener."[5] As I have discussed elsewhere,[6] we may understand God as Divine Eros, the "lure for feeling, the eternal urge

---

2. Cobb, "Wholeness Centered in Spirit," 230.
3. Cobb, "Wholeness Centered in Spirit," 230.
4. This last characteristic is articulated in Kalsched, *Trauma and the Soul*, 169.
5. Jung, *Aspects of the Feminine*, 28, 46.
6. Kling, "God as Eros."

of desire."[7] As the ultimate attractive force, Divine Eros lures everything toward its center and holds the cosmos together. Bringing things toward their own wholeness, then, is a demonstration of relational, Divine Love.

It is an equally powerful demonstration of Love when God lures momentary actualities toward expressions of novelty that "stimulate us to realize new possibilities after the old ones no longer are sufficient to give zest to our enjoyment of being actual."[8] Rabbi Bradley S. Artson writes about the kind of relational transformation where someone "[makes] it possible for you to do something you never thought possible," and describes God as "the One who makes it possible for us to surpass ourselves, the One who inspires us to ever new levels of love and creativity."[9] Therefore, transformation—or positive change—that lures us toward more beautiful, more enjoyable, and more complex expressions of living is inherently relational and powered by Divine Love.

The Power of the Numinous

I have argued at length[10] that one of the driving factors in the fragmentation that opposes our wholeness is the dualism at the heart of the Western worldview. Such dualism splits mind from body and humans from nature and distorts our understanding of our own experience. It bifurcates us from the world in which we reside and from which we receive our sustenance. While there are many compelling paradigms that invite us toward nondualistic ways of looking at life, Michael Zimmerman argues that new cognitive insights alone cannot give us the *experience* of our "membership in the web of all being."[11] Yet, encounters with divine reality, or what Rudolf Otto called the *numinosum*,[12] do seem to have the capacity to radically shift our paradigms and behavior. Such experiences invite us into communion with a sacred Other, and these, argues Chae Young Kim in his exploration of Whitehead's and Jung's views on religion, are the *essence* of religion.[13]

Psychological research into the nature of mystical or religious experience reveals common markers such as a sense of unity, ineffability,

---

7. Whitehead, *Process and Reality*, 344.
8. Cobb and Griffin, *Process Theology*, 59.
9. Artson, "Almighty?"
10. Kling, *Process Spirituality*.
11. Bulkeley, *Visions of the Night*, 40.
12. Otto, *Idea of the Holy*.
13. Kim, "Comparison" 425.

powerful emotion, and paradox.[14] Walter Houston Clark points to mystical or nonreligious ecstatic experience as being uniquely capable of transforming consciousness and behavior and making radical and lasting changes to personality.[15] While such encounters can have a shattering effect on the ego, they ultimately bring us to a greater sense of wholeness and authenticity by connecting the ego or small self to the larger Self that is the foundation of psychological integration. This larger Self in the psyche, according to Jung and Jungians, is its "unifying center."[16] It is what holds the psyche's "disparate, paradoxical, and often conflictual elements" together.[17] According to McGehee and Thomas,

> The Self integrates rather than disintegrates; it creates rather than destroys. It is the part of the psyche that generates and transforms life. It is that aspect of ourselves that urges—even requires—us to continue to evolve as we muddle along in our journey to wholeness . . . To be human is to have a Self, but to be estranged, alienated, or disconnected from this Self is to suffer tremendously.[18]

The fragmentation we see in American culture—sociological, interpersonal, and intrapersonal—shows us that one reason we are suffering so may be our lack of access to the kinds of encounters with the *numinosum* that may heal us.

Form, Freedom, and Uncontrolling Power

When we think with Whitehead and Jung, we can understand the *numinous* as relational, and as an Other that is immanent in both cosmos and psyche. For Whitehead, we encounter this Other at the beginnings of experience and for Jung, we encounter it at our depths. Using their thought gives us a way to understand God or transpersonal Reality as an uncontrolling *relational-imaginal reality of form and freedom*.[19] We reach this conclusion through exploring the functional resonances[20] between Whitehead's eternal

14. Pargament, *Spiritually Integrated Psychotherapy*, 70–71.
15. Clark, "Psychology of Religious Experience," 230.
16. Nicolaus, *C. G. Jung and Nikolai Berdyaev*, 127.
17. McGehee and Thomas, *Invisible Church*, 78.
18. McGehee and Thomas, *Invisible Church*, 78.
19. Kling, *Process Spirituality*, 175–83.
20. Kling, *Process Spirituality*, 29. Here I explain my use of the term "functional resonance," relating it to the musical sense of the word resonance as happens when a vibrating string on an instrument causes an adjacent string to vibrate sympathetically

objects, propositions, and propositional feelings and Jung's archetypes and archetypal images.

Formalism in Whitehead and Jung

Both Whitehead and Jung include transpersonal forms in their systems. Whitehead calls such forms eternal objects and Jung calls them archetypes. Both present patterns and possibilities, are infused with value and meaning, and play a causal role, though neither are determinative. Neither represent any kind of ultimate "ideal" that is of higher value than actualized, embodied realities.

Eternal Objects and Archetypes

It is especially fascinating to tease apart the ways in which eternal objects and archetypes are ahistorical and transcendent, and the ways in which they are historical and contextual. This is achieved through differentiating eternal objects from propositions and propositional feelings, and archetypes from archetypal images. Eternal objects are universally available for actualization but are not active or concrete. In fact, they are only made actual in events. As Susan Shotliff Mattingly writes, "Every eternal object transcends the entity which it forms" because it can recur "at other times and places."[21] They are not time bound but become historically contingent when actualized.

In a similar way, Jung's archetypes are also not ideal forms that are more real. For Jung, the ego is an archetypal complex around which images of one's life experience are collected, and this organizing of images is the central role of archetypes. June Singer understands them as "useful categories for thinking about the vast images which help us to organize our life experience in ways that point toward their ultimate meaning."[22] Jung believed archetypes to be inherited with the brain structure[23] and a part of nature, though unknowable and irrepresentable in their formal concept. Echoing the way Whitehead's eternal object of, say, "horse-ness" or "redness" differs from its instantiation as soon as it is actualized in horses or red balls, so as

---

and harmoniously. "Functional resonance" here suggests congruence and evocation rather than equivalence.

21. Mattingly, "Whitehead's Theory of Eternal Objects," 100.
22. Singer, *Boundaries of the Soul*, 129.
23. Frey-Rohn, *From Freud to Jung*, 97.

soon as what Jung calls the archetypal image arises in a person, it differs from what Jung would identify as an original archetype.

Context and Numinosity: Propositions, Propositional Feelings, and Archetypal Images

We can now look at the aspects of eternal objects and archetypes that are historical, contextual, and carriers of numinous energy. In Whitehead's system, everything comes into being in the same way. A simpler entity does not have a lot of options, though, and typically only repeats its past. Alternatively, more complex entities enjoy supplemental phases of becoming where they can raise up the unconscious data given by the past world to a more conscious comparison between their past and their possibilities for the future. That contrast between past and possible is a proposition, and it carries with it strongly persuasive (but not coercive) meaningful patterns and numinous feelings. All of this happens in a way that is contextual and relevant to that moment's real situation.

In a similar way archetypes present forms that are only activated by concrete life situations. When the archetype is activated in the psyche by something encountered in real life, archetypal images arise that emerge out of the historical context, culture, and personal experience of that individual. They also carry strong numinous energy and fascination that propels us. Although neither eternal objects nor archetypes are determinative, they can both *feel* sovereign[24] because they confront us as powerful energies that seem to come from outside of us.

The archetype is an a priori predisposition to form images,[25] but the archetypal images that arise are filled out by the individual's experience and determined only by that context. The symbols or images that arise are not given or determined by the archetype itself just as the propositions and propositional feelings are not determined by the eternal object. As soon as the image arises, it is already different from the archetype itself, in the same way that when the proposition with its feeling tones and value is integrated in the actual occasion, it is different from the pure possibility that was represented in the eternal object. Here we see that the numinosity that draws us toward transformation and wholeness is not controlling but inviting.

---

24. Wehr, *Jung & Feminism*, 93.
25. Robertson, *Jungian Archetypes*, 194.

PART TWO: FROM THE SPIRIT TO THE POLIS

Uncontrolling Power in God

How do eternal objects and archetypes connect with a relational God that is uncontrolling? For Whitehead, one of the sources for the eternal objects that are available to be actualized in any given moment is God, specifically God's Primordial Nature.[26] For Jung, the psyche is made up of an "almost infinite series" of images that are reproduced by the brain—images that represent unconscious bodily feelings, states, and impressions held together by the "powerful cohesive force" of the conscious ego.[27] The aspect of the psyche that connects the individual unconscious to the collective unconscious and mediates the archetypal material for every human is the archetypal Self. This is what Jung called the God-image in the psyche. Therefore, what lures us toward wholeness and transformation comes from the transpersonal Sacred.

As we have seen, both Whitehead and Jung embrace formalism, seeing forms as having a causal role in the cosmos and in the psyche, but that role is not controlling. At the levels of both cosmos and psyche, we confront a sacred, Transpersonal Other (that we may call God) at the beginnings and depths of our experience, which presents forms for evaluation and consideration. With those forms come powerful, numinous energies that deeply affect us and often lure us toward transformation. The images and feelings arise in us from our historical context with a power that is persuasive but not controlling. Just as God plays an ordering role in terms of presenting possibilities that are relevant to each momentary occasion's actual world, so the archetypal Self (the presence of God in the psyche) plays an ordering or mediating role in terms of the contents that are presented by the unconscious that will serve the growth of an individual.

It is crucial to understand that the presence of form and the need for general stability with the past means that the past exerts real pressure on the present moment. The idea that novelty needs to preserve some general stability with the past may explain why it takes time for novel ideas to gain traction. As more entities actualize novel possibilities, those possibilities then come not only from God's envisioned future but from the past world as well. Possibilities presented by both past and future may have more energy, more numinosity, and may be more persuasive than possibilities that arise from the past or the future alone. That is why social change is possible and why people like Jesus of Nazareth and Siddhartha Gautama, the Buddha, continue to have a strong influence upon the world.

---

26. Eternal objects also are present in the past from which each moment arises.
27. Jung, *Psychology and Religion*, 323.

The Whole-Making Numinous

So far, we have explored what it means to be whole; why we can connect whole-making to Divine Love; the power of the numinous to effect positive change; and form, freedom, and uncontrolling power. By putting Whitehead in conversation with Jung, we glean the integrating resources they offer to address fragmentation. Now we can weave these threads together in the idea that titles this chapter, the Whole-Making Numinous. In this endeavor, we will look at where each thinker situates God and the ways in which the presence and action of God draw humans toward wholeness and greater integration.[28]

Whole-Making in Whitehead

In Whitehead's philosophy, the cosmos is marked by a dance of novelty and order. All actual things are always in the process of becoming, emerging out of a settled past of dead fact to actualize a present possibility, and then perishing to become objective data for the next new moment. Life and all things are made up of moments of experience, and those moments aggregate into what he calls societies of occasions.[29] A person or a dog is such a society.

For Whitehead, a good and whole life is marked by zest, freshness, enjoyment, and actualizing value in the world. In *Process and Reality*, he points out that less complex societies have more stability but less capacity for novelty and therefore less intensity of experience. On the other hand, more complex societies have more intensity of experience but less stability. Therefore, a balance is required for more complex societies between novel responsiveness and stable endurance. Such a balance is achieved through enhancement of the mental pole.[30] He describes two means of enhancing the mental pole: (1) by improving the ability to discern God's initial aims so that entities can then align with those aims and thereby express more creativity and novelty, and (2) by using what he calls transmutation, which means blocking out all the distracting and unwelcome detail in our perception of the world and grasping it as a unified whole through abstraction.[31]

The initial aims offered by God in each moment are given as a lure toward an occasion's highest possibility for that moment—or, if the situation

---

28. Again, some of these ideas have been deeply examined in Kling, *Process Spirituality*. They are summarized here.
29. Loomer, "The Size of God," 40.
30. Whitehead, *Process and Reality*, 101.
31. Whitehead, *Process and Reality*, 101.

is dire, the possibility may only be for what is "best for that *impasse*."[32] This *initial* aim is not coercive, as each entity chooses for itself what will be its own *subjective* aim, its desire "to make something of and for itself."[33] This is the manner in which God draws the world toward novelty and integrated wholeness in an uncontrolling way—through *persuasion*.

Whole-Making in Jung

For Jung, a good and whole life is marked by realizing one's own being in the world and living out one's potentials. He describes the process of individuation as the means through which an individual integrates both conscious and unconscious aspects of personality into a unity. The outcome of this work is access to the dynamic energies that have been repressed in our shadow that help us to become whole individuals who can be in authentic relationship with others. Integrated individuals contribute more value to the world.[34]

God also plays a role in this process. Jung describes an aspect of the psyche he terms the archetypal Self, which "governs" the process of individuation.[35] The Self—or God-image in the psyche—is the "secret dwelling where God resides"[36] and a "unifying center"[37] that draws humans toward individuation and wholeness. Another key point is that as a symbol, the Self—like all symbols—participates in that toward which it points, and so the Self is present in the psyche while also a part of the collective unconscious.[38] Since the collective unconscious is seen by Jung as "empirically indistinguishable"[39] from God, we may understand the Self as the psyche's meeting point between the finite and the infinite.

The Whole-Making Numinous in Cosmos and Psyche

What do we gain when we bring these thinkers together to look at the whole-making numinous in cosmos and psyche? We gain a way to understand the archetypal Self as a *Self in process*, and we can also now identify a practice to

---

32. Whitehead, *Process and Reality*, 244.
33. Hosinski, *Stubborn Fact and Creative Advance*, 84.
34. Jung, *The Basic Writings of C. G. Jung*, 96–97.
35. Wehr, *Jung & Feminism*, 68.
36. Kalsched, *Trauma and the Soul*, 7.
37. Nicolaus, *C. G. Jung and Nikolai Berdyaev*, 127.
38. This idea was explored previously in Kling, "Avoiding a Fatal Error."
39. Odin, *Process Metaphysics and Hua-Yen Buddhism*, 165.

enhance the mental pole in order to achieve Whitehead's sought-after balance between novel responsiveness and stable endurance. Through bringing together these ideas of Whitehead and Jung, we can not only *conceptualize* an ever-present God in both cosmos and psyche who loves us enough to draw us toward wholeness and transformation, but we can embrace a practice that will give us that *experience*.

In bringing together Whitehead and Jung, there is something generative that emerges in the ways in which each fills gaps in the other's system of thought. For example, Whitehead's philosophy gives us no way to understand God's initial aims as related to whole persons, since those aims both arise and perish with each moment, rather than being aggregated in any way for societies of occasions (such as human beings). Jung also offers an archetypal Self that, in dualistic paradigms, runs the risk of being interpreted as a substantial Self. What is gained in the synthesis is an understanding of what I have called a *relational-imaginal God-Self*.[40]

An Archetypal Self in Process

By combining a Whiteheadian view on initial aims as the presence of God within each moment as it arises with a Jungian view of the archetypal Self as the presence of God in the psyche, we can now describe the archetypal Self as a relational-imaginal God-Self in the human psyche that participates in the Transpersonal Sacred, or God. The key to this frame is the connection between *image* and the *aims* that God envisions. The initial aims come from the Primordial Nature of God, and these are received by the actual entity through its mental pole. What might such aims even be, then, if not *images*? They certainly do not enter the occasion in the form of language. In the same way that a person or society is made up of its "historic route" of occasions,[41] I have proposed that Jung's archetypal Self may be made up of that person's historic route of initial aims.[42] In this view, the archetype of the Self is a kind of lattice around which the imaginal initial aims are collected. When we put Whitehead and Jung together, we can see the archetypal Self as a relational-imaginal God-Self in the human psyche that is fluid and processive, and the unifying point in the psyche, a point that relates us directly and intimately to God.

---

40. Kling, *Process Spirituality*, 200.
41. Loomer, "Size of God," 40.
42. Kling, *Process Spirituality*, 202.

PART TWO: FROM THE SPIRIT TO THE POLIS

Dream Work as a Whole-Making Praxis

We return now to Whitehead's idea that a society achieves its balance of stability and intensity through transmutation and aligning with God's initial aims. If initial aims are, in fact, aggregated in whole persons as the archetypal Self, and that Self is the immanent presence of God in the human, then what practices might enable us to discern those aims and thereby live a more creative life? How might we *experience* God's loving, whole-making work in our personal lives? While it is fine to understand that God offers us possibilities through initial aims, how do we come to know what those are? How do we bring that unconscious material and raise it up for conscious evaluation and decision-making? My own experience and that of others shows that spiritual dream work is an effective practice for just this purpose.

I conducted a pilot qualitative study in 2014[43] where I interviewed five individuals active in Christian congregations who use dream work as a spiritual practice. All worked with their dreams to interpret the symbols within them, both on an individual basis and in dream-sharing groups.[44] Five major themes emerged related to the phenomenological experience of these Christian dream workers.[45]

- *First, they all made experiential claims of a mystical nature* that included feeling God's presence, experiencing an inner knowing, a heightened sense of the reality of the spiritual realm, and energy or 'numinosity' in dream images.

- Second, they all claimed, in one way or another, that dream work has *played a significant role in their spiritual lives*, and that dreams themselves hold important meaning and value.

- Third, *they interpreted their dreams (and often synchronicities) as divine communication* that provides insights, guidance, loving support, hope, and healing.

- Fourth, *they saw their dream work as an enriching and transformative practice in relation to their experience of self.* It typically helped to increase their sense of self-acceptance, self-knowledge, and

---

43. I presented the findings of that inquiry in Kling, "God of Their Dreams."

44. Such groups first emerged in the 1970s through the work of psychiatrist Montague Ullman, Unitarian Universalist minister Jeremy Taylor, and others, and is now promoted through the work of the Haden Institute and other organizations and individuals.

45. This inquiry was discussed in detail in Kling, *Process Spirituality*, 221–26.

self-forgiveness, and they described themselves as happier, healthier, more integrated, and more whole as a result.

- *Lastly, they saw their dream work as an enriching and transformative practice in relation to their connections with God and others.* They felt that it helped to broaden their spiritual perspectives, change their images of God, deepen their friendships, heal past hurts, and increase their appreciation of or participation in other traditions.

I have proposed that when we work with our dreams in a Jungian way for the purpose of spiritual growth, such a practice fosters what I call *conscious transmutation*.[46]

Conscious Transmutation: Making the Unconscious Conscious

Whenever I speak about fragmentation, I always speak about trauma. Trauma and abuse seem to set up neural pathways that get entrenched as patterns, so that later, when our outer circumstances resemble the dynamics of our traumatic past, we unconsciously react from that past experience rather than consciously responding to the present moment. This connects to what Jung called psychological complexes. These patterns of reactivity rob us of the dynamism, creativity, and responsiveness that are essential to human life. If we are reacting based on old patterns, we are not truly alive, and God's nearness and whole-making activity are just not as available to us.

As was discussed earlier, the pressure of the past is strong and compelling. Less complex entities have less freedom to actualize novel aims, and more generally can only repeat the past. Human beings are complex creatures, and yet many of us find ourselves fragmented and stuck, in a seemingly endless loop of situations that mimic early life traumas. I wrote in *A Process Spirituality*:

> The creative dance of becoming inherently entails flux, perishing, and loss. This is the wounding reality of embodied existence. Therefore, all of us have things in our past that are painful. Yet many of us find ourselves thinking or behaving in ways that prevent our own flourishing because 'old habits' or old patterns of thinking 'die hard.' For those of us who fight those battles, process thought provides a hopeful vision of reality because it

---

46. Kling, *Process Spirituality*, 216–26.

promises that novelty or positive change—aligned with God's aims—is possible in every moment.[47]

The key to such positive change is making the unconscious conscious. For Whitehead, that involves raising up those propositions and propositional feelings to consciousness, with all their numinous energy, and being willing to choose a future that is in contrast with the past. For Jung, that means bringing the shadow complexes that keep us stuck in the past to consciousness, so they fall apart in the light and we can move forward in a more integrated way.

When we are taken over by a psychological complex—from, for example, a father or mother wound—I argue that we are engaged in a process of *unconscious* transmutation where we block out the details of the present and instead draw only from memories and images of our traumatic past. Rather than seeing the person or situation that is in front of us, we project our past onto the present. Transmuting data unconsciously is a kind of anesthetizing simplification. By putting Whitehead in dialogue with Jung, we realize that we can make transmutation more conscious. So instead of our entrenched patterns from the past pressing us into continuous repetition of our unhealthy behaviors, we can bring those patterns to consciousness and entertain new possibilities.

When we do this—and working with the symbols in our dreams is one way to bring consciousness to shadow material—we can begin to engage the world as it is in the present moment, in the now, rather than projecting our emotional wounds onto our current world and being reactive in an unhealthy way. Engaging the world as it is, we can bring more novelty, originality, and intensity or enjoyment to life. We also contribute more value to ourselves, others, and the world and can engage in healthier relationships.

Conclusion

I began with the claim that if theology does not do real work in the world by transforming people's lives, it is of no value. How do the ideas shared herein do real work in the world and show us something life-giving about Love and uncontrolling power in God?

First, we acknowledged the power of the numinous as a loving lure through which God draws us toward wholeness and transformation by radically changing our understanding of Reality. Next, we engaged Whitehead and Jung to describe God's uncontrolling power as a relational-imaginal

---

47. Kling, *Process Spirituality*, 79.

reality of form and freedom. This is important because it helps us to understand—and maybe forgive—the forceful presence and power of the past while giving us access to freedom, agency, and the novel possibilities that God presents in every moment for our growth and healing. It also helps us to understand why social change takes time.

Finally, I introduced the idea of God as a Whole-Making Numinous, and the relational-imaginal God-Self in the human psyche that is the meeting point between God and human. I also introduced a whole-making praxis of dream work that helps us discern God's initial aims and heal our unconscious reactivity through conscious transmutation. These ideas and practices have tremendous capacity to do real work in the world, as has been confirmed by study participants and the large community of dream workers who attend the Haden Institute's annual Summer Dream & Spirituality Conference.

Yet, even for practices like dream work that are grounded in lived experience, it is still necessary to explain how and why such experience is possible. Without that explanatory framework, experiences of the numinous are reduced to merely individual, subjective, and random experiences. Alternatively, understanding the availability of whole-making encounters with the numinous as woven into the very fabric of existence can be a source of real hope, joy, wholeness, and flourishing for human life.

Therefore, when we think and practice with Whitehead and Jung, we can describe God's uncontrolling whole-making and numinous Love in this way: That for each one of us, God is present to us, internal to us, in every moment of our existence, and offers us the creative possibilities that can move us out of our painful pasts into transformed futures. Dream work is one practice we can use to raise the unconscious, imaginal initial aims to consciousness, allowing us to discern those possibilities, respond freely, and thereby heal our fragmented selves, and maybe even our fragmented society. This is true for each and every one of us because a loving God and God's uncontrolling possibilities for our wholeness are as near to us as our next breath.

Bibliography

Artson, Bradley Shavit. "Almighty? No Way! Coming to Know the God We Already Love." *Jewish Journal* (May 11, 2010): https://jewishjournal.com/judaism/holidays/79290/.

Bulkeley, Kelly. *Visions of the Night: Dreams, Religion and Psychology*. SUNY Series in Dream Studies. Albany: SUNY Press, 1999.

Clark, Walter Houston. "The Psychology of Religious Experience." In *Current Perspectives in the Psychology of Religion*, edited by H. Newton Malony, 227–37. Grand Rapids: Eerdmans, 1977.

Cobb, John B., Jr. "Wholeness Centered in Spirit." In *Spirit-Centered Wholeness: Beyond the Psychology of Self*, edited by H. Newton Malony et al., 225–45. Studies in the Psychology of Religion 2. Lewiston, NY: Mellen, 1988.

Cobb, John B. Jr., and David Ray Griffin. *Process Theology: An Introductory Exposition*. Philadelphia: Westminster, 1976.

Frey-Rohn, Liliane. *From Freud to Jung: A Comparative Study of the Psychology of the Unconscious*. C. G. Jung Foundation Books Series. Boston: Shambhala, 2001.

Hosinski, Thomas E. *Stubborn Fact and Creative Advance*. Lanham, MD: Rowman & Littlefield, 1993.

Jung, C. G. *Aspects of the Feminine*. Translated by R. F. C. Hull. Bollingen Series. Jung Extracts. Princeton: Princeton University Press, 1982.

———. *The Basic Writings of C. G. Jung*. Edited by Violet Staub de Laszlo. Modern Library ed. New York: Modern Library, 1993.

———. *Psychology and Religion: West and East*. Translated by R. F. C. Hull. Corrected. Collected Works of C. G. Jung 11. Bollingen Series 20. New York: Pantheon, 1963.

Kalsched, Donald. *Trauma and the Soul: A Psycho-Spiritual Approach to Human Development and Its Interruption*. London: Routledge, 2013.

Kim, Chae Young. "A Comparison of Alfred North Whitehead's and Carl Gustav Jung's Idea of Religion: Special Reference to Their Lectures on Religion." *Journal of Dharma* 27.3 (2002) 417–28.

Kling, Sheri D. "Avoiding a Fatal Error: Extending Whitehead's Symbolism beyond Language." In *Rethinking Whitehead's Symbolism: Thought, Language, Culture*, edited by Roland Faber et al., 124–43. Edinburgh: Edinburgh University Press, 2017.

———. "The God of Their Dreams: A Qualitative Inquiry into the Lived Experience of Christian Dream Workers and the Mystical Nature of Their Experience." Paper presented at the American Academy of Religion, San Diego, November 2014.

———. *A Process Spirituality: Christian and Transreligious Resources for Transformation*. Lanham, MD: Lexington, 2020.

Loomer, Bernard M. "The Size of God." In *The Size of God: The Theology of Bernard Loomer in Context*, edited by William D. Dean and Larry E. Axel. Macon, GA: Mercer University Press, 1987.

Mattingly, Susan Shotliff. "Whitehead's Theory of Eternal Objects." PhD diss., University of Texas at Austin, 1968.

McGehee, J. Pittman, and Damon J. Thomas. *The Invisible Church: Finding Spirituality Where You Are*. Psychology, Religion, and Spirituality. Westport, CT: Praeger, 2008.

Nicolaus, Georg. *C. G. Jung and Nikolai Berdyaev: Individuation and the Person: A Critical Comparison*. London: Routledge, 2010.

Odin, Steve. *Process Metaphysics and Hua-Yen Buddhism: A Critical Study of Cumulative Penetration vs. Interpenetration*. SUNY Series in Systematic Philosophy. Albany: SUNY Press, 1982.

Otto, Rudolf. *The Idea of the Holy: An Inquiry into the Non-Rational Factor in the Idea of the Divine and Its Relation to the Rational*. Translated by John W. Harvey. 2nd ed. London: Oxford University Press, 1970.

Pargament, Kenneth I. *Spiritually Integrated Psychotherapy: Understanding and Addressing the Sacred.* Paperback ed. New York: Guilford, 2011.

Robertson, Robin. *Jungian Archetypes: Jung, Gödel, and the History of Archetypes.* Rev. ed. New York: iUniverse, 2009.

Singer, June K. *Boundaries of the Soul: The Practice of Jung's Psychology.* Rev. ed. New York: Anchor, 1994.

Wehr, Demaris S. *Jung & Feminism: Liberating Archetypes.* Boston: Beacon, 1987.

Whitehead, Alfred North. *Process and Reality.* Edited by David Ray Griffin and Donald W. Sherburne. Corrected ed. New York: Free Press, 1979.

7

Carl Schmitt's *Political Theology*

A Process Theological Intervention

MATTHEW DAVID SEGALL

This chapter critically engages with Carl Schmitt's antiliberal political theology, offering important interventions from the related perspectives of Alfred North Whitehead's cosmopolitical process theology, philosophical personalism, and Bruno Latour's Gaian political ecology. Schmitt's criticisms of early twentieth-century liberalism are tested against Daniel Dombrowski's admirable defense of a process reading of Rawlsian political liberalism. Since Schmitt was at least nominally Catholic, I also turn to the New Testament for a source of spiritual resistance to his fascist ideology.

As a politically engaged process philosopher, I have found Schmitt's political writing to be disturbingly brilliant. *Brilliant* because his criticisms of liberalism are trenchant (though as we'll see, they are blunted by Dombrowski's process-inflection of Rawlsian liberalism); *disturbing* because his aim, having laid bare the perceived contradictions of liberalism, is to justify fascist dictatorship. Schmitt is usually described as the "crown jurist" of the Nazi Party. Despite being a raging anti-Semite, Schmitt was a member of the Catholic Center Party before Hitler became Chancellor in 1933. In the final year of the Republic's existence he even argued against the constitutionality of the Nazi Party.[1] But following Nazi takeover, he was quick to pledge fealty. Within a few years he would enthusiastically defend Hitler's executions of political enemies. Nonetheless, he was booted from his professional leadership position by the Reich in 1936 because of the perception that he was an opportunistic turncoat. In 1950, he published a memoir, *Ex Captivitate Salus*, comparing himself to a character

---

1. See Schmitt, *Political Romanticism*, x.

in Herman Melville's novella *Benito Cereno* (1855): just as the mutinied captain of Melville's fictional slave ship was forced to do the bidding of the rebellious crew, Schmitt claimed he had been forced to do the legal bidding of the Nazis. Despite his attempt to save face, the posthumous publication of his diaries from the early 1930s show that his support for Nazi rule was hardly feigned. Whatever his reasons for joining the Nazi Party, he only narrowly escaped the Nuremberg trials (trials which he, predictably, found illegitimate) and has since developed something of a cult following among "postliberals" on both sides of the political spectrum.[2]

In this chapter, I focus in particular on Schmitt's book *Political Theology: Four Chapters on the Concept of Sovereignty* (1922/1934), written in Germany during the tumultuous postwar Weimar period when a fragile parliamentary government lurched from one constitutional crisis to the next. The 1934 second edition includes a new preface written after Hitler rose to power and Schmitt joined the Nazi Party. In this preface, Schmitt references his October 1929 lecture "The Age of Neutralizations and Depoliticizations," wherein he unpacks his view of the process of secularization. A few salient ideas from this lecture will help set the stage for my summary of *Political Theology*.

Modern Political Epochs and the Rise of Technological Progressivism

After admitting that "all historical knowledge is present knowledge,"[3] Schmitt briefly recounts European modernity's movement through various political epochs, roughly corresponding to each century. He does not necessarily view these epochal shifts as a progression. They could just as easily be read as a regression. Each epoch in effect "neutralizes" the controversial terms of the prior epoch, resolving disputes by establishing a new regime of truth:

- sixteenth century: the theological epoch
- seventeenth century: the metaphysical epoch (by which Schmitt means the rise of scientific materialism)
- eighteenth century: the humanist/moral epoch (the Enlightenment)
- nineteenth century: the economic/positivistic epoch
- twentieth century: the technological epoch

2. See Wolin, "Cult of Carl Schmitt."
3. Schmitt, "Age of Neutralizations and Depoliticizations," 130.

Schmitt saw the twentieth century becoming increasingly dominated by the "anti-religion" of technological progress. This new epoch is supported by the widespread assumption that the "ultimate neutral ground has been found in technology."[4] But Schmitt rejects the idea of technological neutrality, since the use technology is put to is inevitably shaped by metaphysical, ethical, political, and economic presuppositions. Typified by the rise of Soviet Russia, he described the new anti-religion as implying an "activistic metaphysics," i.e., a belief in the unlimited power and domination of man over nature, even over human nature. He perceived early on the political potential of technologies of mass media (e.g., radio):

> Today we see through the fog of names and words with which the psycho-technical machinery of mass suggestion works. Today we even recognize the secret law of this vocabulary and know that the most terrible war is pursued only in the name of peace, the most terrible oppression only in the name of freedom, the most terrible inhumanity only in the name of humanity.[5]

George Orwell's novel *1984* was published nearly twenty years later, though it is clear from Schmitt's concerns about technological societies that the idea of "Newspeak" was already in the air. Schmitt accepted that the rise of the new technoscientific religion of progress had made the traditional image of an omnipotent deity seem incredible. In the new geological epoch known as the Anthropocene, powers that once belonged only to God have succumbed to hubristic human ingenuity. Nearly a century after Schmitt's lecture, the proliferation of electronic media (whether traditional mass media or social media) has made it no less difficult for liberals to sustain their faith in the power of free speech and a free press to secure and convey the truth. The technologically amplified power of mass suggestion and disinformation has become a major obstacle to the liberal dream of replacing political struggle with legislative proceduralism. Increasingly fragmented social networks have fomented tribalism and ideological capture, making it difficult for democratic polities to agree on what is reasonable in Rawls,[6] much less to agree on the facts or what to do about them. Media technologies were limited to newspapers and radios in Schmitt's day, but having participated in the collapse of the Weimar Republic and the rise of the Third Reich, he was well aware of the vulnerability of liberal democracy to demagogic hijacking.

---

4. Schmitt, "Age of Neutralizations and Depoliticizations," 138.
5. Schmitt, "Age of Neutralizations and Depoliticizations," 142.
6. Rawls, *Political Liberalism*, 48.

Schmitt's Political Theology and Criticism of Liberalism

Schmitt's target in *Political Theology* is what he calls "liberal normativism": Hugo Krabbe (1857–1936), a Dutchman, and Hans Kelsen (1881–1973), an Austrian Jew, author of the Austrian Constitution in 1920, serve as the main representatives of the approach. Schmitt laments the depoliticization resulting from liberalism's attempt at a positivistic purification of legal theory, whereby theorists claim to be politically neutral, unaffected by any personal bias, and capable of securing scientific objectivity by way of a purely formal treatment of law. Unlike liberal theorists, Schmitt was adamant that jurisprudence could have no justification in the absence of philosophical or metaphysical convictions, which legal positivists could only pretend to sidestep. In effect, he accuses liberal theorists of refusing to decide on their true convictions by pretending to have risen above personal political and religious views as if to judge from a superior "scientific" or "objective" position. He rejects the transpolitical status attributed to law by liberals, since any decision about what is not political is itself already political: "the political is the total."[7] Schmitt contrasts the positivistic liberal approach with his own decisionist theory, which refuses to purify law of the personal, instead making the personhood of the sovereign constitutive of both statehood and its legal procedures.

According to Schmitt, "Sovereign is he who decides on the exception."[8] Abstract systems of law cannot encompass or predict the exception, as it represents an emergency that breaks any routine. While the liberal constitutional state "represses" the question of sovereignty, deferring the inevitability of decision by means of endless discussion, Schmitt's sovereign decides not only on the concretely exceptional case but also on the general norm. "There exists no norm that is applicable to chaos. For a legal order to make sense, a normal situation must exist, and he is sovereign who definitely decides whether this normal situation actually exists."[9] Schmitt mocks the liberal political theory of his time as an "interesting spectacle" because of the way its contradictory empiricist and rationalist tendencies are constantly facing off against one another. Though Locke clearly contrasts "law" with the "command" of the monarch (thus rejecting decisionism), Schmitt suggests there remained at least a "vivid awareness of the meaning of the exception" in his precritical conception of natural law. Kant's critical rationalism, on the other hand, simply ignores the exception, since acknowledging it

---

7. Schmitt, *Political Theology*, 2.
8. Schmitt, *Political Theology*, 5.
9. Schmitt, *Political Theology*, 13.

would confound the unity and order required of his transcendental system. Neo-Kantians like Kelsen do what they can to regulate the exception as precisely as possible, to articulate in detail when in an emergency situation it is legitimate for law to "suspend itself." Schmitt objects: "From where does the law obtain this force, and how is it logically possible that a norm is valid except for one concrete case that it cannot factually determine in any definitive manner?"[10]

Schmitt insists that any philosophy that claims to take concrete life seriously must face the exception, the extreme case, since it is more important than the rule: "the seriousness of an insight goes deeper than the clear generalizations inferred from what ordinarily repeats itself. The exception is more interesting than the rule ... In the exception the power of real life breaks through the crust of mechanism that has become torpid by repetition."[11] Here is the first opportunity for dialogue with Whitehead, who certainly took concrete life and creative advance seriously. In *Process and Reality* he claims that "the moralistic preference for true propositions [has] obscured the role of propositions in the actual world." The problem, he explains, is that propositions have been collapsed into logical judgments. "The result is that false propositions have fared badly, thrown into the dustheap, neglected." Instead, propositions, true or false, ought to be distinguished as nonconscious "lures for feeling" that only rarely rise to the level of consciously stated judgments. Thus, "in the real world it is more important that a proposition be interesting than that it be true."[12] Of course, truth is important because of its contribution to interest. But if truth is repetition of the established rule, then the uncompromising prohibition of false propositions would leave us imprisoned in bureaucratic routine. Strictly formal systems aimed solely at the universal and so blind to the personal are, in the words of Whitehead's favorite poet, "rather proud to be/The enemy of falsehood, than the friend of truth."[13] Such systems—content rather "to sit in judgment that to feel"—leave no room for the unpredictably unique expressions of creative process. Schmitt[14] quotes Kierkegaard's *Repetition*:

> Over time, one tires of the interminable chatter about the universal and the universal, which is repeated until it becomes boring and vapid. There are exceptions. If one cannot explain them, then neither can one explain the universal. One generally fails to

---

10. Schmitt, *Political Theology*, 14.
11. Schmitt, *Political Theology*, 15.
12. Whitehead, *Process and Reality*, 259.
13. Wordsworth, *Prelude, or Growth of a Poet's Mind*, 209.
14. Schmitt, *Political Theology*, 15.

notice this, because one does not normally grasp the universal passionately, but only superficially. The exception, on the other hand, grasps the universal with intense passion.[15]

As becomes apparent below, it is important to remember Whitehead's theory of propositional feelings when dealing with the statements of scripture. Even factually false propositions (e.g., about historical human motivations and behaviors) may function in a powerful, world-transforming way as ideals luring us toward greater goodness and beauty. It is also important to note, as Catherine Keller does,[16] that Schmitt conveniently ignores the trajectory of Kierkegaard's dialectic in the above passage, whereby the legitimate exception gains the attention of and becomes reconciled with the universal.

In the real world, unexpected historical events give rise to novel needs and interests, catalyzing reactions against any formulaic treatment of public law. Thus, the law must be self-evolving, the state self-legislating. While philosophers may be tempted to imagine that political truths can be established by way of abstract conceptual dialectics, in historical reality sovereignty and law have more often been defined by bloody power struggles. Schmitt agrees with Rousseau about at least one thing: "The connection of actual power [coercive force] with the legally highest power [which is a mere formula, sign, or signal] is the fundamental problem of the concept of sovereignty."[17] In other words, what is the relationship between the state's monopoly on violence and the symbolic power of a legal order? Neo-Kantian liberal theorists like Kelsen lean on the is/ought distinction in an attempt to subject legal praxis to formal epistemological critique. Legal concepts are thereby thought to be purified of personal political or religious interests. The origin of authority in a liberal constitutional state is therefore not a "sociopsychological power complex" or personal sovereign but rather the ideal unity of a system of norms. Kelsen claims the positivist objectivity of his approach is secured by the fact that the norms he affirms are not his own personal value assessments but belong to the given legal order governing the society he finds himself in. For Kelsen, then, "the concept of sovereignty must be radically repressed," as he himself put it,[18] since there can be no legal decree transcending the unified system of law. Schmitt retorts: "Unity and purity are easily attained when the basic difficulty is emphatically ignored and when, for formal reasons, everything that contradicts the system is excluded as impure."[19]

15. Kierkegaard, *Repetition and Philosophical Crumbs*, 78.
16. Keller, *Political Theology of the Earth*, 40.
17. Schmitt, *Political Theology*, 18.
18. Kelsen, *Das Problem der Souveränität*; quoted in Schmitt, *Political Theology*, 21.
19. Schmitt, *Political Theology*, 21.

Krabbe does not ignore the question of sovereignty, but addresses it by making the law itself sovereign, rather than the state: "However one wants to approach it," he writes,

> the doctrine of sovereignty of law is either a record of what is already real or a postulate that ought to be realized ... We no longer live under the authority of persons, be they natural or artificial (legal) persons, but under the rule of laws, spiritual forces ... These forces rule in the strictest sense of the word. Precisely because these forces emanate from the spiritual nature of man, they can be obeyed voluntarily.[20]

No more can be said about the foundation of legal order and the state, then, than that they spring from our spiritual feelings of what is right. The state thus expresses the legal consciousness emergent from the life of the people. Krabbe is said to converge with the "association theory" founded by Otto von Gierke (1841–1921), which practically eliminates the concept of authoritarian sovereignty, replacing it with the internationalist ideal of a decentralized community of communities constituted from below without need of any centralized monopoly on power. Schmitt resists such conceptions of a self-organizing state, which he seems to associate with the "irrationality" of philosophies of life like Schelling's and Bergson's. He recoils from their organismic intuitions of an evolving mutual immanence between the soul, the world, and God.[21] Whitehead offers another hand here, as his process philosophical project is in part an attempt to "rescue [Bergson's] type of thought from the charge of anti-intellectualism, which rightly or wrongly has been associated with it."[22]

Schmitt is unwilling to relinquish the idea of the sovereign state as the ultimate guarantor of law and order. He zeroes in on the Scholastic concept of the "substantial form" of law, a concept he thinks neo-Kantians misunderstand because of their focus on the subjective transcendental deduction of formal categories. "The legal idea cannot realize itself, it needs a particular organization and form before it can be translated into reality [i.e., by the application of a legal thought to a factual situation]."[23] My colloquial trans-

---

20. Krabbe, *De moderne staatsidee*; quoted in Schmitt, *Political Theology*, 22.

21. See also Schmitt's *Political Romanticism* (1986). Schmitt presumably also rejected the organically differentiating conception of society put forward by his anarchic, esoteric Christian contemporary Rudolf Steiner. Steiner's "social threefolding" movement emerged in the aftermath of the First World War, proposing a differentiation between political/legal, cultural/spiritual, and economic domains guided by the values of equality, freedom, and solidarity, respectively. See Segall, "Urgency of Social Threefolding."

22. Whitehead, *Process and Reality*, xii.

23. Schmitt, *Political Theology*, 28.

lation for what Schmitt means is that law can only be concretely applied by a soul, the substantial form of a person. Schmitt argues that Kelsen contradicts himself by claiming that a critically deduced subjective concept of form could nonetheless objectively unify the legal order through an impersonal act of judgment.[24] This attempt to remove the personal dimension neglects the evident fact that no legal idea says anything about who should apply it.[25] A legal judgment, in other words, is impossible without a personal element. Schmitt thus turns to Thomas Hobbes's *Leviathan* (1651), the classic text in decisionist political theory. Hobbes writes: "autoritas, non veritas, facit legem"/ "authority, not truth, makes the law."[26] On Schmitt's reading, Hobbes advances an argument definitively linking decisionism with personalism, rejecting the rationalist attempt to substitute "an abstractly valid order for a concrete sovereignty of the state." Despite the natural-scientific bent of his thinking, Hobbes realized the legal form could only be located in a concrete decision emanating from a particular personal authority. Schmitt: "What matters for the reality of legal life is who decides ... It does not have the a priori emptiness of the transcendental form because it arises precisely from the juristically concrete."[27]

Schmitt then annunciates perhaps the most influential line in any of his books: "All significant concepts of the modern theory of the state are secularized theological concepts," both for reasons of historical development and because of their systematic structure.[28] In *Process and Reality*, Whitehead adds that the analogy between God concepts and political concepts operates also in the reverse direction: "When the Western world accepted Christianity, Caesar conquered; and the received text of Western theology was edited by his lawyers ... The Church gave unto God the attributes which belonged exclusively to Caesar."[29] While Schmitt argues upon the basis of a transfer from theology to the theory of the state, Whitehead shows that it is equally valid to see a transfer from the theory of state to theology, such that the omnipotent lawgiver became the omnipotent God "fashioned in the image of an imperial ruler." This tragic idolatry, whose violent shadow looms over so much of Western Asiatic and European history, obscures the novel spiritual significance of the life and death of Jesus, who does not at all fit the images of the ruling Caesar, ruthless moralist,

24. Schmitt, *Political Theology*, 29.
25. Schmitt, *Political Theology*, 31.
26. Quoted in Schmitt, *Political Theology*, 33.
27. Schmitt, *Political Theology*, 34.
28. Schmitt, *Political Theology*, 36.
29. Whitehead, *Process and Reality*, 342.

or unmoved mover. Rather, the God-image of Jesus as poetic lurer rather than petty ruler reveals a God who "dwells upon the tender elements in the world, which slowly and in quietness operate by love; and it finds purpose in the present immediacy of a kingdom not of this world. Love neither rules, nor is it unmoved; also it is a little oblivious as to morals."[30] While Schmitt unveils the self-contradictions of liberalism, he fails to see the log in his own eye (Matt 7:3; Luke 6:41): how can he, allegedly a Catholic Christian, theologically define politics as the means by which we distinguish friends from enemies when Jesus calls upon his followers to: "love your enemies" (Matt 5:44)? Further, as Whitehead insists, the "Gospel of Force" is self-defeating because by baring cooperation it stunts social life: "Every organism requires an environment of friends, partly to shield it from violent changes, and partly to supply it with its wants."[31]

Process Political Theology and Personalism

Schmitt's reactionary regression to an idolatrous image of God and solipsist conception of political sovereignty is where the process theological intervention shows its potential. Whitehead urges philosophers to secularize the concept of God's function in the world.[32] In contrast to the Schmittian approach to secularization, whereby an omnipotent interventionist God's *creatio ex nihilo*[33] of the cosmos is translated into to the sovereign decider's capacity to both establish and rupture at will any rationalized system of law, Whitehead's schema of secularization reads the history of Christian empire as a great betrayal of the teachings of Jesus. Whitehead's cosmology is a panentheistic protest against the image of God as totalitarian dictator: "God is not to be treated as an exception to all metaphysical principles, invoked to save their collapse. He is their chief exemplification."[34] In Keller's words:

> What Whitehead's deity exemplifies is the creative process in which anything actual exists only as an interdependent activity of becoming . . . Each actuality, divine included, is a process of embodiment contracting in itself the entangled materializations

---

30. Whitehead, *Process and Reality*, 343.
31. Whitehead, *Science and the Modern World*, 206.
32. Whitehead, *Process and Reality*, 207.
33. See Keller, *Political Theology of the Earth*, 42–43, for an alternative, *deeper* reading of Genesis cosmogony. See also Hogue, *American Immanence*, 31–34 for an analysis of how the ex nihilo metaphor functions to erase the colonial origins of the United States of America.
34. Whitehead, *Process and Reality*, 343.

of the universe . . . [Divine agency] does not coerce, command, or hack its way into the creature [but] lures from inside a within in which we all, *pan*, always together, 'live, and move, and have our being' (Acts 17:28).[35]

Whitehead's secularization of the divine function can be borne out both in speculative cosmology and in political theory. What sort of political organization is implied by his processual, incarnational, panentheistic conception of God as a creature of Creativity like the rest of us? Certainly not a totalitarian dictatorship, whether of the communistic or fascistic type. Whitehead was, as Dombrowski emphasizes, a political liberal committed to deliberative democracy undergirded by a virtue ethic.[36] According to Dombrowski, while political liberalism remains compatible with a variety of comprehensive visions, Whitehead's cosmology "can offer metaphysical support for" it[37]

Is liberal democracy then the secularized transposition of process theology? I don't think it is that simple, at least not if we imagine the liberal individual as an independent substance and "society" as a mere aggregation of such substances, with democracy amounting to little more than the counting of individual votes for or against a prearranged set of representatives or legislative options, the terms of which are set in advance by formal legal procedures. While Dombrowski affirms the importance of individual rights, he also articulates a balanced process critique of abstract individualism *as well as* abstract collectivism, the latter of which reduces individuals to an overarching national, ethnic, or economic whole that they are commanded to serve.[38] Nonetheless, process thought involves a social conception of the universe: "We find ourselves in a buzzing world, amid a democracy of fellow creatures."[39] While I agree with Dombrowski that Whitehead's cosmology is compatible with his process reading of Rawlsian political theory, I see his metaphysical scheme as implying a no less democratic but, somewhat in contrast to liberal formalism, radically *personalist* political ontology. A Whiteheadian conception of the person diverges sharply from the deracinated unity of the Kantian transcendental ego. On Whitehead's account, our own self-consciousness as living personalities arises in the context of complex organic societies (i.e., human bodies and their sociocultural inheritances) that shelter nonsocial nexūs.[40] Within such nonsocial living

35. Keller, *Political Theology of the Earth*, 138.
36. Dombrowski, *Process Philosophy and Political Liberalism*, 156–57.
37. Dombrowski, *Process Philosophy and Political Liberalism*, 24.
38. Dombrowski, *Process Philosophy and Political Liberalism*, 42–43.
39. Dombrowski, *Process Philosophy and Political Liberalism*, 50.
40. Whitehead, *Process and Reality*, 107.

nexūs, which Whitehead suggests hover in the interstices of the brain,[41] the deep character of a person is transmitted from occasion to occasion, not as a simple unity (whether substantial or transcendental), but as a complex intersection of maximally intensified experience issuing from the harmonization of free originality and social canalization.[42] As there is no sharp line in Whitehead's account between the rational and the bestial, nonhuman animals with continuity of character are also persons (and thus moral *patients*), even if the creative intensity of human personality may be especially pronounced (to the point where moral *agency* becomes applicable).

Dombrowski argues cogently for a process interpretation of Rawls's method of reflective equilibrium, whereby we are counseled to bring our experience of particular beliefs into coherent balance with our theoretical reflection upon universal principles. But the reliance of this method upon the abstract thought experiment of an original position of deliberation behind a veil of ignorance risks privileging the rigidly formal over the creatively personal to such an extent that the latter comes to seem an impediment to rather than the principal strength of political liberalism. On Dombrowski's reading of Rawls, the deeper the political conflict, the higher the level of philosophical abstraction that is required to sort it out.[43] Clearly, however, in the real world passionate emotion easily overflows our capacity to abide by rational procedures. Further, as William James recognized in his reflections upon the social basis of moral psychology, "probably no one can make sacrifices for 'right,' without to some degree personifying the principle of right for which the sacrifice is made." Our conscience, in other words, is compelled not by formal principles but by a desire to be loved by an "ideal social self," that is, by "the true, the intimate, the ultimate" interpersonal judge: God, "the 'Great Companion.'"[44]

The process-inspired theory and praxis of public administration from Mary Parker Follett (1868–1933) would greatly contribute to fleshing out more deliberative and participatory forms of democracy that go beyond mere voting and parliamentary proceduralism in their concrete realization of power-sharing decision-making processes.[45] Follett invites experimentation with a novel method of human association beyond both market domination and political compromise that she called "integration":

---

41. Dombrowski, *Process Philosophy and Political Liberalism*, 105–6.
42. Dombrowski, *Process Philosophy and Political Liberalism*, 109.
43. Dombrowski, *Process Philosophy and Political Liberalism*, 159.
44. James, *Principles of Psychology*, 315–16.
45. See Stout and Staton, "Ontology of Process Philosophy."

> An individual as an abstraction does not meet another individual as an abstraction; it is always activity meeting activity . . . What happens when I meet another person for the first time? . . . I have different wants to integrate; you have different wants to integrate. Then there are your wants and my wants to be joined. But the process is not that I integrate my desires, you yours, and then we together unite the results; I often make my own integration through and by means of my integration with you.[46]

Follett, writing in the early 1920s, could observe the "disintegration" (also a creative force) of the German empire in 1918 "as a signal sign of advancing liberalism."[47] Unfortunately, raw emotion and power politics soon won out over abstract parliamentary procedure, the fragile constitutional order being no match for the competing ideological interests of a war ravaged, economically hamstrung nation. One wonders what may have transpired if liberals in Germany were able to apply Follett's administrative theory.

Whitehead may not agree with more philosophically idealist personalists on all points, but his intuition given condensed gnomic expression on the final two pages of *Process and Reality* concerning the intimate connection between human personality and the consequent nature of God[48] suggest a deeper consonance. For French personalists like Emmanuel Mounier (1905–1950), the political conflict and metaphysical confusion following the First World War called for something more than an uncritical endorsement of liberal democracy. He worried that the consumerism, individualism, and mass culture that flourished under and were even encouraged by liberal states made these polities especially vulnerable to totalitarian takeover, whether from the communist Left or fascist Right.[49] This is because on his view the abstract, formal definition of human freedom defended by liberal theorists could only function as a debasement of the true nature and moral value of the human person. Western liberals remain embarrassed by the deep moral roots of their own political values, namely the Biblical idea of the human being created in the image of God (Gen 1:27), believing instead that human rights originate in and are endowed by secular human institutions and associations. Personalists do not at all begrudge the development of human rights: witness Jacques Maritain's role in the drafting of the 1948 United Nations Universal Declaration. But they warn that a failure to affirm the truly divine value of persons leaves an inviting vacuum to be filled by

---

46. Follett, *Creative Experience*, 177.
47. Follett, *Creative Experience*, 178.
48. Whitehead, *Process and Reality*, 350.
49. Williams and Bengtsson, "Personalism"; Mounier, *Personalism*, ch. 5.

objectifying concepts of the human being, whether as *Volk* mystically identified with the *Führer*, as material-economic products in need of communist reeducation, or as hedonistic consumers enjoying a life of untrammeled private freedom in service of capital accumulation.

Dombrowksi notes the Rawlsian distinction between theoretical conceptions and moral ideals of human persons, insisting that "conceptions of the human person underdetermine moral theory" (e.g., Catholics all accept the *imago Dei* principle but vary dramatically in their political application of it, ranging from the personalism of Mounier and Maritain to Marxist liberation theology, to Opus Dei fascism, to political liberalism); as a result of this underdetermination, liberal democracies must remain neutral as regards "competing conceptions of the human person."[50] Of course, there are limits to liberal tolerance of such conceptions, namely that all parties no matter their metaphysics agree to mutually respect one another as rational agents and to fair decision-making procedures. But deeper than this sort of tolerance, and indeed grounding of the mutual respect required for the functioning of its institutions, is the metaphysical affirmation of *natural rights* rooted in the *imago Dei* principle or some similar spiritual source (rough translations of this principle, though obviously not equivalencies, can be found in nontheistic wisdom traditions, e.g., the Mahayana Buddhist concept of Buddha-nature/*tathagatagarbha*). Dombrowski[51] cites Rawls' footnote[52] wherein the latter affirms a source "established independently from social conventions and legal norms" that affirms "the concept of natural rights . . . assigned in the first instance to persons."

While it is true, as Charles Hartshorne often put it, that "a liberal is someone who knows that he or she is not God,"[53] it appears that Rawls himself ultimately holds individual rights to be inalienable, thus the human person inviolable, because we are created in God's image. Secular liberals may object that this sort of religious reasoning has no legitimate place in a pluralistic democratic society. The source of our rights to life and liberty must either be bracketed or institutionally constructed. But is such quietism or formalism sufficient to protect a democratic order from the threats it faces from the comprehensive doctrines motivating both left- and right-wing extremes? If one accepts Whitehead's secularization of the concept of God's function in the world, including his amendments to the traditional divine attributes of omnipotence and omniscience, I would argue the *imago*

---

50. Dombrowski, *Process Philosophy and Political Liberalism*, 15.
51. Dombrowski, *Process Philosophy and Political Liberalism*, 9–10.
52. Rawls, *Theory of Justice*, 442–43n30.
53. Dombrowski, *Process Philosophy and Political Liberalism*, 154.

Dei principle (or a similar spiritual principle from nontheistic traditions) enhances rather than pollutes public reason. If God is love rather than force and knows only as much as creativity allows, then "we do not make ourselves more like God by utterly rejecting [epistemic and ontic] anxiety."[54] To affirm that liberal political values stem from a spiritual source is not to impose one comprehensive doctrine in the face of a plurality of other reasonable doctrines, but simply to admit that there is no such thing as a neutral starting point for the derivation of such values. Liberals committed to individual rights and reasonable pluralism should be more forthright about the metaphysical grounds of their values. Whitehead's open and relational process theism provides an especially helpful guide in this respect. Liberals can also turn to personalists like Martin Buber[55] or Emmanuel Lévinas[56] for examples of how these values can be grounded in the experiential immediacy of face-to-face encounters, rather than in discursive theoretical arguments. Follett offers her own such vision:

> The essence of experience, the law of relation, is reciprocal freeing: here is 'the rock and substance of the human spirit.' . . . We are all rooted in that great unknown in which are the infinite latents of humanity. And these latents are evoked, called forth into visibility, summoned, by the action and reaction of one on the other. All human intercourse should be the evocation by each from the other of new forms undreamed of before, and all intercourse that is not evocation should be eschewed . . . The test of the validity of any social process is whether this is taking place—between one and another, between capital and labor, between nation and nation . . . To free the energies of the human spirit is the high potentiality of all human association.[57]

As Mounier has it, the nature of the human person cannot be systematized, nor its moral status reduced to the terms of any legal form or political program. It is not institutions that create our natural rights or freedom, but our freedom that creates (and destroys) institutions. The introduction to Mounier's *Personalism* (1952) resonates deeply with Whitehead's account of human self-consciousness (see footnotes):

> The person is not the most marvelous object in the world, nor anything else that we can know from the outside. It is the one

---

54. Dombrowski, *Process Philosophy and Political Liberalism*, 156; summarizing Malone-France, *Faith, Fallibility, and the Virtue of Anxiety*.

55. Buber, *I and Thou*.

56. Lévinas, *Totality and Infinity*.

57. Follett, *Creative Experience*, 303.

reality that we know, and that we are at the same time fashioning, from within. Present everywhere, it is *given* nowhere ... A fount of experience, springing into the world, it expresses itself by an incessant creation of situations, life-patterns and institutions. But the essence of the person, being indefinable, is never exhausted by its expression, nor subjected to anything by which it is conditioned. Nor is it definable as some internal substratum, as a substance lurking underneath our attitudes, an abstract principle of our overt behavior ... It is a living activity of self-creation, of communication and of attachment, that grasps and knows itself, in the act, as *the movement of becoming personal.* To this experience, no one can be conditioned or compelled.[58]

Whitehead could easily affirm this view of human experience as "the movement of becoming personal." In light of the personalist emphasis on indefinability, it is essential that the process liberal keep their abstract deliberations in the original position honest and realistic by refusing to stray from consideration of concrete experience, as Dombrowski himself affirms.[59]

Gaian Political Ecology

According to Richard Wolin, Schmitt was present at the University of Munich in 1921 when Max Weber delivered his famous lecture on "Science as a Vocation." On Wolin's reading,

> Schmitt agreed wholeheartedly with Weber's characterization of modernity as an 'iron cage': a world in which the corrosive powers of 'rationalization' and 'disenchantment' had precipitated a crisis of 'meaninglessness.'[60]

Bruno Latour (1947–2022) made a career as a sociologist of science, calling this myth of modernity into question. While it may be true that contemporary liberal societies are faced with something of a "meaning crisis"

---

58. Mounier, *Personalism*, 3 (italics original). Whitehead affirmed a reformed subjectivist principle that saw human experience as an exemplification of a more generic texture of experience pervading the cosmos: "Our datum is the actual world, including ourselves; and this actual world spreads itself for observation in the guise of the topic of our immediate experience" (Whitehead, *Process and Reality*, 4). "The body ... is only a peculiarly intimate bit of the world. Just as Descartes said, 'this body is mine'; so he should have said, 'this actual world is mine.' My process of 'being myself' is my origination from my possession of the world" (Whitehead, *Process and Reality*, 81).

59. Dombrowski, *Process Philosophy and Political Liberalism*, 14.

60. Wolin, "Cult of Carl Schmitt," 1.

(as cognitive scientist and philosopher John Vervaeke refers to it[61]), Latour argues compellingly that modern science has not, in fact, purified itself of religion nor disenchanted the world. In alignment with Whitehead's claim in *Science and the Modern World*[62] that "faith in the possibility of science . . . is an unconscious derivative from medieval theology," Latour reveals how the scientific worldview is more mixed up with religion than moderns like to admit: in the course of lengthy battles in the seventeenth century, science borrowed the traditional theological idea of "matter" to invent a "material world" governed by an overtly religious view of the nature of deterministic causation, wherein all the action is placed in the antecedent such that "it hardly matters . . . whether the antecedent is called an omnipotent Creator or omnipotent Causality."[63] In Latour's view, science did not so much disenchant the world as *learn to sing a different song*.[64] His task as sociologist was to disentangle the exact methods of the various sciences from the still too theological origin story of capital-S Science.

> We have known all this, of course, we who for a long time have been studying this curious obsession of the Moderns with deanimating the world in which they have nevertheless been causing unexpected and surprising agents to proliferate. We were well aware that the rationalizing style had no relationship with the sciences as they are practiced. This was even what had allowed me to assert, twenty-five years ago, that 'we have never been modern.'[65]

Whitehead similarly rejects the modern scientific image of nature as valueless, deterministic material that might be entirely subdued by human technologies. Latour shares and amplifies Whitehead's protest against "the bifurcation of nature," a protest first annunciated in *The Concept of Nature*.[66] The bifurcation of nature enforced by scientific materialism has led modern societies to deanimate the nonhuman natural world, deeming it little more than a collection of inert objects, and to overanimate the human, deeming it the sole possessor of subjectivity and creative freedom.[67]

---

61. Vervaeke Foundation, "What Is the Meaning Crisis?"
62. Whitehead, *Science and the Modern World*, 13.
63. Latour, *Facing Gaia*, 71. Dombrowski's neoclassical process theism leads him to an identical criticism of what, following Hartshorne, he calls "etiolatry," or worship of causes. Dombrowski, *Process Philosophy and Political Liberalism*, 44.
64. Latour, *Facing Gaia*, 72.
65. Latour, *Facing Gaia*, 72; referencing Latour, *We Have Never Been Modern*.
66. Whitehead, *Concept of Nature*, ch. 2.
67. Latour, *Facing Gaia*, 85.

In *We Have Never Been Modern*, Latour paints the picture this way: Modernity in its liberal and communist forms had a twin mission, "the double task of emancipation and domination."[68] The emancipatory task was political: to end exploitation of humans by humans. The task of domination was technoscientific: to become masters and possessors of nature. These two tasks depend upon one another, such that challenging the image of nature as raw material to be owned and reverse engineered to serve human purposes also challenges the liberatory project of modern politics.

Like Schmitt, Latour returns to Hobbes, but he draws a somewhat different lesson in light of the planetwide ecological mutation now undeniably underway (remember, as Schmitt says, "all historical knowledge is present knowledge"). Hobbes's *Leviathan* remains important to technoscientifically-minded moderns as a reminder of the inescapably entangled history of modern science, politics, and religion.[69] Natural science was not then and is not now purified of sociological and theological elements. Amid the seventeenth-century's religious wars and scientific revolution, Hobbes sought to achieve a lasting peace by replacing the "immortal god" invoked by various religious fundamentalists with the "mortal god" of the sovereign state. He drew up a treaty to be signed on the basis of a new metaphysics, one that distributed agency according to the new materialism. Among the agencies were an inert matter governed by mechanistic laws of nature known with scientific certainty, a society driven solely by the passion of interest, and a strictly controlled interpretation of the figurative language of the Bible. Hobbes sought to extract human society from the state of nature by means of a social contract. Latour's Gaian political ecology, arising at the terminal moment of the Cenozoic era, cannot but scramble Hobbes's early modern attempt to purify these categories. James Lovelock's concept of Gaia is a muddle, the exact opposite of Hobbes's Leviathan. Unlike "nature" or "the material world" as moderns had conceived of it, Gaia is not the inert background of human history but animate, vibrating underfoot, a proliferation of responsive nature-culture hybrids. Human beings, too, find themselves in quite a muddle. Social authority has become increasingly scattered and diffuse; science has become increasingly mixed up with technoindustrial capitalism; and the pope has found himself attempting to lay claim to ecology. Humanity has been overcome with political inertia just as what used to be called "matter" has come to life in the form of Gaia's reaction to our industrial provocations. In Latour's words:

---

68. Latour, *We Have Never Been Modern*, 10.
69. Latour, *Facing Gaia*, 147–49.

> We can no more indulge in the belief that the question of nature has been resolved, that religion is a thing of the past, that science offers an unquestionable certainty, that we can fool ourselves into believing that we know the driving forces that agitate humans or the goals of politics.[70]

From Latour's nonmodern perspective, neither "nature" nor "society" can survive the ecological mutation unscathed. The theater of modern history has been destroyed and must be reconstructed from the ground up. Gone is the passive stage, "nature," upon which the actors, "rational animals," have for so long waged their wars and signed their peace treaties. The Anthropos is no longer *in* nature, nor *outside of* nature. Latour heralds the coming of an entirely new kind of political animal, a novel form of political body. They are a people to come, the people of Gaia, agents of an impatient planet. That the supposedly incontestable category, "human," does not apply universally could not be made more evident than by the notion of "human-caused climate change." Responsibility for the climate catastrophe is obviously not evenly distributed among members of our species. Unfortunately, its effects will not be evenly distributed, either. Sea-level rise, food shortage, disease, and other disasters will disproportionately affect precisely those sectors of the world population that are least responsible for causing the catastrophe. Today climate change is perpetuated by certain industrialized sectors of the human population, that is, by a particular people (consumer-capitalists) summoned by a particular God: Mammon (i.e., the capitalist market). Gaia, now fully sensitive to the presence of the people of Mammon, is growing increasingly impatient with that presence.

Latour does not believe Gaia provides some sort of political magnet that might swiftly, as if by magic, unify us into a global people. Even climatology has become politically contested, not to mention the questions of who should pay for climate change mitigation or what to do about untold millions of climate refugees who are already seeking resettlement in the Global North. So far Gaia is more likely to divide than to unite us. Latour[71] compares Gaia to Jesus, who says: "Do not suppose that I have come to bring peace to the earth. I did not come to bring peace, but a sword" (Matt 10:34 NIV). In other words, Gaia is not here to reason with us but forces us to *decide* on fundamental cosmopolitical questions: "What people are you forming, with what cosmology, and on what territory?"[72] The need for such decision is putting

---

70. Latour, *Facing Gaia*, 150.
71. Latour, *Facing Gaia*, 144.
72. Latour, *Facing Gaia*, 143–44.

tremendous pressure on liberal political institutions, severely challenging their superficial universality and supposed metaphysical neutrality.

Latour finds it difficult to secularize "nature," since the Science claiming knowledge of it already has so much religion in it. Modern science is the inheritor of the Axial monotheisms' "counter-religiosity," i.e., their negligence of the ultimate concerns and absolute authorities affirmed by the plurality of other people's religions.[73] Like monotheism, which insisted on One True God, modern Science insisted on objective Nature. Latour argues that the Gaian muddle we find ourselves in calls for a more diplomatic pluralism that is "at once post-natural, post-human, and post-epistemological."[74] For Latour, secularizing the modern idea of nature means replacing it with the Lovelockean vision of Gaia. "With Gaia, Lovelock is asking us to believe not in a single Providence, but in as many Providences as there are organisms on Earth."[75]

Cosmopolitical Theology

Latour's Lovelockean secularization of nature finds its polar complement in Whitehead's secularization of God, a feat he accomplishes by divinizing the cosmos. God is not an omnipotent *dēmiurgós* above the world, but becomes "the judge arising out of the very nature of things, redeemer or goddess of mischief," an incarnate love providing "the particular providence for particular occasions."[76] Whitehead's is a *depth democracy*, deeper than most modern liberalisms and socialisms. He rejects modern anthropocentric individualism, totalitarian collectivism, and technoscientific materialism in favor of a cosmopolitical vision of each of us as individuals-in-community, or in Paul's terms, "members one of another" (Rom 12:5).

Whitehead's clearest articulation of the political relevance of his process philosophy occurs in the first "sociological" part of *Adventures of Ideas* (1933). He operates under the assumption that human civilization has profound cosmological and theological significance. The fact that civilized beings have emerged in the course of the evolution of the universe tells us something important about the nature and perhaps even the purpose of this universe. Whitehead's speculative hypothesis is that the rise of human civilization exemplifies the effective lure of ideas in the adventure of cosmogenesis. While the issue of novel ideas into practical consequences may be slow, the upward adventure of life on Earth testifies to their persuasive power.

---

73. Latour, *Facing Gaia*, 152.
74. Latour, *Facing Gaia*, 144.
75. Latour, *Facing Gaia*, 100.
76. Whitehead, *Process and Reality*, 351.

For Whitehead, history is far more than a collection of facts. Were we to be presented with the bare facts, devoid of any theoretical interpretation, we would have merely sound vibrations and the motion of colored shapes.[77] History is a story told in the present, often to serve as material for the formation of our own self-understanding and moral motivation. Further, our imaginations of history are inseparable from our metaphysical and cosmological presuppositions.

Whitehead's philosophical study of history reveals a general dichotomy, that between senseless, often violent, compulsion and consciously formulated aspiration. People "are driven by their thoughts as well as by the molecules in their bodies, by intelligence and by senseless forces."[78] Whitehead lists environmental conditions and the brute necessities of technological production (e.g., the socially transformative effects of coal, steam, electricity, and oil) among the senseless forces, and Axial religion and democratic equality as examples of intelligent aspiration.[79]

While Whitehead was himself a progressive liberal (he was involved in the women's rights and educational reform movements of his day), he cautions against the impetuous insistence upon imposing new ideas in the wrong season. Sometimes in the rush to implement social improvements, attendant complexities are ignored, and the attempt to remove an evil ends up releasing further evils.[80]

> A great idea is not to be conceived as merely waiting for enough good [people] to carry it into practical effect ... The ideal in the background is promoting the gradual growth of the requisite communal customs, adequate to sustain the load of its exemplification.[81]

Ideals may be well-intentioned, but due to the complexities of both nature and culture (and the complex interplay and overlap between them), the actual effects of their untimely implementation often far outrun any conscious intent.

Whitehead dwells on the institutions of human sacrifice and slavery long accepted among supposedly civilized peoples as examples of the power of inherited instinctive behaviors to override higher ideals. "Freedom" was almost a meaningless notion for earlier societies, such as the Egyptian or

77. Whitehead, *Adventures of Ideas*, 3.
78. Whitehead, *Adventures of Ideas*, 46.
79. Whitehead, *Adventures of Ideas*, 7.
80. Whitehead, *Adventures of Ideas*, 20.
81. Whitehead, *Adventures of Ideas*, 21.

Babylonian.[82] Whitehead tasks philosophy with seeking to consciously entertain and articulate those ultimate intuitions, obscured by habitual customs, that nonetheless guide human beings toward civilized order, that is, toward a world wherein the persuasion of free beings has emerged victorious over coercive force as the prime agent of history.[83]

Whitehead offers an updated rendering of Plato's suggestion in the *Republic*—that the ideal state would be run by philosopher-kings:

> Today, in an age of democracy, the kings are plain citizens pursuing their various avocations. There can be no successful democratic society till general education conveys a philosophic outlook.[84]

Such a philosophical outlook would marshal wisdom as a "modifying agency" upon the two streams that feed into our consciousness, that is, inherited instincts/routines and intellectual ferment/spontaneity.[85] Wisdom functions to coalesce these streams into some self-determining (i.e., free) and integrative judgment. Wise decision-making is limited by the limitations of our consciousness: "We do not initiate thought by an effort of self-consciousness. We find ourselves thinking, just as we find ourselves breathing and enjoying the sunset."[86] Nonetheless, few are willing to deny the role of knowledge and freedom in human life, though admittedly they tend to come in brief and unexpected flashes. Civilization advances, if it does, because wisdom kindles these flashes into the flame of virtue, which melts and makes malleable inherited customs to light the way toward juster futures.

Whitehead sees little evidence that humanity's inborn mental capacities have increased during the historical period. Rather, he points to "the outfit which the environment provides for the service of thought," that is, to the impact of various media technologies (e.g., literary and mathematical symbolisms, communication methods, etc.). The downside is that technologically mediated intelligence is liable to get locked into its favored abstractions, "[dismissing] the baffling aspects of things" in favor of the certainty provided by logical system. "Wisdom," Whitehead suggests,

> is persistent pursuit of the deeper understanding, ever confronting intellectual system with the importance of its omissions

---

82. Whitehead, *Adventures of Ideas*, 49.
83. Whitehead, *Adventures of Ideas*, 25.
84. Whitehead, *Adventures of Ideas*, 98.
85. Whitehead, *Adventures of Ideas*, 47.
86. Whitehead, *Adventures of Ideas*, 47.

... The folly of intelligent people, clear-headed and narrow-visioned, has precipitated many catastrophes.[87]

Writing in the early twentieth century, Whitehead thought that the economic sphere constituted the "most massive problem of human relationships."[88] He maintains high hopes for commerce, since ideally "it is the great example of intercourse in the way of persuasion," while "war, slavery, and governmental compulsion exemplify the reign of force."[89] But difficulties stand in the way of realizing the ideal. Whitehead decries the invention of corporate personhood, which he believes totally undermined classical liberal political philosophy, wherein freedom belonged to individual human beings, rather than to fictional corporate entities. He also questions the hazy notion of private property, which with the expansion of monopolistic corporate rule and competitive market dynamics has come to signify little more than "the will of the stronger."[90]

Whitehead admits that the classical liberal idea of "absolute individuals with absolute rights" is both metaphysically and politically inadequate: "The human being is inseparable from its environment in each occasion of its existence."[91] His process-relational understanding of reality has it that individuals, while they constitute the real loci of aesthetic and moral value, are nonetheless emergent from their social relations. Similarly, societies are shaped by the decisions of their members. The emergence of individuals from their social relations means that *custom* forms the instinctive basis of our behavior. But determination by custom is not total, as individuals are also free to emphasize novel intuitions of alternative courses of action, and to consciously agree to mutually beneficial transactions with one another. In the end,

> nothing is effective except massively coordinated inheritance. Sporadic spontaneity is composed of flashes mutually thwarting each other. Ideas have to be sustained, disentangled, diffused, and coordinated with the background. Finally they pass into exemplification in action.[92]

Obviously, much work remains to be done in nominally democratic societies to translate the ideal of freedom into the economic domain.

87. Whitehead, *Adventures of Ideas*, 47–48.
88. Whitehead, *Adventures of Ideas*, 62.
89. Whitehead, *Adventures of Ideas*, 63.
90. Whitehead, *Adventures of Ideas*, 63.
91. Whitehead, *Adventures of Ideas*, 63.
92. Whitehead, *Adventures of Ideas*, 64.

Whitehead traces the rise of the ideal of freedom in the history of human societies. Once a negligible fancy, it has gradually become the founding value of democratic societies. But he warns us against conceiving of freedom in purely cultural terms, as freedom of thought and speech, of the press, or of religious practice; that is, it is shortsighted to conceive of restraints on our freedom as stemming merely from the conflicting desires of other human beings. It is not our fellow human beings, but the "massive habits of physical nature" that constrain our freedom and set the scene for our suffering: "birth and death, heat, cold, hunger, separation, disease . . . all bring their quota to imprison the souls of women and of men."[93] Process-influenced political philosopher William Connolly recounts the catastrophic Lisbon earthquake in 1755, which provides as striking an example as we could ask for of what Whitehead means. Connolly describes how the senseless shock of this terrible natural disaster fed into the emergent Enlightenment mentality represented by Voltaire, who in his satirical book *Candide* (1759) ridiculed both traditional religious consolations as well as Leibniz's rationalist conception that we inhabit the best of all possible worlds. In Connolly's terms, the Lisbon earthquake, like all natural disasters, exemplifies the way "the human estate is both imbricated with and periodically over-matched by a cosmos composed of multiple, interacting force fields moving at different speeds."[94]

Rather than adopting an atheistic position in response to nature's vicissitudes and the fragility of human life, Whitehead affirms the role of Ideas in history, believing that we can directly intuit an eternal Good beyond all changing circumstances. Without such ideal intuitions to stir the soul toward higher life and deeper relation, he sees no reason why civilized beings should have come to exist in the first place.

Whitehead critiques the socioeconomic consequences of the Malthusian doctrine and the attendant Darwinian notion of "the survival of the fittest," which he believes are at best an oversimplification and, at worst, when compared with the recent facts of European history, demonstrably false. The doctrine naturalizes the inequalities of capitalist society, with its "fortunate few, and . . . semi-destitute many," forcing us to abandon "hope of improving the social system by a humane adjustment of social . . . conditions."[95] Connolly demonstrates the continued effect of these doctrines in his discussion of neoliberalism, an ideology seeking to use state power to inject market dynamics into all domains of human life.[96] The assumption is that the

---

93. Whitehead, *Adventures of Ideas*, 66.
94. Connolly, *Fragility of Things*, 7.
95. Whitehead, *Adventures of Ideas*, 73.
96. Connolly, *Fragility of Things*, 21.

self-organizing dynamics of the market will result in the best of all possible worlds. Neoliberalism is thus a kind of capitalist Panglossianism[97] (Pangloss is Voltaire's caricature of Leibniz).

Though Whitehead emphasizes the selective agency required for the evolution of civilization out of nonhuman nature, he rejects the prevalent dichotomy between humanity and nature. "Mankind is that factor in Nature which exhibits in its most intense form the plasticity of Nature."[98] Life itself is about more than mere survival, as living beings are constantly groping toward novelty and expansion of their powers. In the human sphere, it follows that "a policy of sociological defense is doomed to failure."[99] "In a live civilization, there is always an element of unrest. For sensitiveness to ideas means curiosity, adventure, change."[100]

Whitehead's speculative scheme extends some degree of subjectivity and self-creativity beyond the human to every creature in the cosmos, such that our sense of moral ideals—of what has value and how it ought to be treated—cannot be separated from our sense of scientific fact or ontology—of what there is and how it comes to exist:

> The basis of democracy is the common fact of value experience, as constituting the essential nature of each pulsation of actuality. Everything has some value for itself, for others, and for the whole. This characterizes the meaning of actuality. By reason of this character, constituting reality, the conception of morals arises. We have no right to deface the value experience which is the very essence of the universe. Existence, in its own nature, is the upholding of value intensity. Also no unit can separate itself from the others, and from the whole. And yet each unit exists in its own right. It upholds value intensity for itself, and this involves sharing value intensity with the universe. Everything that in any sense exists has two sides, namely, its individual self and its signification in the universe. Also either of these aspects is a factor in the other.[101]

Whitehead's politics is thus a cosmopolitics, a "democracy of fellow creatures" that calls humans to dramatically expand our circle of ethical concern not only to include all members of our own species, but also the nonhuman persons belonging to all species of life. Humans may still be unique at least

97. Connolly, *Fragility of Things*, 6.
98. Whitehead, *Adventures of Ideas*, 78.
99. Whitehead, *Adventures of Ideas*, 81.
100. Whitehead, *Adventures of Ideas*, 83.
101. Whitehead, *Modes of Thought*, 111.

in our heightened capacity for reflective abstraction[102] and self-consciousness of imaginative participation in the divine nature (by whatever name we refer to it), even if the divine image or Logos enlivens every creature in turn. "We, who are many, are one body in Christ," as Paul put it (Rom 12:4). Politics is thus not about the friend/enemy distinction, but a means of coming, through ongoing diplomatic encounter, to understand and sympathize with the values and experiences of others. The only reason any of us exist as we do today is because our ancestors found some way of coexisting, of composing common worlds together. Cosmopolitics is about finding a way to continue and deepen our existing relationality, and is thus a compositional, cocreative activity, as far from Hobbes's "war of all against all"(*Bellum omnium contra omnes*)as could be imagined.

Carl Schmitt links the historical development of liberal constitutionalism to a kind of Jeffersonian deism. Just as God was, as it were, *neutralized* by being conceived of as "wholly other" to the natural world, genuine sovereignty becomes neutralized by being equated with the constitutional order. Just as the deistic God cannot break the laws of nature, no authoritarian ruler can break the laws of the state. All miracles are banished from the world, and with them any concrete legal conception of the sovereign decision about when protection of the legal order requires an exception. The machine of the liberal state, like the machine of nature, is supposed to run automatically without exception. Eventually, even deism became unbelievable and was replaced either by a more pantheistic or atheistic immanence or by a positivist indifference to metaphysics as such. Political revolutionaries began to replace God with man, insisting that all that stood in the way of human freedom was traditional religious dogmas and the political forms these dogmas supported. As Friedrich Engels put it: "The essence of the state, as of religion, is mankind's fear of itself."[103]

Whitehead rejects both the deist's separation of an absolutely transcendent God from an entirely immanent nature as well as the positivist's pretense to have no need for metaphysics (all the positivist means when they deny metaphysics, Whitehead would say, is that they don't like having their own covert metaphysics criticized). Whitehead's processual panentheism invites us to imagine God as both beyond *and* within the world: "The world lives by its incarnation of God in itself," as he puts it.[104] In other words, Whitehead's secularization of the concept of God invites us to perceive every instance of worldly creativity—each actual occasion of

---

102. Whitehead, *Modes of Thought*, 102–3.
103. Quoted in Schmitt, *Political Theology*, 51; from *Schriften aus der Frühzeit*, 1920.
104. Whitehead, *Religion in the Making*, 149.

experience—as itself a miracle made in the image of God.[105] Such a vision, if it *commands* anything, calls us to attend reverentially to every creature and to each unique human person, who in innumerably diverse ways reflects and embodies the infinite love and wisdom of God.

Prospects for Process Liberalism

Carl Schmitt's *Political Theology* climaxes with his turn to the book's principle protagonist, the Catholic counterrevolutionary political theologian Juan Donoso Cortés. Donoso began his life as a liberal diplomat advocating for constitutional monarchy, but gradually grew more conservative as Europe's political situation grew more chaotic. The revolutions of 1848 marked his definitive turn away from liberalism toward Catholic dictatorship. Schmitt praises Donoso's intense consciousness of "the metaphysical kernel of all politics."[106] Just as the liberal positivists could not grasp the significance of the personal element in decisionist concepts of state sovereignty, Donoso could not grasp the scientism shaping their mechanistic conceptions of political order. His political and cosmological imagination remained resolutely medieval.

While Donoso's love of all things medieval led some to consider him a product of Romanticism, Schmitt insists that this is a reductive misreading. Schmitt sees Romantics, like liberals, as too easily satisfied with endless conversation and at best with merely aesthetic resolutions.[107] Donoso and other counterrevolutionary Catholic thinkers argued, like Schmitt, that the times demanded a firm decision. Neither the syntheses of Hegelian dialects nor the evolving potencies of Schellingian *Naturphilosophie* were adequate to the moral disjunction—the either/or—that Donoso insisted upon. Donoso rejected "the strange pantheistic confusion" he perceived in the German idealists. For the decisionists, there can be no higher third or complex identity of identity and difference, no mutual immanence between the soul, the world, and God. It is either the omnipotent Being of the traditional Catholic God, or the abyss of nihilism; either good or evil, life or death.

Schmitt's claim that "Every political idea in one way or another takes a position on the nature of man"[108] is difficult to dispute. Are we good or sinful by nature? This decisive issue, on Schmitt's reading, can only be clouded by educational or economic explanations, the terms in which liberals and

---

105. Whitehead, *Process and Reality*, 85.
106. Schmitt, *Political Theology*, 51.
107. See Schmitt, *Political Romanticism*, 139.
108. Schmitt, *Political Theology*, 56.

socialists may prefer to discuss the matter. Fichte, for example, saw the state as little more than a tyrannical "educational factory," while Marx just denied outright that humanity has a fixed nature, since we are molded always by the socioeconomic conditions of a given historical epoch. In general, the atheistic anarchists insisted that humanity is basically good, and that all evil stems from theology or the state authority it justifies. Donoso, predictably, bases his political theology on an anthropology of original sin: "Had God not become man, the reptile that my foot tramples would have been less contemptuous than a human being."[109] He is so convinced of the utter depravity of human nature, the stupidity of the masses and the vanity of their leaders, and the near complete disaster of history that even Schmitt recoils from Donoso's pessimism, seeking a more doctrinal view of sin as an injury that can be repaired.

Schmitt relays Donoso's mid-nineteenth-century apocalyptic conviction that "the bloody decisive battle" between Catholicism and atheist socialism had arrived.[110] Donoso disdained bourgeois liberalism precisely because it shrunk from decisiveness in the face of this battle, retreating instead into the evasiveness of everlasting discussion. In Schmitt's view, "A class that shifts all political activity onto the plane of conversation in the press and in parliament is no match for social conflict."[111] Schmitt then enumerates the "curious contradictions of liberalism" as he perceived them during the Weimar period:

> Although the liberal bourgeoisie wanted a god, its god could not become active; it wanted a monarch, but he had to be powerless; it demanded freedom and equality but limited voting rights to the propertied classes in order to ensure the influence of education and property on legislation, as if education and property entitled that class to repress the poor and uneducated; it abolished the aristocracy of blood and family but permitted the impudent rule of the moneyed aristocracy, the most ignorant and the most ordinary form of an aristocracy; it wanted neither the sovereignty of the king nor that of the people. What did it actually want?[112]

While some liberal theorists tried to construe this metaphysical indecisiveness as an expression of the organic life of a pluralistic democratic society, these contradictions contributed to liberalism's growing irrelevance as

---

109. Quoted in Schmitt, *Political Theology*, 58.
110. Schmitt, *Political Theology*, 59.
111. Schmitt, *Political Theology*, 59.
112. Schmitt, *Political Theology*, 60.

communist and fascist extremes vied for total power over the German state. Since Schmitt, like Donoso, accepted that the idea of the divine right of kings had become incredible, he did not reject democracy but sought to anoint a demagogue to corral the will of the people in devotion to the sovereign *Führer*. The secular liberal miracle of truth emerging naturally from free speech and a free press did not occur. Instead, Hitler harnessed the new psychotechnology of radio—the *Volksempfänger* or "people's receiver"[113]— and raised an army of committed national socialists. In a state of emergency, faced with the existential threat of what he perceived to be radical evil, Schmitt sought legal justification for fascism. The choice, as he saw it, was anarchy or authority, and he was decisive. The Nazi projection of radical evil onto a perceived enemy motivated the Holocaust, perhaps the most singular and systematic evil committed in all human history.

Fortunately, Schmitt's is not only a forced but a false choice. As we've seen, on Dombrowski's reading,[114] Rawlsian political liberalism must be distinguished from liberalism as a comprehensive metaphysical doctrine, the latter being just one among a plurality of potentially reasonable comprehensive doctrines (some theological, others not). Politics is thus not the place to debate human nature or other matters of ultimate concern, but rather an arena wherein reasonable, rational agents adhering to varying comprehensive doctrines can nonetheless agree on a fair decision-making procedure that respects the equal rights of all to life and liberty (i.e., "the right is prior to the good"). At the same time, and contrary to Schmitt's caricature of liberalism, Dombrowski shows how Rawls did not seek to entirely purify political theory of the personal, but rather emphasized that rights arise precisely from the mutual recognition of moral personhood in and by each member of society, independently of any linguistic convention or legal procedure. Despite first appearances, Rawls' theory of justice is, on his own admission, rooted in some version of natural rights theory[115] and perhaps ultimately even in some version of the *imago Dei* principle.[116]

In place of any pretense to positivist neutrality, the core of my argument is that process liberals are better positioned to admit and to rationally defend the metaphysical grounds of their political values than Rawls, who remained something of a fideist.[117] As Whitehead himself warned,

---

113. Meier, "Affordable Radio." For a Whiteheadian look at the metaphysical implications of twenty-first-century media technologies, see Segall, "Whitehead and Media Ecology."

114. Dombrowski, *Process Philosophy and Political Liberalism*, 21.

115. Dombrowski, *Process Philosophy and Political Liberalism*, 8–10.

116. Dombrowski, *Process Philosophy and Political Liberalism*, 3.

117. Dombrowski, *Process Philosophy and Political Liberalism*, 28.

liberalism without metaphysics loses its intelligible justification.[118] I agree wholeheartedly with Dombrowski that "the fact that [political liberalism] either encourages or requires [metaphysical views] should be more widely known."[119] I also accept that in a pluralistic society the political arena as such is not the place to debate the ultimate nature of reality, with the important exception that the liberal ideal of mutual respect among equals presupposes the spiritual ground of human personhood (as the image of a loving God, or Buddha-nature, etc.). Whitehead did not hold it to be possible, nor desirable, for those of diverse comprehensive doctrines to agree on all the details of their views. But he did believe that it was possible, despite differences in sympathetic intuitions and stresses on various metaphysical insights, "to reach a general agreement as to those elements, in intimate human experience and in general history, which we select to exemplify that ultimate theme of the divine immanence."[120] That human persons are divinely endowed with inalienable rights to life and liberty (and divinely expected to respect these rights in others) is one such element, essential for the healthy functioning of any liberal political project.

As Dombrowski makes clear, a Rawlsian process liberalism is decisive that democratic values require the just economic distribution of all basic goods within a society: "formal liberties like freedom of speech do not amount to much if there is not also material freedom from hunger."[121] Process liberalism is thus decisive in its rejection of neoliberal capitalism as a system predicated upon injustice and "the curse of money"; but it is just as decisive in its rejection of centralized communism as a system insensitive to the democratic rights of individuals.[122] In addition to moving beyond both neoliberal capitalism and state communism, process liberalism implies an expansion of the narrowly anthropocentric confines of modern political theories to embrace a cosmopolitical "democracy of fellow creatures." Finally, process liberals can decisively affirm that in the self-consciousness of our own freedom is revealed also the *parousia* of an all-loving God: "For the kingdom of heaven is with us today."[123]

---

118. Whitehead, *Adventures of Ideas*, 36.
119. Dombrowski, *Process Philosophy and Political Liberalism*, 72.
120. Whitehead, *Adventures of Ideas*, 161.
121. Dombrowski, *Process Philosophy and Political Liberalism*, 136.
122. Dombrowski, *Process Philosophy and Political Liberalism*, 137, 144.
123. Whitehead, *Process and Reality*, 351.

Bibliography

Buber, Martin. *I and Thou*. Translated by Ronald Gregor Smith. Bloomsbury Revelations. London: Bloomsbury Academic, 2013.

Connolly, William. *The Fragility of Things: Self-Organizing Processes, Neoliberal Fantasies, and Democratic Activism*. Durham: Duke University Press, 2013.

Dombrowski, Daniel A. *Process Philosophy and Political Liberalism: Rawls, Whitehead, Hartshorne*. Edinburgh: Edinburgh University Press, 2021.

Follett, Mary Parker. *Creative Experience*. New York: Longmans, Green., 1924.

Hogue, Michael S. *American Immanence: Democracy for an Uncertain World*. Insurrections: Critical Studies in Religion, Politics, and Culture. New York: Columbia University Press, 2018.

James, William. *The Principles of Psychology*. American Science Series. New York: Holt, 1890.

Keller, Catherine. *Political Theology of the Earth: Our Planetary Emergency and the Struggle for a New Public*. Insurrections: Critical Studies in Religion, Politics, and Culture. New York: Columbia University Press, 2018.

Kelsen, Hans. *Das Problem der Souveränität und die Theorie des Völkerrechts: Beitrag zu einer reinen Rechtslehre*. Tübingen: Mohr Siebeck, 1920.

Kierkegaard, Søren. *Repetition and Philosophical Crumbs*. Translated by M. G. Piety. Oxford's World's Classics. Oxford: Oxford University Press, 2009.

Krabbe, Hugo. *Die moderne Staats-Idee*. Belgium: Scientia, 1919.

Latour, Bruno. *Facing Gaia: Eight Lectures on the New Climatic Regime*. Translated by Catherine Porter. Cambridge: Polity, 2017.

———. *We Have Never Been Modern*. Translated by Catherine Porter. Cambridge: Harvard University Press, 1993.

Lévinas, Emmanuel. *Totality and Infinity: An Essay on Exteriority*. Translated by Alphonso Lingis. Martinus Nijhoff Philosophy Texts. Dordrecht: Kluwer Academic, 1979.

Malone-France, Derek. *Faith, Fallibility, and the Virtue of Anxiety*. New York: Palgrave Macmillan, 2012.

Meier, Allison C. "An Affordable Radio Brought Nazi Propaganda Home." In *JSTOR Daily*. Politics and History. (2018): https://daily.jstor.org/an-affordable-radio-brought-nazi-propaganda-home/.

Mounier, Emmanuel. *Personalism*. Translated by Philip Mairet. Notre Dame: University of Notre Dame Press, 1952.

Rawls, John. *Political Liberalism*. Exp. ed. The John Dewey Essays in Philosophy 4. New York: Columbia University Press, 1993.

———. *A Theory of Justice*. Rev. ed. Cambridge: Belknap, 1999.

Schmitt, Carl. "The Age of Neutralizations and Depoliticizations (1929)." *Telos* 1993 (96) 130-42.

———. *Ex Captivitate Salus: Experiences, 1945-47*. Edited by Andres Kalyvac and Federico Finchelstein. Translated by Matthew Hannah. Cambridge: Polity, 2017.

———. *Political Theology: Four Chapters on the Concept of Sovereignty*. Edited and translated by George Schwab. 1934. Reprint, with a new foreword by Tracy B. Strong. Chicago: University of Chicago Press, 2005.

———. *Political Romanticism*. Translated by Guy Oakes. Studies in Contemporary German Social Thought. Cambridge: MIT Press, 1986.

Segall, Matthew T. "The Urgency of Social Threefolding in a World Still at War With Itself." *Cosmos and History: The Journal of Natural and Social Philosophy* 19.1 (2023) 229–48. https://cosmosandhistory.org/index.php/journal/article/view/1069.

———. "Whitehead and Media Ecology: Toward a Communicative Cosmos." *Process Studies* 48.2 (2019) 239–53.

Stout, Margaret, and Carrie M. Staton. "The Ontology of Process Philosophy in Follett's Administrative Theory." *Administrative Theory & Praxis* 33.2 (2011) 268–92.

Vervaeke Foundation. "What Is the Meaning Crisis?" Web page. https://vervaekefoundation.org/what-is-the-meaning-crisis/.

Whitehead, Alfred North. *Adventures of Ideas*. 1st Free Press paperback ed. New York: Free Press, 1967.

———. *Modes of Thought*. 1st Free Press Paperback ed. New York: Free Press, 1968.

———. *Process and Reality*. Edited by David Ray Griffin and Donald W. Sherburne. Corrected ed. New York: Free Press, 1979.

———. *Religion in the Making: Lowell Lectures, 1926*. 1st paperback ed. Cambridge: Cambridge University Press, 2011.

———. *Science and the Modern World*. Lowell Institute Lectures 1925. New York: Free Press, 1967.

Williams, Thomas D., and Jan Olof Bengtsson. "Personalism." In *The Stanford Encyclopedia of Philosophy* (Summer 2022 Edition). Edited by Edward N. Zalta: https://plato.stanford.edu/archives/sum2022/entries/personalism/.

Wolin, Richard. "The Cult of Carl Schmitt." *Liberties* 3.1 (2022).

Wordsworth, William. *The Prelude, or Growth of a Poet's Mind*. 2nd ed., corrected by Stephen Gill. Oxford Paperbacks. Oxford: Oxford University Press, 1970.

8

Prehending Political Potentials

Reconstituting American Liberal Democracy

Timothy C. Murphy

A long with the other chapters in this edited collection, this chapter responds to the original conference theme: "Power and the God of Love." It may therefore be surprising to see a chapter dedicated to doing what is, in effect, a political science analysis. Some may approach this topic from the mindset of the twentieth-century Christian Realist Reinhold Niebuhr, who said that love has no business in the realm of politics, which is instead about balances of power. However, we can also recall that as the public theologian Cornel West has famously stated, "Justice is what love looks like in public."[1] Having healthy systems that respond to people's needs, and give them opportunities to experience their agency and collaborate with others, help make space for the possibility of justice in our world. Over millennia, different political systems have been tried, and of the options thus far felt, some version of democracy comes closest to the initial aim of this justice-love in public. However, not all democracies are equal, as some are more responsive, some less so, and some are stuck in dysfunctional patterns that diminish the potential for just policies to be implemented, which are needed to benefit people's quality of life, moving them to not simply live, or live well, but live better.[2]

To begin with an understated lament, the political system of the United States is somewhat dysfunctional. One does not need to do academic research to know this is true. All it takes is to read the news and observe

---

1. West, "Justice Is What Love Looks Like in Public."
2. Whitehead, *The Function of Reason*, 8.

the results.[3] Two-party systems are supposed to prevent extremists from gaining political power by forcing parties to have crossover appeal. This compromise has unraveled, and the United States has one of its two major political parties facing rapid decline in its commitments to democracy and representation of the people.

While the US system is designed to thwart despots from concentrating power, currently federal election outcomes do not lead to the resolution of policy debates, resulting in the gradual decline in popular trust in democratic systems to solve problems. Once officials are in power or are reelected, they are largely unable to implement their political platforms. In 2021 and 2022, there was, at least formally, unified control of Congress and the presidency by the Democratic Party. While they achieved some of their policy objectives, few if any people would argue that they held a consistent, governing, and working majority. After the 2022 US midterm elections concluded, control of the federal government once again became divided, resulting in renewed gridlock. All but the most basic laws concerning government operation and funding have become next to impossible to pass. Even must-pass legislation such as keeping the government open and raising the debt ceiling to pay for already-existing debt obligations have become contentious.

Any substantive policy changes are now in reality deferred until after the 2024 election. However, that election itself does not guarantee an outcome that will result in a working majority. Eras of unified political control are few and far between. Since the end of 2010, there were only four years where one party held both chambers of Congress as well as the presidency. During the brief time frame of Republican unified control in 2017 and 2018, the most significant piece of legislation was a tax cut in 2017. Regardless of one's ideological commitments and instincts on whether that was a compelling use of political power, those in power were not able to pass any other substantive legislation to demonstrate their political priorities or why they should remain in office. During the 2021 and 2022 legislative session with unified Democratic control, the United States saw more legislative activity. However, ambitious policy goals were limited to what could get through the Senate. For well over a decade, most major policy challenges in US society have been deferred or tweaked along the margins since then. This impasse would include issues that have had overwhelming popular majorities at one time or another, including reforming the system of immigration since the mid-2000s, making direct financial assistance to families with children permanent in 2021, reforming the criminal justice system since the mid-2010s, increasing the minimum wage since 2009, and addressing climate change

3. Porter, "Threat to U.S. Democracy."

since the mid-1990s. However, the system does not readily respond to these popular majorities, because they do not result in political majorities, and the political majorities that are created cannot decisively exercise political power. If you believe as I do that our political system needs to address challenges in our society in a timely manner, this is a major problem. The United States' political system is almost perfectly designed for gridlock.

A second problem is one that can be harder to see, but it has to do with how unrepresentative the United States' voting system is. The results do not reflect the actual will of the people in terms of who is elected. Most people are familiar with this situation in terms of gerrymandering. For example, I currently live in the state of Indiana. It is a relatively conservative state, demonstrated by how it was the first to ban by legislation practically all access to abortion in the summer of 2022, despite ongoing court challenges. No one should consider Indiana a purple or swing state. By popular vote, it is more of a 55–45 state, with Republicans significantly outnumbering Democrats in registration and voter preferences. It is reasonable to expect Republicans to have a working majority most of the time. But when you look at its assembly and senate, that ten-point spread becomes far more skewed. As of the most recent election, representatives in those two houses are 70 percent and 80 percent Republican, respectively.[4] So while there is a strong working majority, it does not reflect the will of the population in general. Bills like the abortion ban would not likely have passed if Indiana's assembly and house more accurately reflected the political preferences of the state. Without an option to vote by popular referendum in Indiana, the popular majority was unable to stop legislation that it opposed.[5]

After every decennial census, both the federal government and state governments reallocate their distribution of legislative seats. Federally, some states lose seats in the House of Representatives while some gain them. No state can have less than one representative in this house with no upper cap. Whether a state gains, loses, or keeps the same number of seats, the locations of those seats are adjusted, most often by those in political power. Because there are those in power who have an incentive to maintain their power, and because of the advancement of computer models predicting how people will vote, legislators have become increasingly sophisticated in how seats are divided spatially.

This power can have major consequences. For instance, the 2021 redistricting of Indiana's state senate was greatly impacted by partisan

---

4. Wikipedia, s.v. "Indiana General Assembly."

5. Kansas is another conservative state that is somewhat unrepresentative in its legislative configuration, but it had the option for popular referendums, which is how abortion access was protected there at that time.

gerrymandering. I live in Allen County, with a population of around 390,000 people, with the city of Fort Wayne lying at its center with a population of about 270,000. Based on that population, Allen County was entitled to more than one senate seat. Fort Wayne itself could have received two Senate representatives. However, four seats were created during 2021 redistricting, dividing up Fort Wayne into four pieces and assigning them to senate districts with outlying areas of the county and even surrounding rural counties.[6] Based on where I live in Fort Wayne proper, the result is that I reside within two miles of two other senate districts, with parts of my own district extending over fifty miles away to the south. In this way, Allen County is left with 100 percent Republican representation despite that not reflecting the collective votes of the county.

Situations like this one are not exclusive to Indiana. Other states have similar situations with unfairly allocated seats, such as Nashville, Tennessee, which used to have one federal House of Representatives seat for the city. However, since the most recent redistricting process was completed, Nashville was redrawn from one Democratic seat into three Republican-leaning districts.[7] This issue is not exclusive to one party, either. In Maryland, despite a Republican receiving over one-third of the votes for governor, in both legislative chambers, the Republican Party received less than 28% of the seats. It was worse for federal representation, where districts are larger and easier to manipulate by gerrymandering. Despite an approximate 2:1 ratio between Democrats and Republicans statewide in Maryland, the federal House of Representatives results were an 8:1 ratio.[8] In Allen County, Democrats are underrepresented, while in Maryland, Republicans are underrepresented. The fact that both parties are overrepresented elsewhere in the country does not make up for the lack of opportunity for millions of citizens to have representatives that reflect their voting priorities. Officials in Maryland have no interest in what I have to say any more than Allen County officials are interested in receiving a call or visit on an issue of concern from a conservative in Maryland.

A third problem is that single-district, first-past-the-post voting systems lend themselves to a binary, two-party system. Whoever receives the most votes wins, which structurally creates strong disincentives for alternative parties or candidates at federal and state levels. A candidate can win with a simple plurality even if the majority of the population would prefer

6. "2021 Indiana Senate Districts."

7. Gainey, "GOP Redraws Nashville from 1 Democratic District into 3 Republican-Leaning Districts."

8. "Maryland Election Results."

someone else. If one votes for a third- or fourth-party candidate, there is rarely a reasonable chance that this candidate can win. For instance, an ideological Leftist may find the Democratic candidate too beholden to corporate interests and feel compelled to vote for a Green Party or Democratic Socialist option if available. However, if they don't have a chance to succeed, this effectively benefits the ideologically opposite party, which is all too glad to see more liberal votes be split among multiple candidates. One only has to recall the 2000 presidential election result in Florida vis-à-vis Ralph Nader, who was blamed for the loss of Al Gore there, with 100% of the Electoral College results eventually going to George W. Bush.[9] From that third-party voter's perspective, a refusal to vote for a binary lesser-evil option results in the greater evil benefiting. Thus, third- and fourth-party candidates are strongly discouraged from running or are blamed for unfavorable plurality results. A similar dynamic is brewing ahead of the 2024 US Senate election in Arizona, which risks a three-way contest with liberal-and-moderate-leaning voters splitting votes between a Democratic candidate and the current senator, Kyrsten Sinema, the former Democrat who may run as an independent. Third and fourth voting options effectively benefits one's ideological opponents in competitive elections for such single-member, first-past-the-post elections.

What I want to attempt is to review some alternative formulations of representative liberal democracies. There are many problems within the United States that need addressing, and it would be possible to make what I believe are compelling arguments around particular policies for the United States and why certain laws should be passed. However, that would move beyond the scope of what I aim to do here. To make this analysis manageable, I need as process philosophy would say, a principle of limitation. Therefore, I will not be focusing on any particular economic, social, or environmental policy recommendations, regardless of how much I personally believe they are urgently needed. Rather, I want to exclusively examine how the structural limitations of America's political system can be reconfigured. I will do so by comparing it to other existing liberal democratic models for future potential incorporation. For the sake of my argument here, these options need to be actual rather than theoretical models. I have a few reasons for this choice.

Process philosophy distinguishes between what we can call pure possibilities and real potentials. The former may not have ever been instantiated in a particular occasion or event. While they are potentials for future occasions, they are often not actualizable in the moment, because they lack

9. Dao, "2000 Elections."

a relevant world in which to be felt. There may be a world where they can transition from pure possibilities to real potentials, but it is not in this moment. On the other hand, real potentials are readily available for other occasions to prehend and be actualized in a new way. While they may also be abstract, they are more easily felt and thus made concrete. They are present in actual entities that can be prehended and find their way into the formation of new occasions or events.

The same is true for political systems. Some systems exist, and some do not. Some can be seen and felt in our world, and some have never existed before, even if they are an abstract possibility in an unknown future. There may be pure possibilities of revolutionary political systems like biodemocracy, anarchosocialism, a pure direct democracy, or some other model that would serve as a radical breaking in of novelty, expanding the range of what is possible. A few of these alternatives have existed in a localized way with small-scale communities, communes, or villages. Others have existed as radical experiments that have endured for a brief temporal moment, but have collapsed within a generation, if not sooner. The most innovated political systems can only be found on a piece of paper or as an idea in a thinker's mind. They are possibilities, true, but they do not exist on a scale of countries and states and generations. For my purposes here, it is not enough that something is interesting; it needs to be available as a potential to be actualized on the time frame and scope of political societies as they currently are configured. It is not sufficient to say that a classless system of voluntary cooperation should exist; what matters is whether it can exist in an imminent time-horizon. The best evidence for that potential is to see whether it *does* exist anywhere. If not, I will exclude it as an option. It is not a real potential in the same way that other models can be prehended around the world. Therefore, I will limit myself to existing democracies that use *some* form of representation.[10]

To prehend is to feel one's relevant world, positively or negatively, for potential incorporation as a novel event. That is what I aim to do here, and it is analogous to what the Founding Fathers did when they developed the current political system of the United States. They prehended the data that was available to them. One of the biggest differences is that when the

---

10. For those particularly interested in more a more direct democracy option, the closest example would be Switzerland, which is a hybrid between direct democracy and representative democracy. In that system, any law can be challenged through a popular referendum if a sufficient number of people petition to have it brought up for consideration. While that may be an option at a statewide level, given that Switzerland's population is closer to the size of a US state at 8.7 million, it would be very difficult to implement for a population of over 330 million.

United States' constitutional system was being designed, its creators had limited options from which to draw. Throughout the world, there were no full democracies at a state level. Thus, the potentials from which they could positively prehend were *narrow* compared to today. The Founding Fathers incorporated elements from the British parliament, sought lessons from the records of the Roman Republic and its fall, and admired city-state-sized Athenian democracy. They drew from the writings of political philosophers, most famously John Locke. They saw the Haudenosaunee Confederacy and other Native governments as positive examples of federalism, which helped them envision the possibility of governing a large geographic area.[11] For both historical and aristocratic reasons, they were keenly aware of the risk of democracy falling into despotism and sought to reduce those risks by creating multiple checks and balances within the federal system and between federal and state governments. Their plan has been in place now, with some modifications, for over 230 years. Thanks to their efforts, the United States is lauded as the oldest continually existing constitutional democracy in the world. However, there is a negative corollary to this longevity. It means that what they designed through imitation and inspiration, not to mention political compromise, had the least to work with when it was formulated.

In the intervening two centuries, multiple other models and examples of durable representative democratic systems have emerged. Today, there are dozens of vibrant liberal democracies in existence. Some of them are more stable than others. While the United States is the oldest example of a representative democratic system, no new democracy takes the United States' system as the model to emulate. This lack of emulation is true even when US representatives have been in charge of the process of forming a democratic system. This is the case in such disparate examples as post-war Germany, Japan, or Iraq. Therefore, it is not simply the matter of others having some anti-US bias. Even when Americans are in charge, they do not use our presidential system with single-member congressional districts and first-past-the-post winner-take-all seats as the primary model to replicate.

While we can look anecdotally at stable, just, and enduring systems in the news or our lived experience, it helps to have a metric to rank countries based on their democratic bona fides. The Democracy Index evaluates countries based on expert assessments of several categories: electoral process and pluralism, civil liberties, functioning of government, political participation, and political culture.[12] It then lists countries as full democracies, partial democracies, or autocracies. In 2021, the top ten countries that each were

11. Little, "Native American Government"; Cottier, "How Native Americans"; and Grindle and Johansen, *Exemplar of Liberty*.
12. Wikipedia, s.v. "Democracy Index."

ranked as full democracies were as follows: Norway, New Zealand, Finland, Sweden, Iceland, Denmark, Ireland, Taiwan, Australia, and Switzerland.[13] By contrast, the United States is ranked as a flawed democracy. When we examine these top-performing countries, it is possible to notice that these full democracies have a few things in common.

By and large, these countries have parliamentary systems instead of presidential systems, meaning that the executive power grows out of the legislative wing rather than being a fully separate branch of government. This is in the form of a prime minister, who runs the government, and a separate head of state, who holds primarily ceremonial duties. In the United States, control of Congress and the presidency are often held by different parties as noted earlier. Both can declare a mandate from those who elected them. But in a parliamentary system, the designed paralysis found in the United States is absent. One other risk that they avoid is the tendency of presidential systems to slide towards autocracy. Presidents or their equivalents around the world have often moved into becoming strongmen or autocrats. Some of the weaker-performing formal democracies of Central America and central Africa hold such presidential systems, as does Russia. Alternatively, prime ministers are less known to centralize power around their person; they are more dispensable.

A second similarity of successful democracies is that instead of having single winner-take-all districts for their legislatures, they allocate representatives proportionally. Some modify this slightly with what is called a mixed-proportional system, which combines first-past-the-post representation with additional seats allocated to give a proportional final result. By doing so, they encourage multiparty systems. Parties that surpass a certain threshold, such as 5 percent, automatically receive seats and representation. A winning party with a majority or a ruling coalition can govern so long as they maintain a working majority. By definition, they can pass the legislation their respective parties ran and won on. If they no longer have a governing majority, the government falls, new elections are called, and a new prime minister is installed. There is no gridlock by design.

The second benefit of either proportional or mixed-proportional voting is that it solves not just the effect but even the incentive of gerrymandering. Some states within the USA, like California, have tried to reduce the political influence that leads to gerrymandering by forming independent commissions. Such commissions are an improvement over partisans drawing boundaries, but they have structural limits. They cannot fix the geographic sorting or overconcentration of voters of a party in a single area,

---

13. *Economist Intelligence Unit*, "Democracy Index 2021."

which leads to votes being effectively wasted. But a proportional system is a more systemic solution, because there are no wasted votes. Even the best independent commission cannot remedy the natural sorting of people into affinity communities and geographic proximity. A proportional system or one similar to it results in there being no incentive to gerrymander districts. This is because gerrymandering does not affect the partisan composition of the legislature at all. The percentage of people who vote for a party will be that party's percentage of the seats, regardless of where the votes came from.

Another observed similarity of successsful representative democracies is that these top-performing states tend to have unicameral instead of bicameral legislative bodies, resulting in fewer obstacles for legislation to pass. Where there is a second legislative body, its role is one of review or perhaps delay of legislation. It can slow down and help improve hastily written bills, but it cannot prevent bills from coming to a vote like the United States Senate can. Examples of bicameral systems with review-only would be the United Kingdom's House of Lords or Canada's Senate. Both the United Kingdom and Canada are still ranked below the top-functioning democracies, in part because of their first-past-the-post seats. However, for all their challenges, they still function better than the United States on account of having one less roadblock for legislation.

Problems in the United States such as legislative gridlock, gerrymandering, and a partisan duopoly would be resolved with these political features found elsewhere. However, they would need to be done in conjunction. Only a portion of these modifications could result in something akin to the democracy in India, which is a multiparty, parliamentary system but utilizes first-past-the-post voting with single-member districts in the lower house. In some ways, this is the worst of both worlds, as it allows for almost unfettered passage of legislation that is not representative of the broader population. For instance, the Bharatiya Janata Party (BJP), a Hindu nationalist party, holds an absolute majority despite only receiving 37 percent of the vote in the 2019 general election.[14]

One concern that precludes unconditional support is that there are flawed democracies that are fairly unstable even though they have these systems in place, such as Italy and Israel. Both countries are highly fragmented, and coalition governments tend to be unstable, resulting in their frequent collapse as has been the case for both in recent years. An independent judiciary is key to ensuring that minority rights endure and are not overthrown by a crude majoritarianism, and that very prospect is at risk in the Knesset's efforts to pare back judicial oversight of their proportional parliamentary

---

14. Wikipedia, s.v., "2019 Indian general election."

political system. Some might rightly question whether the United States would suffer the same experience. It is impossible to know for sure, though I believe that our current system actually exacerbates polarization by keeping issues unresolved where strong majorities exist as well as driving Americans to binary voting decisions with only two parties.

While a combination of these systems found in other democracies may be preferable to the existing formulation in the United States, there exists an almost insurmountable problem when it comes to implementation. Most of these changes would require a change to the United States Constitution, which historically has been exceedingly difficult to amend outside of short bursts of national upheaval. Of the twenty-seven amendments to the US Constitution (out of eleven thousand proposed), twelve of them passed in the first fifteen years after its initial approval. There have been huge time lapses between later amendments. Sixty-one years passed until the civil rights amendments were ratified after the end of the Civil War. Following those three, it was another forty-three years until more passed during the Progressive Era including things like a federal income tax, direct Senate elections, and women's suffrage. These occurred in intense periods of social activism and institutional reform. Other than an amendment concerning congressional pay raises in the 1990s, it has been over fifty years since the last substantive constitutional amendment in the United States.

Thus, the United States Constitution is considered by many scholars to be one of the hardest constitutions in the world to amend, if not the hardest. There are only two ways to do so: by Article 5, which requires a two-thirds vote of approval in both houses of Congress followed by ratification by three-quarters of all state legislatures, or alternatively by a constitutional convention called by two-thirds of the states. The problem with the former is that it is not possible to fix Article 5 through the method that Article 5 prescribes, resulting in a catch-22. The problem with the latter option is that most of the energy around a constitutional convention is among the far right, where all constitutional rights that are currently protected would be up for debate and decided by one vote per state regardless of population. Given that the largest dozen states make up half the USA's population, any decisions by a numerical minority would once again be unrepresentative and could yield an even worse result than the current dysfunctional system. Thus, many people prefer the devil they know to the devil they don't. Aziz Rana, professor of law at Cornell Law School, laments that "Americans are essentially stuck with a document that distorts democracy and feeds institutional paralysis, due to the disproportionate power that the Electoral College, the Senate, and the Supreme Court all give to small pockets of the population."[15]

15. Kapczynski et al., "New Year, New Amendments."

One recent proposed solution to this roadblock comes from Ryan Doerfler of Harvard, and Samuel Moyn of Yale. They suggest that Congress pass a Congress Act that reorganizes the legislature by reducing the Senate to an advisory and revision body without the power to obstruct laws.[16] This would solve at least one element of institutional paralysis and the structural bias of the Senate that gives more weight to populations of smaller states. More radical solutions include packing the union with many new states, which could be added with a simple congressional majority, and whose congressional representatives would ally with the existing majority to ratify new amendments to fix the problem of unequal representation. Fixes might include transferring the Senate's powers to a body that represents citizens equally, replacing the Electoral College with a popular vote, and modifying the amendment process itself.[17]

If we look further at the experiences of other nations, we note that the country of Chile recently struggled with its own obstacles of changing its constitution, one that was developed in 1980 during the Augusto Pinochet dictatorship. Over three-quarters of voters approved a 2020 referendum to rewrite that constitution, but the details of the proposal split that support, with a referendum to approve it failing in September of 2022. As of this writing, Chileans are going back to the drawing board to try again with a new constitutional proposal for popular consideration. While some of the reasons for failure were likely due to demagoguery around the initial proposal's contents, it is the case that the first proposal would have been one of the most progressive constitutions in the world.[18] One lesson for the United States to consider would be that it is less important to have the on-paper ideal constitution and preferable to have a constitution that has built-in achievable rules to allow for its amendment down the road. That way, it is flexible enough so it can be changed when priorities arise. One example of that latter phenomenon is the already-existing ability to change state constitutions in the United States. None of them have the high barriers that the US Constitution has, with most requiring only 50 percent to become law. With our unrepresentative chambers, this is a problem, but it would not be such a problem in a proportional system. Likewise, stable countries like Germany amend their constitution almost every year, and France amends its constitution every few years.[19] Rather than seeing the constitution as a sacred, eternal entity, it is better to see it as a process that is open-ended and ongoing.

16. Doerfler and Moyn, "Constitution Is Broken."
17. "Pack the Union."
18. Otis, "Chileans have rejected."
19. Posner, "U.S. Constitution Is Impossible to Amend."

So where does that leave us? To paraphrase the process-relational theologian Marjorie Suchocki, God works with the world as it is in order to help it become what it could be. Likewise, citizens of the United States have to work with what we have. In the short term to the midterm, it seems clear that state experiments are far more likely to be successful than a broader federal restructuring. A starting point could be for a state heavily committed to expanding democratic values to redraw its *state* legislature into a proportional, multiparty system. While it is needed very much in places like my state of Indiana, such locales are unfortunately the least likely to implement reforms as they move along an anti-democratic trajectory. Moreover, I do not think it would be wise for states to have their federal representatives elected this way in isolation from other states acting similarly, for while it would alleviate intra-state unrepresentative structures, it would exacerbate inter-state disparities. If only some of the states made these changes, and they tended to be represented by the same party, it could make the federal imbalance even worse.

I have not mentioned up to this point the usual popular suggestions for short-term patches, but they are worth a brief reference. These options include abolishing or circumventing the Electoral College for presidential elections. This could be done with a collection of states holding the majority of electoral votes. All they need to do is vote to give their electoral votes not to the winner of their state but to the winner of the popular vote, having it go into effect only once the number of states worth equal to or greater than 270 electoral votes pass similar legislation. This option is called the National Popular Vote Interstate Compact, which as of 2023 had 195 of the needed 270 votes to pass.[20] Given the aforementioned near impossibility of amending the US Constitution, this option would formally leave the Electoral College in place but would neutralize its effect. Secondly, even if we cannot abolish the Senate, make it an advisory-only body, or delegate its powers to a more representative institution, the Senate could at a minimum end the filibuster with just fifty-one votes, removing one of several excessive gridlock mechanisms. Finally, without the possibility of constitutional amendments, the interpretation of the existing Constitution becomes high-stakes political warfare in terms of the current lifetime appointments of Supreme Court justices. Following other healthy countries' approaches, the United States could move away from our unique system of lifetime appointments to the Supreme Court, with one possibility being that judges have eighteen-year terms so that each president can select two per term.[21] This maintains

20. *National Popular Vote*, "Agreement among the States."

21. Johnson, "Is It Time to Reconsider Lifetime Appointments to the Supreme Court?"

judicial independence by having longevity and assures parties that different presidents who serve the same length of time do not have an arbitrary number of appointments.[22]

There are many ideas out there, and despite the obstacles, we do see small experiments within the United States that are learning from other democratic examples. These should be encouraged, and lifting them up as potentials to be prehended reminds us that another world is indeed possible. Let me end with one final example: ranked-choice voting or single-transferable vote systems. This option is particularly useful when there is a single office to be filled. The states of Alaska and Maine have begun implementing this model for offices like governor races. This solves the problem of a "wasted vote" found in our first-past-the-post plurality system. With a ranked-choice option, there are no wasted votes as people are free to rank their first choice as a first choice, their second as a second choice, and so on, until through a process of removing lower-ranking results and transferring votes to secondary picks, one candidate eventually receives an absolute majority. This would be a positive switch for statewide elections for governors, senators, and for statewide congressional seats in low population states like Vermont, Wyoming, Delaware, or other places where a statewide proportional system would not impact the result. Local elections for mayor would be viable and perhaps easier to implement in municipalities. Finally, presidential elections that included a ranked-choice option alongside a popular vote would end the disincentive for people to not consider third and fourth parties as viable options.

This has been a brief overview of some of the alternative systems to strengthen representative liberal democracy in the United States, based on models from around the world that are improvements to our often binary and dysfunctional system. It is my assertion that the United States, which from the beginning has claimed that it ever seeks to be a more perfect union, should positively prehend these models as real potentials for concrescence into a yet more perfect union.

Bibliography

Cottier, Cody. "How Native Americans Shaped U.S. Democracy." Planet Earth. *Discover*, Oct. 10, 2022. https://www.discovermagazine.com/planet-earth/did-native-americans-shape-u-s-democracy/.

---

22. For instance, both President Clinton and President Obama served for two terms and each appointed two Supreme Court justices, while President Trump served only one term and yet appointed three justices.

PART TWO: FROM THE SPIRIT TO THE POLIS

Dao, James. "The 2000 Elections: The Green Party; Angry Democrats, Fearing Nader Cost Them Presidential Race, Threaten to Retaliate." *New York Times*, Nov. 9, 2000. https://www.nytimes.com/2000/11/09/us/2000-elections-green-party-angry-democrats-fearing-nader-cost-them-presidential.html/.

Doerfler, Ryan D., and Samuel Moyn. "The Constitution Is Broken and Should Not Be Reclaimed." Opinion. Guest Essay. *New York Times*, Aug. 19, 2022. https://www.nytimes.com/2022/08/19/opinion/liberals-constitution.html/.

Economist Intelligence Unit (website). "Democracy Index 2021: The China Challenge." *Economist Intelligence Unit* (website) (2022): https://www.eiu.com/n/campaigns/democracy-index-2021/.

Gainey, Blaise. "GOP Redraws Nashville from 1 Democratic District into 3 Republican-Leaning districts." *All Things Considered*, NPR, July 26, 2022. https://www.npr.org/2022/07/26/1113810519/nashville-s-3-u-s-house-districts/.

Grindle, Donald A., Jr., and Bruce E. Johansen. *Exemplar of Liberty: Native America and the Evolution of Democracy* (1990). https://ratical.org/many_worlds/6Nations/EoL/index.html#ToC/.

"Pack the Union: A Proposal to Admit New States for the Purpose of Amending the Constitution to Ensure Equal Representation." *Harvard Law Review* 133.3 (Jan. 2020) 1049–70. https://harvardlawreview.org/2020/01/pack-the-union-a-proposal-to-admit-new-states-for-the-purpose-of-amending-the-constitution-to-ensure-equal-representation/.

Johnson, Carrie. "Is It Time to Reconsider Lifetime Appointments to the Supreme Court?" Politics. NPR, February 17, 2016. https://www.npr.org/2016/02/17/466976937/is-it-time-to-reconsider-lifetime-appointments-to-the-supreme-court/.

Kapczynski, Amy, et al. "New Year, New Amendments." *Law and Political Economy Project*, January 10, 2022. https://lpeproject.org/blog/new-year-new-amendments/.

Little, Becky. "The Native American Government That Helped Inspire the US Constitution." *History*, Nov. 10, 20020, updated July 12, 2023. https://www.history.com/news/iroquois-confederacy-influence-us-constitution/.

"Maryland Election Results." *New York Times*, Dec. 14, 2022. https://www.nytimes.com/interactive/2022/11/08/us/elections/results-maryland.html.

National Archives Foundation. "Amendments to the U.S. Constitution." *National Archives Foundation* (website). https://www.archivesfoundation.org/amendments-u-s-constitution/.

National Popular Vote. "Agreement among the States to Elect the President by National Popular Vote." *National Popular Vote*. https://www.nationalpopularvote.com/written-explanation/.

Otis, John. "Chileans Have Rejected a New, Progressive Constitution." *Morning Edition*, NPR, Sept. 5, 2022. https://www.npr.org/2022/09/04/1121065756/chile-constitution-referendum/.

Porter, Eduardo. "A Threat to U.S. Democracy: Political Dysfunction." *New York Times*, Jan. 3, 2017. https://www.nytimes.com/2017/01/03/business/economy/trump-election-democracy.html/.

Posner, Eric. "The U.S. Constitution Is Impossible to Amend." *Slate.com* (website), May 5, 2014. https://slate.com/news-and-politics/2014/05/amending-the-constitution-is-much-too-hard-blame-the-founders.html/.

"2021 Indiana Senate Districts." https://cdn.zephyrcms.com/a6cfab54-1ed2-41e6-9e90-706924b4eb0e/-/inline/yes/2021-senate-district-map-as-adopted-oct-12021-counties-townships-cities.pdf/.

West, Cornel. "Justice Is What Love Looks Like in Public." Lecture presented at Howard University, Washington, DC, April 2011.

Whitehead, Alfred North. *The Function of Reason*. Louis Clark Vanuxem Foundation Lectures 1929. Beacon Paperbacks 72. 7th printing. Boston: Beacon, 1971.

Wikipedia, s.v. "Democracy Index." https://en.wikipedia.org/wiki/Democracy_Index/.

———, s.v. "Indiana General Assembly." https://en.wikipedia.org/wiki/Indiana_General_Assembly/.

———, s.v. "2019 Indian General Election." https://en.wikipedia.org/wiki/2019_Indian_general_election/.

Part Three

To Pluralism, Axioilogy, and Apocalypse

9

The Buddha's Pedagogical Power

The Unlimited Capacity to Love and Liberate All Sentient Beings

JOHN J. THATAMANIL

Incommensurability, sameness, or opposition—three temptations that beset judgments about the relationship between religious traditions. The incommensurability temptation posits that traditions have such distinctive myths, motifs, meanings, practices, and logics that their adherents cannot make themselves mutually understood (not even to engage in conflict as they are simply unintelligible to each other) across religious boundaries. Understanding a tradition requires insider status because it comes only through conversion, which enables participation in the rules of the game, and participation generates comprehension. Otherwise, the difference between traditions is too vast for meaningful translation across religious boundaries. The contrasting temptation—often articulated in popular culture—is that the traditions are, at bottom, the same. Despite apparent differences in vocabularies, traditions lead to and offer a shared understanding of a single reality. An alternative formulation of this position runs as follows: despite exoteric differences, there flows within all religions the selfsame underground esoteric stream. Differences are, thus, only superficial. In their depths, traditions are identical—it is the same water in all underground reservoirs. So, the options for assessing how religious traditions interrelate appear to be either their incommensurability, their essential identity, or (a final possibility) their opposition one to another. We know well what they are saying, and it is radically opposed to what we affirm. Hence, conflict is unavoidable.

The comparativist's task is, well, to compare, which is to say, to see what there is to see and not to posit in advance of investigation what there is to be found. Sweeping prejudgments are sure to mislead where only inquiry will do. If there is a provisional working assumption to be ventured, it would be analogy. Take traditions to be in a relation of difference-in-sameness and sameness-in-difference.[1] We are, after all, not members of alien species, and virtually all of our traditions have been in contact and conversation. Understanding takes time, nuance, judgment, and sustained conversation. Building from these working assumptions is likely to issue in comparison that neither assumes nor generalizes.[2]

The question of the relationship between "love" and "power" presents intriguing and demanding challenges when thinking from a Buddhist starting point. Given my opening cautionary notes, it should be unsurprising to stipulate that English-language terms such as these can be deployed for conventional purposes alone; conversation must begin somewhere. But we would do well to acknowledge that the terms carry quite distinctive meanings within Buddhist vocabularies. The terms can only be understood as vague categories that require further specification that is attentive to meanings to be discovered within specific vocabularies.[3]

Buddhist religious texts have much to say about love, or at least cognate concepts, but Buddhists in core religious texts do not have much to say about power as customarily understood in theistic traditions for the simple reason that a divine being possessing "omnipotence" is not a core Buddhist theme or motif. Subject to correction, I will venture this twofold claim: Power, for Buddhist thinkers, has two core meanings. First, power is at root the capacity to awaken and see reality clearly. By extension, power is the capacity to awaken innumerable, countless other living beings and thereby to lead them out of their captivity to greed, hatred, and delusion and into liberation. Second, power is the vigor (*virya*) required to sustain the path toward such other centered liberation and the resolve to maintain that quest over numberless lifetimes. Before I spell out this twofold claim, let me offer some quick observations.

Questions of power in concrete and sociopolitical forms are also thematized in Buddhist texts and contexts. Siddhartha Gautama's royal lineage

---

1. This way of putting things is particularly characteristic of David Tracy. See, for example, his classic book, *The Analogical Imagination*.

2. This posture of openness does not rule out either incommensurability or opposition. In particular cases, comparison may well come up against these possibilities. That said, given the intense disagreements within traditions, there is no reason to suppose that opposition will be encountered only across the lines between traditions.

3. On the use of vague categories in comparison, see the work of Robert Neville, who uses the work of Charles Peirce to develop his theory of comparison. For one helpful locus among many, see Wildman and Neville, "How Our Approach to Comparison Relates to Others."

and visions of Emperor Ashoka as ideal Buddhist ruler introduce themes of kingship into Buddhist thought quite early on. Key texts such as the *Rajaparikatha-ratnavali* or just *Ratnavali* in short, attributed to Nagarjuna, offers concrete advice to kings.[4] Moreover, the question of the relationship between the monastic community, the sangha, and the ruler in particular Buddhist countries is richly addressed in a wide variety of concrete historical studies. There is much rich material to be mined there that will bring readers very quickly to concrete questions of political power. Accounts of what an ideal king ought to look like are readily available, and one can explore accounts of the proper use of power from these texts and contexts. Nonetheless, central to Buddhist imagination is the Buddha's renunciation of political kingship for *another kind of sovereignty*. The Buddha most assuredly remains a world-conqueror, one who turns the wheel of universal rule (*cakravartin*), but the world he conquerors is samsara, the entire transmigratory realm. So, a discourse of power and sovereignty still applies, albeit in a soteriological key. Because he has conquered the veil of ignorance that keeps all beings trapped in the cycle of transmigration, the Buddha does indeed possess incalculable power, even if it is a power that is not of a political order.

With those observations offered, I return to the heart of my twofold argument, which is made from a broadly Mahayana perspective. I begin with a core comparative generalization which is perhaps obvious but nonetheless worth articulating: the question of the relationship between love and power will necessarily take on a different cast within a nontheistic setting than in a theistic one. When Christians set about thinking about the relationship between love and power, there is no way to disentangle those two notions from their theistic frame. The question of the relationship between love and power is always at first a question about the relationship between God's love and God's power, and as is quite clear in the other chapters in this volume, that question is impossible to think apart from contending with notions of omnipotence and divine sovereignty. Political theology too is inevitably shaped not just by discourses of providence but by the political figuring of God and Christ as King and Lord.

Within a theistic frame, theological reflection is routinely bound to figure the divine as a being, the most perfect being perhaps, but a being all the same. This register of discourse is, of course, qualified by the venerable indeed ancient history of insisting that God is not a being of any sort but being-itself or even the Good beyond being. These ancient theological motifs notwithstanding, the narrative frame of the tradition, rooted in

---

4. Readers should keep in mind the new translation offered by Sara McClintock and John Dunne of *Nagarjuna's Precious Garland*.

scripture, has always retained and been determined by accounts of God as an agential being figured as Lord. An all-powerful divine agent enjoys a centrality within the Christian symbolic repertoire that it does not enjoy within Buddhist repertoires.

Within Buddhist frames—here we can generalize across Theravada and Mahayana traditions—ultimate reality, although variously conceived, has very rarely been understood *primarily* in personal or agential terms. Nirvana, *dharmakaya*, emptiness (*sunyata*), and *pratityasamutpada* are all best understood as impersonal or transpersonal realities or even as no sort of reality at all.[5] Agential figures—even celestial Buddhas and Bodhisattvas—are indeed present, but always as second- or third-tier manifestations of an underlying transpersonal ultimate reality. This priority of the transpersonal means that the power—even quite considerable power—of Buddhas and Bodhisattvas will always be connected to empowering beings to recognize ultimate reality as transpersonal. *Who* these figures are is far less important than *what* they can teach or show. With this framing contrast in mind, we return to the question of the role of kingship, sovereignty, and power in Buddhist and Christian traditions.

If the story of the Buddha revolves around Siddhartha's refusal of political kingship (more on this below), it is worth signaling that an analogous refusal also conditions Christian traditions. Just as Siddhartha Gautama renounces kingship of a conventional political sort, Jesus too renounces that temptation as presented to him by the devil in the wilderness. Recall the critical verses in Matthew's Gospel (Matt 4:8–11):[6]

> Again, the devil took him to a very high mountain and showed him all the kingdoms of the world and their glory, 9 and he said to him, "All these I will give you, if you will fall down and worship me." 10 Then Jesus said to him, "Away with you, Satan! for it is written,
> 'Worship the Lord your God,
> and serve only him.'"
> 11 Then the devil left him, and suddenly angels came and waited on him.

Jesus' refusal of royal power recurs also in the Gospel of John in his climactic encounter with Pilate, Caesar's delegate. Here too, Jesus insists that he

---

5. The phrase "or no reality at all" is likely to be perplexing to the uninitiated. What I mean is that it is possible to argue that emptiness (*sunyata*) is not any sort of reality whatsoever—whether personal or impersonal—but rather a characteristic of whatever there is, of all realities, namely, that no thing whatsoever has intrinsic existence.

6. All translations from the Bible are from the New Revised Standard Version Updated Edition.

is no sort of worldly king when Jesus affirms that "My kingdom is not of this world" (John 18:36). Arguably, then *both* traditions in their treatments of power are compelled to contend with conceptions of sovereignty that carry over but also contradict or surpass conventional political sovereignties. Soteriological sovereignties operate on a different register than that of kingship even when saving figures are called King and Lord. However, the Christian case is distinguished by the fact that, quite apart from Jesus' own ambivalent relation to political power, God's power appears to include, even if it surpasses, political power. God is routinely figured as cosmic King and Ruler. Hence, Christian theologians, particularly process thinkers, do not have the luxury of thinking about love and power apart from these conceptual entanglements even or especially when their goal is to break the stranglehold of omnipotence.

From the first, Buddhist reflections on love and power will not be marked by the framework of divine omni-power. The broader Indic context is replete with divinities, but in Buddhist cosmologies, these deities pay homage to the Buddha, not the other way around. Buddhist narratives are certainly not devoid of divinities, even the narrative of Siddhartha's awakening is narrated as aided by divine beings who take the form of the Four Sights (a sick person, an old person, a dead body, and a wandering renunciant) that jar Siddhartha into a realization of impermanence. Likewise, narratives are present in which divine beings facilitate Siddhartha's escape from his castle compound as he begins his life as a renunciant. But the miraculous powers possessed by these divine beings is not of religious import or significance save for the way in which they enable the Buddha-to-be on the road to his awakening. Hence, attention to themes of power in Buddhist discourse must focus instead on the kinds of "power" possessed by Buddhas and Bodhisattvas.

In time, a variety of omnidiscourses do emerge in Buddhist traditions, and these omnidiscourses eventually focus on celestial Buddhas and Bodhisattvas, not the divine beings of the Hindu pantheon. But even these discourses are preeminently in the key of omniscience, namely the omniscience of the Buddha who understands the nature of every dharma by understanding their emptiness. This discourse does build in time and Mahayana traditions do ascribe to the Buddha infinite cognitive power, including prophetic and miraculous powers, but the Buddha's movement into quasi-divine status in Mahayana traditions is always understood primarily as the power to liberate beings from their captivity to suffering (*dukkha*). Such cognitive power is never construed as controlling power. The power that Buddhas and Bodhisattvas possess is their power to set suffering beings free from the causes of their ensnarement, and as that ensnarement is always at root a matter of our ignorance (*avidya*), the human failure to understand the nature of reality as it truly is. Hence, the kind of power that the Buddhas possess is *pedagogical power*. The power enlightened beings possess is their power to teach with consummate skillful means (*upaya kausalya*) and thus grant to each being what that particular being needs to emerge from captivity to ignorance.

There is in Mahayana texts a deep-rooted awareness that while a generic diagnosis of the human predicament is easily accomplished—craving driven by a root ignorance regarding emptiness—the peculiar psychic configurations that such ignorance takes are as various as the beings captive to them. That each student has very distinctive impediments on the road to awakening is probably not news to classroom teachers. Moreover, Buddhist wisdom is never a matter of transmitting information in propositional form. What is needed is wisdom resulting from the transformation of patterned reactivities generated by habits, propensities, attachments and aversions built up over multiple lifetimes. To trace out how the skeins of tangled patterns operate in any particular person requires unusual powers of penetrating vision. This capacity to see just what is going on in the particular person before you and then to skillfully offer to that person just what she needs is a core meaning of Buddhist power.

Even when Bodhisattvas and Buddhas are granted miraculous powers, those powers are never separable from their liberating through teaching function. Consider the particularly famous account of the powers of the Buddha's toe in *The Vimalakirti Sutra*.[7] Which toe in particular is left unspecified, but I am guessing it must have been his big toe. After a cosmic vision in which the Buddha's disciple Shariputra beholds that all the other cosmic Buddhas and Bodhisattvas inhabit radiant bejeweled Pure Lands, Shariputra wonders if there's something wrong with our Buddha given that our realm is well, to use a technical phrase, so shitty: "When I look at this land, I see it full of knolls and hollows, thorny underbrush, sand and gravel, dirt, rocks, many mountains, filth and defilement." A Brahma king explains that the fault lies in the beholder: "It's just your mind has highs and lows and does not rest on Buddha wisdom. Therefore you see this land as impure." Skipping a bit, the Buddha, namely our Buddha, knowing what Shariputra is thinking, performs a miracle.

> The Buddha then pressed his toe against the earth, and immediately the thousand-millionfold world was adorned with hundreds and thousands of rare jewels ... All the members of the great assembly sighed in wonder at what they had never seen

7. Watson, *Vimalakirti Sutra*.

before, and all saw that they themselves were seated on jeweled lotuses . . .

. . . The Buddha said to Shariputra, "My Buddha land has always been pure like this. But because I wish to save those persons who are lowly and inferior, I make it seem an impure land full of defilements, that is all . . . If a person's mind is pure, then he will see the wonderful blessings that adorn this land.[8]

The text then goes on to conclude this episode by stating the result of this display, namely that among others, "eighty-four thousand persons all set their minds on attaining *anuttara-samyak-sambodhi*, unsurpassable perfect enlightenment. The Buddha then released the supernatural power that he had exercised with his toe and the world returned to its former appearance."[9]

In this passage, the miraculous powers of the Buddha are inconceivably vast; in fact, those powers seem equivalent to the powers likely to be possessed by any divine being inasmuch as the Buddha is responsible for how almost all human beings perceive this world. To conceal an inconceivably radiant world as radically impure is an enormous ongoing act of supernatural power. But it nonetheless remains a steadfastly pedagogical power. The Buddha is always teaching, both when he hides the truly glorious nature of this Buddha realm—which presumably is what he is always doing—*and* when he discloses its true nature with his toe. And, when this disclosure is made, those gathered are enabled to see themselves as seated upon jeweled lotuses, which is another way to say that they are enabled to recognize their own Buddha-nature. In short, the Buddha is always deploying his powers to motivate human beings to strive for liberation by making it seem that this glorious realm is riddled with defilement and so driving us to seek escape from that realm.

Buddhist iconography often represents the Buddhas and Bodhisattvas with multiple arms—customarily a way of representing omnipotence in Hindu deities for example—but in the Buddhist case, these many arms signify the skillfulness and extensive compassionate reach of these beings. Admittedly, some Buddhas and Bodhisattvas are recognized as having miraculous powers to effect various forms of mundane help and rescue from danger, but at root, their core power remains the power to reach and to teach innumerable beings in just the way they need. Power remains pedagogical in its true nature, the power to illumine.

The mention of multiple arms brings me to a second feature of power in this context—namely, the unlimited reach and extension of the Buddhas

---

8. Watson, *Vimalakirti Sutra*, 30–31.
9. Watson, *Vimalakirti Sutra*, 31.

and Bodhisattvas in their *desire* to set free all sentient beings. For most of us, the range of our capacities for care are relatively limited. We find we have time and resources for our partners and family and a few others, but the ambit of our capacities to care are acutely limited. Moreover, our care for beings beyond that circle remains largely notional rather than vivid and extensive. The powers of the divine or semidivine beings of Buddhist cosmologies are, by contrast, unlimited, but again, this power is not understood as the powers of an omnipotent God are. The power of Buddhas and Bodhisattvas just is their capacity to care for and reach out to *all sentient beings* and provide the conditions that will in time set those beings free from captivity to wheel of suffering (*samsara*).

The capacity to have compassion (*karuna*) and loving-kindness (*maitri* in Sanskrit or *metta* in Pali) is in principle without limit but practically constrained by our particular capacities. The Buddhas and Bodhisattvas, by contrast, set their mind on liberating all beings and then assiduously cultivating the disciplines necessary to make their compassion anything but merely notional. I'll offer more on this in a moment; but first, let's move back to the Buddha—now not the enormously powerful Buddha described in the *Vimalakirti Sutra*, but the Buddha we know from the earliest available narrative traditions.

Recall that despite the enormous diversity of global Buddhisms, the starting point of the tradition—a single human figure attaining to awakening—sets the context for thinking about the nature of power and love within a Buddhist narrative frame. The unambiguous and emphatic articulation of early Buddhists—that the Buddha was most assuredly not a divine being—removes divine omnipotence from the picture. Even when Mahayana Buddhists imagine figures like the Buddha whom we just met and Amida Buddha who have the power to create entire Buddha realms such as the Pure Land, that power is still configured as the power to illumine and to love. The source of this power is acquired by karmic merit. This merit, acquired over countless lifetimes of virtuous living, grants them the power to create realms with the propitious conditions necessary for beings to be in their presence and thereby liberated. The power of their tremendous karmic merit (a distinct kind of power indeed) thus remains a power to set free. Their capacity resides in their wisdom and their compassion, or put otherwise, their omnipotence resides precisely in their omnibenevolence. Their power is their loving wisdom.

Here is a further note on the importance of Buddhist beginnings. As already noted above, the core narrative of Siddhartha Gautama's life begins with his father receiving a prophecy that his son would be *chakravartin*—"a wheel-turner." This wheel is characterized as a mutually exclusive twofold;

he will *either* turn the wheel of universal political and military conquest or turn the wheel of dharma, of liberating teaching, but not both. We know from the stories what the Buddha's father wants. And hence, the Buddhist narratives of young Siddhartha closeted in splendid sensual luxury on palace grounds lest an encounter with suffering prompt religious questions. But we know that thanks to the Four Sights, young Siddhartha leaves the palace and enters into his religious quest. Hence, from the first, Buddhist tradition begins with Siddhartha's refusal of royal power. This double absence—the absence of an omni-God and the Buddha's own refusal of sovereign power—illumine and set the unfolding preconditions for Buddhist constructive reflection regarding the kind of power that the Buddha possesses.

But does the refusal of kingship amount to a refusal of sovereign power altogether, or a reconfiguration of the same? As the Buddha is indeed a *chakravartin*—one who turns the world-conquering wheel—the Buddha is regarded in many if not most textual and practice traditions as sovereign but now again in a liberative and pedagogical key. Having liberated himself from enslavement to karmic bondage to existence as such, he has indeed conquered the universe. The conquering power the Buddha now commands is the power he wields to set other beings free from the wheel of suffering. Because he possesses and exercises this liberating power, he is regarded as sovereign conqueror but in a decidedly emancipatory key. Moreover, the Buddha's distinctive sort of sovereign power is not his alone. His power to illumine and liberate all beings also extends to those who aspire to become Buddhas themselves. Consider the following verse from Santideva's *Bodhicaryavatara*, the classic treatise on the Bodhisattva path: "For I must conquer everything. Nothing should conquer me. This pride should be wedded to me, for I am the son of a lionlike conqueror" (7:55).[10]

I will return to the broader context of this verse in a moment, but the verse itself should suffice to indicate that both the Buddha and the Bodhisattvas possess or aspire to possess immense power, but that power remains resolutely soteriological and pedagogical. It is the power to liberate oneself and, in principle, all sentient beings from captivity to the round of suffering. In the broad Mahayana tradition, one begins to access this power by committing oneself to the Bodhisattva way. A common version of that vow in contemporary practice traditions takes the following form:

> Beings are numberless; I vow to free them
> Delusions are inexhaustible; I vow to end them
> Dharma Gates are boundless, I vow to enter them
> The Buddha Way is unsurpassable; I vow to embody it.[11]

10. Santideva, *Bodhicaryavatara*, 72.
11. For more about these vows, see the following illuminating link on these vows

The aspiration to free all beings, extinguish all delusions, enter boundless dharma gates, and become Buddha is manifestly a longing for immense power. But it hardly needs to be said that this power, to put it in Whiteheadian terms, is persuasive power and not coercive power. Neither the Buddha nor his dharma sons and daughters relinquish sovereignty altogether, but they do transmute it. World conquering is accomplished not as political power but as soteriological power. *Sovereign are they who are liberated and who have the power to liberate.*

This religious account of sovereignty remains cognitive in character. What binds beings to the samsaric cycle are their delusions. Delusion is itself rooted in the core failure to realize that nothing whatsoever has intrinsic existence (*svabhava*) or own-being. To pursue this project of liberative teaching for countless beings requires enormous resolve. That resolve must be cultivated by the disciplined quest for *virya-paramita*, the perfection of vigor. The word *virya*, related to the English words "virtue" and "virile," names the power to persist in the pursuit of awakening.

Santideva's *Bodhicaryavatara* 7:1–2 define *virya* as follows:

1. Patient in this way one should cultivate vigour, because Awakening depends on vigour. For without vigour there is no merit, just as there is no movement without wind.

2. What is vigour? The endeavour to do what is skilful. What is its antithesis called? Sloth, clinging to what is vile, despondency and self-contempt.[12]

Those who cultivate vigor configure themselves as heroes by overcoming innumerable obstacles. These obstacles (as are their contraries) are mental factors such as sloth and despondency. Figured as participants in a battle between negative and positive factors, those who aspire for their own liberation and the liberation of others join the fray and refuse to be cowed by innumerable obstacles to be overcome even across countless lifetimes. Hence, no account of the notion of "power" in Buddhism would be complete without accounting for the disciplined cultivation and practice of vigor over the course of many lifetimes.

Many other questions remain to be plumbed. What is it that makes it possible for Buddhas and Bodhisattvas to access such immense liberating power? Mahayana traditions answer: *dharmakaya*. Buddhas and Bodhisattvas do what they do because they have come to realize their own Buddha-nature. What Buddha-nature is exactly is contested across Buddhist

---

within Japanese Buddhism: https://terebess.hu/zen/szoto/vows.html/.

12. Santideva, *Bodhicaryavatara*, 67.

traditions, with some holding Buddha-nature to be a kind of primordial nondual but nonsubstantial consciousness that is the union of wisdom and compassion. Still other traditions remain resolutely wary of any positive discourse about ultimate reality, worried that Buddhists will reinstitute a duality between the changeless absolute and the changing world, a dualism that, as it happens, Alfred North Whitehead worried about. Regardless of how it is conceived, ultimate reality for Buddhists is radically inseparable from conventional reality or just is conventional reality rightly seen.

Hence, nondual ontologies undergird the aforementioned discussion of Buddhist power. Recall that bodhicitta—the mind (*citta*) of awakening (*bodhi*)—is at once both the desire or aspiration for awakening and also one's true nature. Here, as an aside, it should be noted that conventional translations of *citta* as "mind" may instigate in the English-language reader a mind-versus-heart opposition and bifurcation. No such duality is presumed in Sanskrit usage. This is why the bodhicitta can be in the aspirant at once both a desire for enlightenment and the mind of enlightenment. In the realized person, bodhicitta is the union of infinite wisdom and compassion; the cognitive and the affective are never set at odds.

Those who come to see rightly do wield enormous power, but that power just is the power to love and liberate all beings so that they come to recognize their own most true nature. Power remains resolutely pedagogical power first and foremost, and then the secondarily the vigor or assiduousness necessary to commit oneself to the liberation of all sentient beings.

A Brief Concluding Gesture toward a Comparative Theology of Pedagogical Power

Time does not permit a full-fledged comparative reflection in which this discussion of the Buddha's pedagogical power—the power to teach, illuminate, and set innumerable beings free from their ignorance—is brought into conversation with Christian accounts of the kind of power wielded by Jesus the Christ. We have already noted that both figures renounce standard political sovereignties and therefore have no interest in wielding conventional political power. Both Buddha and Jesus have this much in common. Might this mean that Jesus too can be regarded as wielding pedagogical power rather than political power? Indeed! No reader of the Second Testament can fail to notice that what Jesus creates is a pedagogical community, a community of learning and teaching. One can hardly fail to notice that Jesus is routinely addressed as Rabbi and his followers are disciples, that is to say, those who learn. Hence, the structure of their community is one of teaching and learning. Thus, our reading of Buddhist materials and excavating from within those materials the category of "pedagogical power" has the promise to generate new Christian readings of the kind of power that Jesus wields. "Pedagogical power" can function as a vague comparative category which is likely to be differently specified within the two respective traditions.

Given how much of the Gospel narratives is given over to Jesus' teaching ministry, comparative readers might well wonder why it seems Christian theologies generally undervalue and neglect to articulate Jesus as one possessed of extraordinary pedagogical power. Even the category of pedagogical power as such seems largely absent from Christian commentarial and theological literature. This neglect is despite the fact that gathering disciples and teaching them by means of preaching and parable form the work and content of Jesus' ministry. What sets Jesus apart is that he too is, like the Buddha, a master teacher. Interestingly, his chief rivals, the Pharisees, are a rival teaching and learning community. Jesus' many confrontations with Pharisees are meant to demonstrate Jesus' superior pedagogical power.

Consider, for example, the concluding verses of Jesus' Sermon on the Mount, the pinnacle of Jesus' teaching. Here, Matthew recounts Jesus' concluding words as follows:

> 24 "Everyone, then, who hears these words of mine and acts on them will be like a wise man who built his house on rock. 25 The rain fell, the floods came, and the winds blew and beat on that house, but it did not fall because it had been founded on rock. 26 And everyone who hears these words of mine and does not act on them will be like a foolish man who built his house on sand. 27 The rain fell, and the floods came, and the winds blew and beat against that house, and it fell—and great was its fall!" 28 Now when Jesus had finished saying these words, the crowds were astounded at his teaching, 29 for he taught them as one having authority and not as their scribes.

Matthew presents Jesus as an exemplary teacher of wisdom. What Jesus has to offer to those gathered is precisely his teaching (*didache*). His core community of disciples and the wider assembly around them are invited to listen and then put into practice Jesus' teachings. Jesus' words are the words of life, words that articulate the values and norms of the coming kingdom of heaven/God. Jesus is both the herald and inaugurator of that kingdom, and this is the source of his astonishing power or authority (*exousia*). He does not speak as other teachers do. He speaks with distinctive pedagogical power because he understands himself—and his listeners recognize this—as one who is in some way intimately and inseparably related to the kingdom he proclaims. Hence, his distinctive and singular power. Even Jesus' miracles are in the Gospel narratives taken to be signs which are meant to aid and be in service of his primary work of teaching. The Buddha is one who teaches what he has himself learned—the way to awakening. The Buddha and what he has to teach may be distinct—others too can learn what he has learned—but inseparable. Jesus too as herald, inaugurator, and even exemplar of the kingdom he proclaims is a master teacher who teaches with power. If anything, Jesus and the kingdom he proclaims are inseparable in a more profound way that the Buddha and his teaching. Others can enter the kingdom, but Jesus is the one who brings in that kingdom.

And yet, despite the shared emphasis on extraordinary pedagogical power, the two traditions diverge. To begin with, the human predicament to which the Buddha's teaching is directed is understood as ignorance (*avidya*). This ignorance cannot be narrowly construed as a mere lack of information that the teacher can readily transmit. Hence, *avidya* has both cognitive and affective dimensions. Total transformation is required; information alone is insufficient. Nonetheless, because ignorance is the root of the Buddhist analysis of the human predicament, teaching has a singular power in generating escape from that predicament.

By contrast, in the case of Christian analyses of the human predicament, the emphasis is placed on the bondage of the will rather than on ignorance. Here too, much comparative work is needed to tease out the nuances implied by this distinction. Remaining simply with the frame of Matthew's Gospel, the presence of "kingdom discourse" cannot be overlooked. Jesus might have renounced claims to political power and sovereignty, but he is nonetheless one who proclaims a coming kingdom. That kingdom is clearly meant to embody and counter the values of the kingdom of Caesar. Jesus invites his disciples to learn and then put into practice the values of the coming kingdom that he proclaims, inaugurates, and embodies. Hence, the work of this pedagogical community does seek to interrupt, even if nonviolently, the kingdom of Caesar. And hence, a contestation of powers—the power of God versus the power of Caesar—is constitutive of Jesus' message. Jesus' pedagogical power is in the service of ushering in that kingdom. Hence, his pedagogical power is in the service of generating a transformed sociality. Further comparative work is needed to follow through on these distinctions.

How does the Buddha's pedagogical power operate? How does pedagogical power operate within a nondual frame, a frame in which the learner already is possessed of Buddha-nature to which the teacher is pointing? By contrast, how does pedagogical power work when it is in the service of a kingdom yet to come? What is the relationship between the pedagogical powers of the Buddha and Jesus and the political power exercised by sovereigns and states of their respective times? These and many other questions remain to be pursued. But none can even be articulated let alone explored without developing the formal category of pedagogical power, and that limited task has been the work launched in this chapter.

Bibliography

McClintock, Sara, and John Dunne, trans. *Nagarjuna's Precious Garland: Ratnavali*. Classics of Indian Buddhism. New York: Wisdom, 2024.

Santideva. *The Bodhicaryavatara*. Translated by Kate Crosby and Andrew Skilton. The World's Classics. Oxford: Oxford University Press, 1996.

Tracy, David. *The Analogical Imagination: Christian Theology and the Culture of Pluralism*. A Herder & Herder Book. New York: Crossroad, 1998.

Watson, Burton, trans. *The Vimalakirti Sutra*. New ed. Translations from the Asian Classics. New York: Columbia University Press, 2000.

Wildman, Wesley J., and Robert C. Neville. "How Our Approach to Comparison Relates to Others." In *Ultimate Realities*, edited by Robert C. Neville, 211–36. the Comparative Religious Ideas Project. Albany: State University of New York Press, 2001.

10

The Elephant Is Loving

Pluralism and Diversity as the Embodiment of God's Love

BRUCE G. EPPERLY

A well-known parable describes a group of sight-impaired persons gathered around an elephant. The creature is new to them, and they are curious about its identity and character. Each one feels a certain part of the elephant's body and then assumes that the part they are touching is the totality of the creature. Each one believes that their experience accurately describes the elephant while their neighbors are in error.

The intention of this ancient story is to remind us that we only experience a small portion of the Divine and are tempted to claim that the section we touch describes the Infinite Whole. The Divine is much larger than we can imagine, and we would do well to be humble in describing Ultimate Reality. For the sincere spiritual seeker, there are many honest and insightful perspectives on the Divine, and there are many helpful paths to wholeness and enlightenment provided we recognize their limitations and our own.

The parable's message is the same if we substitute blindfolded, culture-bound, or religiously committed persons for sight-impaired persons. We experience the Holy through the lenses, histories, experiences, and biases of our communities and faith traditions. Accordingly, we should not equate our spiritual path with the totality of God. Put positively, we can celebrate the fact that there is always more to learn about the Holy, and our vocation is to be adventurous in our quest to experience a reality we can never fully encompass.[1] The spiritual journey is a Holy Adventure of discovery and innovation.

---

1. I appreciate the insights of another "elephant" author, John Thatamanil, *Circling the Elephant*. Although we came to our titles independent of one another and have different goals in our respective works, we both employ the elephant as an image of the divine,

In my book *The Elephant Is Running*, I suggested that the image of an elephant standing still, passively letting itself be touched, is inadequate to describe either an elephant or the Ultimate Reality.[2] A living elephant is always on the move—twitching, stomping, flapping its ears, waving its trunk and tail, and running. We too are on the move in relationship to the elephant. We need to hang on for dear life to stay in contact with the part of the elephant we are currently touching. Moreover, if the elephant is running, we must grab at new and unfamiliar aspects of the elephant as we try to keep up with her movements. We may even need to take the hand of our neighbor to stay in touch with the lively creature. In so doing, we discover that the elephant is far more mysterious and multidimensional than we previously imagined.

A living elephant, however, does more than run. It communicates to humans and other elephants with low rumbles, roars, touching, odors, and visual expressions. We'd better be attentive to its changing expressions and behaviors if we are to know our companion elephant's feelings and intentions.

Those who follow the path of the Divine Elephant, whether it is known as Ganesha, God, Allah, Tao, Great Spirit, or by any other name, must be prepared to make changes to widen their religious perspectives and spiritual traditions to reflect their experiences of the changing reality they experience.[3] Further, a healthy response to the running elephant or a living divinity is to expand our vision not only by continuing our ongoing journeys into the Divine but also by listening to the descriptions of our companions on the spiritual search.

One more amendment may be necessary in the parable of the blindfolded or sight-impaired persons and the elephant. Elephants are more than their bodily movements and physical characteristics. They are more than their obvious communications. They have intentions and emotions and can communicate them directly or subtly to us and their companions. Moreover, unseen to us, except in terms of the elephant's external communications, is the elephant's emotional, intellectual, and spiritual life. There will always remain a mystery to the elephant we experience and describe.

Real-life elephants are active, creative, and adaptive in relationship to their kin, progeny, and the world around them. Observation tells us that elephants care for their calves, develop relationships with human beings,

---

and counsel humility and adventure in the quest to describe and experience the Divine.

2. Epperly, *Elephant Is Running*.

3. Ganesha, or Ganesh, the elephant deity in the Hindu pantheon, is the god of new beginnings, and the remover of obstacles. Ganesha breaks down the barriers placed between us and the Divine and all that stands is the way of spiritual growth and abundant life.

and experience joy and grief. The elephant is not only running; the elephant is also loving and playful. Elephants bond, protect, nurture, adapt, and give their young space to grow. Unambiguous in caring, the goal of a mother elephant is her offspring's survival and flourishing.[4] Yet, there is a hidden elephant spirit and species memory that we can intuit but never fully know.

While we cannot make a literal one-to-one correspondence between a living elephant and a living divinity, I believe that many of the same realities apply to the spiritual seeker and the Divine Reality they seek. We see in a mirror dimly, as the Christian spiritual teacher and mystic Paul of Tarsus notes (1 Cor 13:12). *Plus ultra!* There is always more to the divine than we can imagine or fathom, and the quest for the Divine will always be, for sincere and honest seekers, a holy adventure, in which the horizons of divinity recede as we move forward. Further, the reality we seek, whether we see it as primarily personal or impersonal, has a certain liveliness and intentionality—an abundant creativity and energy—that makes the quest not only endless, but also an adventure in encountering a reality that is also seeking us, motivated by the love that moves the stars and planets, and calls forth universe upon universe. The divine elephant speaks to us and also within us, as the murmurings of our deepest self and the insights of those around us, including those of the nonhuman world. The living elephant is also the remover of obstacles, most especially those that separate our spiritual traditions from one another and ourselves from the Divine. This is good news, theologically, spiritually, and communally, for our relationship with the Divine is a novel and endless holy adventure.

My Life with the Elephant

You can't have theology without theologians and their communities. The concrete and personal nature of theological reflection is an obvious but often neglected truth of the theological journey. Theologians seek to describe the divine, and yet all their descriptions are shaped by their personal experiences and the traditions, rituals, and theologies of their community, as well as by the personal initiative of the Divine. Accordingly, even when a theologian has a direct mystical encounter with the Divine, any theological descriptions of the Divine that may derive from it are shaped by the concrete experiences and histories of religious traditions and their communities; so for those of us who find meaning in them, theological articulations always

---

4. I recommend the following films, describing elephants in loving relationships with humans and their elephant kin: Birkhead, *Echo: An Elephant to Remember*; and Gonsalves, *Elephant Whisperers*.

have an autobiographical element often as important as the movements of the Divine Reality we seek in shaping our spiritual lives and our communities of faith experientially and theologically. We may seek to be self-transcendent, and theologians should try to go beyond the limitations of their culture and community in their search for the Divine, but even our most expansive quests are still finite and earthbound. Theology without concreteness is abstract and irrelevant to the hopes and dreams of humankind.

It is inevitable that our visions of God reflect the interplay of the experiences and insights of our community and our personal quests. My understanding of the living elephant, and the Living God, has emerged from the interplay of spiritual experience and theological reflection as an evolving Christian, and my personal encounter with religious pluralism. Those of us who describe ourselves as interspiritual pilgrims, that is, persons whose spiritual lives have been shaped by encounters with many religious paths, give witness to the many facets of the living elephant as well as to our unique personal and communal quests.

As spiritual pilgrims, we are always rooted in particular cultural, historical, and spiritual traditions. We may also experience spiritual growth by our participation in the rituals and spiritual practices of other faiths. These experiences profoundly shape and expand the contours of our commitments to our own faith tradition and can be the catalysts for constant creative transformation. In the spirit of an ever-widening holy adventure, I share a few snapshots of my own story to illuminate the global quest to encounter the Holy in all its mysterious liveliness and to give witness to the infinite and intimate love of God. As a reflection of my own faith as a follower of Jesus, I will refer to the Ultimate as "God," the personal reality that Jesus addressed, who is also the Intimate-Infinite "in whom we live and move and have our being." (Acts 17:28) While my experience is finite, imperfect, and sometimes sinful and self-interested in the context of a 13.7-billion-year, trillion-galaxy universe, the affirmation by Saint Bonaventure and Nicholas of Cusa that God is an "infinite sphere whose center is everywhere and whose circumference is nowhere," gives every seeker confidence that our deepest intuitions touch something of the nature of the Divine Reality.

I am a cradle Christian, and cannot be otherwise than a follower of Jesus, regardless of how far I sojourn from my spiritual beginnings. My first spiritual stirrings occurred in the parsonage of a small-town Baptist preacher in King City, at the time a village in the Salinas Valley, California. I was my father's son—deeply religious, prayerful, and prone to nature mysticism. I experienced Jesus as a companion who, in the words of a favorite hymn of my childhood, "walked with me and talked with me and told me I was his own."[5] Jesus came to me not only "in the garden" but walking along the Salinas River. His presence was palpable when I said my prayers at night and gave thanks when I awakened in the morning. I prayed to a personal God, known through God's Son Jesus, about anything and everything, from the outcomes of golf tournaments and Little League games to the health of the elders in our church and my own success in elementary school.

At age nine, I formally accepted Jesus as my personal savior at a revival meeting, "The Roundup for God," led by cowboy evangelist Leonard Eilers. While I don't remember all the details of this datable conversion experience, as we Baptists called it, I do remember the feeling tones of this experiential rite of passage: shedding tears of grace, coming forward, saying yes to Jesus as my savior, and being baptized a week later. I remember the evangelist's boots and chaps, lariat, and a song I've never heard anywhere since that time:

> Put your foot in the stirrup,
> Climb up on the horse,
> The roundup for God is on.

Though evangelical in spirit, my father was never doctrinaire. Although he embraced conservative Christian understandings of God (the Trinity, sin, and survival after death), I never heard him arguing theology or preaching about hell. The intricacies and controversies of theology and doctrine were penultimate for him. What was important to my father as a pastor and believer was our relationship with God and our neighbors, which occasionally got him in hot water when he invited migrant workers experiencing houselessness to sleep in our garage, when he provided haven for peace marchers on pilgrimages from Los Angeles to San Francisco, and when he refused to ratify racist attitudes toward the Mexican farmworkers who lived in migrant camps on the outskirts of town. While being intellectually astute, my father was a true evangelical, when the word "evangelical" meant being an intimate follower of Jesus, devoted to his "Lord and Savior," very much in the spirit of the bhakti yogis and the followers of Pure Land Buddhism. In times of peril, my father believed that when you call on Jesus—as others call on Krishna or Amida—God will find a way where you perceived no way forward. The God of my father comforted, healed, and challenged, and compelled him to see his relationship with Jesus as an invitation to welcome outsiders as God's beloved children, regardless of politics, race, or religion.

Everything changed in 1963, the summer after the revival meeting, when my father was asked to leave his pastorate, and our family moved to

---

5. Miles, "In the Garden" (1913).

San Jose, California. At ten years old, I found myself spiritually rootless, so traumatized by the experience of my father's dismissal and the change in our social standing that attending church elicited mild panic attacks and feelings of suffocation and imprisonment. While frightening to me, these feelings of physical emergency and threat may actually have been the harbingers of an emerging spirituality, one I had no words for at the time—a spirituality without walls, fences, or roof; a spirituality defined by imaginative pilgrimage and unlimited love. I needed an elephant's spirit, the spirit of Ganesha, to spiritually deconstruct the faith of my childhood, and break down the prison walls of small-town conservative Christianity, to experience the wider vistas of God's loving presence. I also needed the spirit of Jesus to heal the trauma caused by narrow visions of God and authoritarian and punitive religion.

Moving to San Jose turned my religious, cultural, and relational world upside down. While I lost the certainty of small-town spirituality, and a world defined solely in terms of Protestant and Catholic Christianity, I gained over the next few years the cosmopolitan creativity, freedom, and spiritual and cultural pluralism of the San Francisco Bay Area. By my sophomore year in high school, I was immersed in a spiritual adventure with Tolkien's Gandalf, Frodo, and Bilbo; Herman Hesse's Steppenwolf and Siddhartha; Carlos Castaneda's spiritual guide Don Juan Matus; and the insights of American Transcendentalism, Alan Watts, Buddhism, and Hinduism, along with the magical mystery tour of the San Francisco scene and weekly psychedelic excursions. As the lines from the Chambers Brothers' "Time Has Come Today," still one of my favorites of the Summer of Love, proclaim, "my soul [had] been psychedelicized."[6] Somehow, I survived the '60s. Perhaps through the interplay of a hidden providence in my spiritual quest and the wisdom associated with Ganesha, I evaded the substance use addiction that victimized many of my friends.

My world changed and my mind expanded once more when I took another spiritual route. In October 1970, I learned Transcendental Meditation at the Berkeley, California, ashram of the Students International Meditation Society. In many ways, learning the simple mantra meditation taught by Maharishi Mahesh Yogi brought about a second revival and datable conversion experience. God works in mysterious ways, and to my amazement, two weeks later, I returned to church, discovering a progressive congregation on the edge of San Jose State's campus. I was welcomed by the two pastors, who saw a theologian and spiritual leader in a long-haired hippie kid and gave me an opportunity to lead worship and to discover the riches of process theology; by the time I graduated from college, I regularly taught courses in

6 Chambers Brothers, "Time Has Come Today."

process theology to adults three times my age! I once more could claim to be a follower of Jesus, although the God of Jesus was far more expansive and innovative than the God of my childhood Baptist church.

Over the nearly five decades since college, I have lived an interspiritual adventure, deepening my personal relationship to Jesus and commitment to the Christian movement as a pastor, university chaplain, seminary administrator, and professor, while joining Christian practices with global spirituality. Transcendental Meditation inspired my personal and scholarly interest in Christian mysticism.[7] While Christ remains my spiritual center, the circumference of Christ's spiritual path is, as Saint Bonaventure asserted, nowhere. As a young professor, I became interested in the New Age and new spiritual movements initially through the study of attitudinal healing taught by Jerry Jampolsky and Susan Trout, which deepened my understanding of the Bible as a book of spiritual affirmations.[8] From the Hindu mystic activist Mahatma Gandhi I was inspired to study contemplative activism and encounter the spiritual foundations of the civil rights movement as embodied in the lives of Howard Thurman, Martin Luther King Jr., John Lewis, and Fannie Lou Hamer.[9] Later learning Reiki healing touch, with its emphasis on the healing power of chi or ki, revived my interest in the healings of Jesus and the healing ministry of the church and invited me to go beyond horizontal and unimaginative biblical scholarship to recognize that Jesus' healing power is alive in our world and that we can become God's partners in healing the world—personally, communally, and spiritually.[10] I discovered that the center of Divine revelation, inspiration, and healing, is everywhere, touching and inspiring everyone, and excluding no faithful spiritual quest.

Now in my seventh decade, I am living out the spirit of *plus ultra*, the affirmation that "there is more" to God and revelation than we can ever fathom. Theological reflection on God's love is not an abstract intellectual exercise for me; it is a concrete and embodied personal adventure. I have come to see a pattern of providence in my life, grounded in the interplay of the Infinite and Intimate, in which the love of God has both centered me and called me to expand the circumference of faith to embrace the varieties of spiritual experience.

The loving and barrier-breaking elephant has called me to grow in wisdom and stature. Rooted in her spiritual DNA, which is unique to every

---

7. For more on process-relational mysticism, see Epperly, *Mystic in You*; Epperly, *Become Fire!*; and Epperly, *Mystics in Action*.

8. Jampolsky, *Love Is Letting Go of Fear*; and Trout, *To See Differently*.

9. Epperly, *Prophetic Healing*.

10. Epperly, *Reiki Healing Touch*; Epperly, *Energy of Love*; Epperly, *Healing Marks*; Epperly, *God's Touch*.

person and culture, the divine mother elephant calls us to go beyond our religious beginnings and current spiritual perspectives to embody what Bernard Loomer described as S-I-Z-E:

> By size I mean the stature of a person's soul, the range and depth of his love, his capacity for relationships. I mean the volume of life you can take into your being and still maintain your integrity and individuality, the intensity and variety of outlook you can entertain in the unity of your being without feeling defensive or insecure. I mean the strength of your spirit to encourage others to become freer in the development of their diversity and uniqueness.[11]

While I cannot abandon my spiritual DNA, reflected in my childhood and everyday adult experience of Jesus walking beside me, challenging and guiding me, and surrounding me with protective love, I have discovered that Jesus' Parent, the personal reality revealed in Jesus as Christ, is known by many names, and embodied in diverse spiritualities. God is One and yet Many, unified but not homogenous. There are many paths, reflected in the many dimensions of Divine Reality and Inspiration. In listening to the wisdom of these spiritualities and participating in their practices, I have come to know more fully my Divine Parent and follow her ways. I have discovered that religious, cultural, and ethnic diversity is the gift of Divine Love, and not a fall from grace. In the spirit of another hymn of my childhood, one often forgotten by the adults of my church, I have experienced the infinite and intimate love of God revealed in the wondrous pluralism of the world's spiritual traditions:

> There's a wideness in God's mercy,
> Like the wideness of the sea;
> There's a kindness in God's justice,
> Which is more than liberty.
> But we make God's love too narrow
> By false limits of our own,
> And we magnify its strictness
> With a zeal God will not own.
> For the love of God is broader
> Than the measures of the mind,
> And the heart of the Eternal
> Is most wonderfully kind.[12]

---

11. Loomer, "S-I-Z-E is the Measure," 70.
12. Faber, "There's a Wideness in God's Mercy" (1862).

Lions and Tigers, and Bears, Oh My!

One of the best-known scenes from the film version of L. Frank Baum's *Wizard Oz* occurs in response to Dorothy's question to the Tin Man when Dorothy and her companions find themselves in a dark wood along the Yellow Brick Road, "Do you think we'll meet any wild animals?" The Scarecrow frets anxiously, "Animals that eat straw?" To which the Tin Man responds, "Mostly lions and tigers and bears." The Tin Man's speculation throws all three into a panic, and they begin fearfully chanting, "Lions and tigers, and bears, oh my! Lions and tigers, and bears, oh my!" Their anxious chant awakens the cowardly Lion, who tries to disguise his fear with growls, roars, and threats. To their relief and eventual good fortune, the Lion drops his fearsome façade, joins in the adventure, and eventually realizes his true nature as a loyal companion and protector.[13] What initially appeared to be a weakness becomes a saving strength.

Many images of God and doctrinal statements resemble the threatening "lions and tigers, and bears" imagined by Dorothy and her companions. Divine supplicants view God not only as the reality who sets the universe in motion and determines its course but also as the sovereign who separates humankind into saved and unsaved, orthodox and heretic, and demands absolute obedience. Omnipotent, God determines the rules of salvation, and there is nothing we can do about it. If we turn from God's appointed path and stray from orthodox doctrine, we jeopardize our souls. By God's predestining wisdom, the souls of those who have never heard of God's true path are also in jeopardy. In contrast, those whom God has chosen, and who obey what they perceive to be God's admonitions have heaven as their destination, regardless of the quality of their ethical lives. While faith in this sovereign God centers on the sacrificial Jesus who died for our sins, paying the price for humankind's primordial disobedience, the omnipotent sovereign has determined that there is only one way to salvation, and that way is to be found in accepting the rules and doctrines of God's chosen path, regardless of how ludicrous and mean-spirited they appear to be. Woe unto the unbeliever, agnostic, stranger, or adherent of another faith tradition, who will be condemned by divine fiat to eternal torment in the land of "lions and tigers and bears." Saved and unsaved are alike truly "sinners in the hands of an angry God." Deserving punishment, the saved hang by the slender thread of divine predestination, sacrament, or doctrinal orthodoxy, while the damned are condemned to roast eternally in hellfire and brimstone. Questioning, innovation, and adventure are discouraged, and punished, by

---

13 Fleming and Vitor, *Wizard of Oz*.

this backward-looking, authoritarian faith. As a student once told me, "My parents are good people, but if they don't accept Jesus as their savior, they are destined for hell along with good people like Gandhi and Buddha."

The fearsome God of threat and division has chosen to open only one path to salvation, and that divine authoritarianism and divisiveness becomes the model for his followers' relationships to dissenters, agnostics, and persons of other faiths. In their quest for certainty, salvation, and power, the omnipotent and divisive God's most ardent followers claim that their particular and limited perspective on the Divine is the only true path to salvation. In fact, these true believers thrive on limitation and particularity, scorning anything that resembles universality and hospitality. Believing that any doctrinal change is a threat to the one true faith they control, they have determined the limits and nature of the path to salvation and preached that the one way involves (some variation and combination of) making a confession of faith in Jesus as Savior, sharing in the clergy-controlled sacraments of the church, and obeying a particular human or scriptural authoritarian conduit of God's revelation.

While there are nuances in this vision of God in terms of fearsome "lions, tigers, and bears," the versions of this vision share the belief that beyond the loving Jesus is the hidden and punitive will of God, whose righteousness cannot tolerate either the sinner or the sin. They claim that Jesus loves us, but they fear that as the result of our inherent sinfulness, God is out to get us if we don't follow the prescribed path of salvation. The loving and welcoming Jesus is penultimate, while the judgmental, divisive, inscrutable, and threatening God is ultimate in worship, reality, and relationship with humankind.

The otherwise-angry God, whose sovereignty must not be questioned, creates a theological and ethical world of insiders and outsiders. An undeserving sinner who does not come to the true faith is not one of "us" and is expendable to God and to God's true believers unless they choose to toe the line, join the one true faith, and embrace their theological and cultural prejudices. As a placard held by a protester at a Pride march threatened, "God destroys all who forsake him."

The God of "lions, tigers, and bears" can be feared but cannot be loved. Despite their good-heartedness in interpersonal relationships, people who worship this God often rely on fear and ostracism as a primary motivation for living out their faith and sharing it with others. Deep down this God's followers know that, despite Jesus' love, we are still offensive to God's sovereign perfection. The Father God rules by the power of fear and not the power of love, and encourages his followers to do likewise. Woe unto spiritual adventurers, who color outside the lines, and discover deeper aspects of God than those authorized by God's holy books and representatives.

A More Graceful Option

Yet, there is another theological and relational option, grounded in the biblical affirmation that perfect love casts out fear. (I John 4:18) The amipotent and uncontrolling love of God, reflected in the relational universalism of Paul's christological hymn in Philippians 2:5-11 is grounded in the contrasting images of God's companionship, solidarity, and love that inspires similar loving and affirming values in God's followers.[14]

> Let the same mind be in you that was in Christ Jesus,
> who, though he existed in the form of God,
> did not regard equality with God
> as something to be grasped,
> but emptied himself,
> taking the form of a slave,
> assuming human likeness.
> And being found in appearance as a human, he humbled himself
> and became obedient to the point of death—
> even death on a cross.
> Therefore God exalted him even more highly
> and gave him the name
> that is above every other name,
> so that at the name given to Jesus
> every knee should bend,
> in heaven and on earth and under the earth,
> and every tongue should confess
> that Jesus Christ is Lord,
> to the glory of God the Father.

From this perspective, there is no ambiguity or contrast between the character of God and the Beloved Son Jesus Christ. Jesus Christ is the incarnation of God's pure, unbounded love. Christ is the loving elephant mother, the all-embracing companion, who becomes one of us, letting go of threat and coercion, and ruling by loving relatedness. There is no "hidden," threatening will of God, nor is God out to get us. While God is the wisdom behind the moral and spiritual arcs of history, God's judgment in history is that of the Great Physician, seeking healing and not sickness, reconciliation and not punishment. Like the mother elephant, God even protects God's wayward and authoritarian children. When the children go astray, they are not punished or abandoned by their Mother. Rather they are lovingly chastened and challenged by God's presence in the moral and spiritual arcs of history, in order to be brought back to a path of justice and compassion. We bow out

14. Oord, *Death of Omnipotence*.

of gratitude and praise, not out of fear of punishment, to the divine elephant who breaks down every barrier between God and us. We reflect the ways of God in reconciliation and not destruction, becoming barrier breakers ourselves. The relational creativity of God inspires respectful and supportive relationships with persons of other faiths and cultures.

New Testament scholars note that the apostle Paul's first-century readers would have contrasted this *kenotic,* self-emptying, and relational divine power with the power of Caesar, under whom any disobedience brought death. Paul tells his readers to live as Christ did, placing the power of love and community, sacrifice and solidarity, ahead of the love of power. To have the mind of Christ is to live lovingly, to serve faithfully, and to rule relationally, whether in religious, political, or relational life. In our time, we contrast this vision of the amipotent God[15] with authoritarian and legalistic religion and the walls it builds to separate us from the "other," whether the "other" appears in our own faith tradition or within and among the various spiritual traditions of humankind. A mother elephant is powerful, and its power is aimed at nurture and protection, and education and inspiration, of all her offspring.

Diversity as Grace

The parable of the divine elephant and the blindfolded or sight-impaired pilgrims describes the Ultimate Reality and the journey toward God as multifaceted and ever expanding. God's nature, like that of the elephant, is complex and intricate, not homogenous. The Divine is living, moving, and changing, and constantly revealing new aspects of itself. While we honor the apophatic, mysterious, ineffable, and changeless aspects of God, their reality is but one aspect of the concrete, moving, and loving God. Diversity, concreteness, and change are ultimate, while changelessness is subsumed within the ever-changing experience of the Holy One, the personal mystery we call God. In contrast to many approaches to mysticism, the living elephant Deity, similar to Saguna Brahman and Amida Buddha, is the God of history, diversity, and transformation, who invites us to plunge into the world of change, finding enlightenment and salvation in the ever-flowing fountain of divine love, toward which the beauties of this word point. Indeed, the myriad beauties of this world reflect the manifold wisdom and creativity of Divine Beauty, who gives direction to the beauty-creating teleology of the universe, described by philosopher Alfred North Whitehead. The quest of mystics and believers, accordingly, is not for eternal, unchanging, and

---

15. See Oord, *Death of Omnipotence.*

disembodied life but for everlasting, incarnate, and ever adventuring life, grounded in the gentle interdependence of God. The God of all universes takes us beyond words and doctrines in the concreteness of divine grace. The God of wondrous diversity inspires followers to move from self-interest, even interest in enlightenment and salvation, to world loyalty—to be Little Christs and Bodhisattvas who place the healing of the world and its creatures above their own well-being.

Theologians and their political followers have privileged uniformity and changelessness and accordingly have viewed diversity and change as inferior aspects of divinity and the universe. In so doing, they have cultivated individualism and apathy toward the pain of others, rather than interdependence and empathy to the experiences of others. They have also aspired to uniformity as the basis of faith, rather than the relational interplay of unity and diversity. In contrast, the image of the living elephant, and the Christian image of divine trinity or triunity, sees relationship and the production of diversity as essential to God's nature and the nature of the universe. The multifaceted living God parents forth a diverse universe with diverse creatures, cultures, theologies, and spiritual paths. While our spiritual adventures touch different aspects of the divine, it is also the case that God intentionally reveals different aspects of God's own self, creating and responding to various cultural and religious experiences.

The loving and companioning God is the Word and Wisdom made flesh in history and embodiment. This God also embodies the loving spirit of parenting and grandparenting, and deep friendship as well as the intimate protectiveness of nurturing mother elephants: our love is expressed in many ways depending on the particular context and seasons of life. Love, whether human or divine, can take the form of challenge and comfort, and confrontation and compassion, with the goal of healing and self-realization in relationship with God and one another. God loves diversity, whether in human experience or religious expression. After all, God is the fountain from which diversity flows!

The apostle Paul's vision of Christ, described in Philippians 2, and by Thomas Jay Oord's word "amnipotence," lovingly reveal those aspects of God's presence that are most helpful to salvation and healing of persons and cultures. While God takes the initiative gracefully inspiring all creation, God constantly shapes God's presence to address the concrete realities of our lives and contexts. God is the ultimate intimate, personalist, and anamcara, friend of the soul, relating Godself to persons and communities.

The love of God varies in energy and emphasis from one person and one moment to another and constantly shifts in relationship to context, age, character, and previous decisions. Diversity is expected and promoted, not denied or suppressed.

The great trinitarian insight, whether seen in terms of Father, Son, and Holy Spirit, Creator, Christ, and Spirit, or Brahma, Vishnu, and Shiva, is that Divinity is diverse, and so is the world emerging from divine creativity. God delights in diversity and praises pluralism, providing pathways of the spirit as a reflection of God's own wondrous artistry. As the ultimate model for human existence, God's nature invites us to seek unity in diversity and diversity in unity, always attentive to the holiness of God's beloved children. Accordingly, in times of social stress, we can picket and pray, knowing that our alignment with God's vision of wholeness includes protester and oppressor alike.

A Final Word

The practical implication that my lyrical and autobiographical approach to the parable of the elephant as representing the all-embracing love of God is that we can celebrate our spiritual limitations and delight in the growing edges of religious experience. Our spiritual limitations reflect the concreteness of our spiritual experiences and our unique personal and communal experiences of God. They reflect God's intimate presence in our lives and the world. The world lives by the incarnation of God, and God is incarnate in the many spiritual paths we take. We can also celebrate the liveliness of the elephant, calling us to run alongside and join hands with spiritual companions of other faith communities, cultures, races, ethnicities, sexual orientations, and gender identities. A living God and a running elephant both reveal new and expansive vistas of spirituality and call us to new experiences and to humbly share our insights.

Limitation and concreteness are the womb of possibility constantly inviting us to spiritual growth. The horizon is infinite, provoking a holy adventure celebrating the insights of our spiritual companions. We need not fear "lions and tigers and bears" of the coercive and authoritarian God and its followers, for we travel with the divine elephant who removes every barrier to love on the way to wholeness, healing, and reconciliation for creation in its manifold wonder and beauty.

Bibliography

Birkhead, Mike, dir. *Echo: An Elephant to Remember*. A documentary film written by Daniel Bernstein et al. Starring Martyn Colbeck et al. Produced by Rubin Tarrant Productions. Released on October 2, 2010 (in the US). See https://www.imdb.com/title/tt1713800/?ref_=fn_al_tt_1/.

Chambers Brothers. "Time Has Come Today." On *The Time Has Come*, side 2, song 5. Columbia CS 9522, 1967, LP.

Epperly, Bruce G. *Become Fire! Guideposts for Interspiritual Pilgrims*. Vestal, NY: Anamchara, 2018.

———. *The Elephant Is Running: Process and Open and Relational Theologies and Religious Pluralism*. Grasmere, ID: Sacra Sage, 2022.

———. *The Energy of Love: Reiki and Christian Healing*. Topical Line Drives 26. La Vergne, TN: Energion, 2017.

———. *God's Touch: Faith, Wholeness, and the Healing Miracles of Jesus*. Louisville: Westminster John Knox, 2001.

———. *Healing Marks: Healing and Spirituality in Mark's Gospel*. Gonzales, FL: Energion, 2012.

———. *Prophetic Healing: Howard Thurman's Vision of Contemplative Activism*. Richmond, IN: Friends United, 2020.

———. *Mystics in Action: Twelve Saints for Today*. Maryknoll, NY: Orbis, 2020.

———. *The Mystic in You: Discovering a God-Filled World*. Nashville: Upper Room, 2018.

———. *Reiki Healing Touch and the Way of Jesus*. Kelowna, BC: Northstone, 2005.

Faber, William Austin. "There's a Wideness in God's Mercy." Hymn (1862). See https://hymnary.org/text/theres_a_wideness_in_gods_mercy/.

Fleming, Victor, and King Vidor, dirs. *The Wizard of Oz*. Written by Noel Langley et al. Starring Judy Garland et al. Produced by MGM. Released on August 25, 1939. See https://www.imdb.com/title/tt0032138/?ref_=fn_al_tt_1/.

Gonsalves, Kartiki, dir. *The Elephant Whisperers*. A documentary film written by, Kartiki Gonsalves et al. Starring Bellie and Bomman. Produced by Sikhya Entertainment. Released on December 8, 2022 (in the US). See https://www.imdb.com/title/tt23628262/.

Jampolsky, Gerald G. *Love Is Letting Go of Fear*. Berkeley: Celestial Arts, 2004.

Loomer, Bernard. "S-I-Z-E Is the Measure." In *Religious Experience and Process Theology: The Pastoral Implications of a Major Modern Movement*, edited by Harry James Cargas and Bernard Lee, 69–76. New York: Paulist, 1976.

Miles, C. Austin. "In the Garden." Hymn (1913). See https://hymnary.org/text/i_come_to_the_garden_alone/.

Oord, Thomas Jay. *The Death of Omnipotence and the Birth of Amipotence*. Grassmere, ID: SacraSage, 2023.

Thatamanil, John J. *Circling the Elephant: A Comparative Theology of Religious Diversity*. Comparative Theology: Thinking across Traditions. New York: Fordham University Press, 2020.

Trout, Susan. *To See Differently: Personal Growth and Being of Service through Attitudinal Healing*. Washington, DC: Three Roses, 1990.

11

God, Value, and Ontological Gratitude

On the Axiological Foundations of Worship

Andrew M. Davis

In the development of modern process-relational thought, key figures have continually returned to the question of God's worthiness of worship. They have done so for a variety of reasons and through a variety of resonant proposals. At least in part, they have been indebted to Whitehead's own concerns on the matter. Writing in the 1920s, it is clear that the question of worship was central to Whitehead's own religious and existential angst with respect to God. "The immediate reaction of human nature to the religious vision is worship," he states; true "worship of God" is not a "rule of safety," but an "adventure of the spirit."[1] Concerns for the proper mode of worship upheld Charles Hartshorne's own theological proposal in the late 1940s, which sought to "express and enhance reverence or worship" for God "on a high ethical or cultural level." Indeed, he was deeply concerned with "whether and how" God might be conceived "as having such a character" so that an "enlightened person may worship and serve" with "whole heart and mind."[2] In the late 1980s, David Ray Griffin insisted that the claim that God alone be "worthy of worship" is not only essential to the "generic idea of God" that has spanned civilizations, but also vital to any postmodern naturalistic theism.[3] So too in the early 1990s, C. Robert Mesle, in perhaps

---

1. Whitehead, *Science and the Modern World*, 192.
2. Hartshorne, *Divine Relativity*, 1.
3. Griffin, *God and Religion in the Postmodern World*, 77. Later, Griffin would remove this criterion from his list of generic features of God because of its tautological nature: "It would have rendered tautological my conclusions that the being described is worthy of the name God." Griffin, *Reenchantment without Supernaturalism*, 166n27. For Griffin's further considerations in dialogue with key critics, see Appendix B, current volume.

the best-known introduction to process theology, comments on worship and poses the question directly: "To worship properly is to center our lives around something, to see it as the proper focus of our ultimate commitment ... My worship awaits something, or someone, worth giving my life to. What kind of God, then, is worthy of worship?"[4] In the mid-1990s, Rabbi Harold S. Kushner, author of the bestselling book *When Bad Things Happen to Good People* (1981), would also raise this question in direct debt to his interactions with process thinkers: "What sort of God is worthy of worship?"[5]

These are a few examples of the historical importance of this question within open, relational, and process circles. It seems fully natural, however, for the question of God's worthiness of worship to be raised yet again, and for a new time. As is the case with great questions, they are not easily exhausted; they must be posed and reposed anew such that each generation might build upon the past in novel and relevant ways. Any question worth asking again is worth answering again. Although the question might be the same, answering again in a new context and in a new way might cast fresh light upon old insight.

In this chapter, I consider this question anew and in dialogue with the resonant insights of key figures within open, relational, and process traditions (Alfred North Whitehead, Keith Ward, and Nicholas Rescher), as well as with those outside these traditions (John Leslie and A. C. Ewing). I approach the question through a deeper, meditative inquiry into the nature of divine necessity and advocate a particular axiological approach differently supported and expressed by these figures.

In my estimation, taking this question seriously requires one to meditate upon it and all its implications. Sinking into its reflective depths awakens something undeniably "there" in human experience, something both existentially and philosophically significant, something that is—dare I say—*worthy* of consideration. It is a question that at once challenges us to clarify what it is we mean by "God"; what it would possibly involve for something to be "worthy"; and what it is we actually refer to when using this curious word "worship." I offer then a kind of philosophical meditation in hopes that the relationship between these notions might find some manner of novel illumination. In doing so, I request that readers also sit with the reflections and questions that unfold toward a reframed answer as to the axiological foundations of God, the world, and human worship.

4. Mesle, *Process Theology*, 15.

5. Kushner, "Would an All-Powerful God be Worthy of Worship?," 90. For John Cobb's 1984 Center for Process Studies interview with Kushner on the theme of "Human Suffering and the Power of God," see: https://www.youtube.com/watch?v=EdO12ovwAM8/.

The Question below the Question

Let me first lay out the contours of my approach. It is my conviction that one cannot begin to consider the question "What kind of God is most worthy of worship?" without first addressing another more fundamental question, namely: "Why it is that God, and perhaps anything at all, should exist in the first place?" This is a fantastic question; and it does not, per se, seek arguments for God's existence. However related they are, it is one thing to argue *that* God exists and another to answer *why* God exists. What I am seeking is a coherent and plausible reason as to why God and a world such as ours should exist as opposed to not exist.

This is not an easy theological question. Answering it requires both imagination and application. "Theology is not merely a rehearsal and translation of tradition," Gordan Kaufman rightly states: "It is (and always has been) a creative activity of the human imagination seeking to provide more adequate orientation for human life."[6] To use Whitehead's phraseology, theology, like philosophy, involves "imaginative generalization" from our concrete experience.[7] I realize too that this may seem a rather strange and perhaps unrelated way to approach the question of God's worthiness of worship; yet I've come to see that no question could be more important. It is not unrelated; to the contrary, I would submit that one cannot even answer the question before us without first answering this one.

That God is *necessary* is likely the first response a reflective consideration might come to. "Necessity," of course, is another one of those curious and difficult notions of philosophical theology. In part, I remain fully confident in the tradition: if God exists, then God does so necessarily. But what is the *nature* of divine necessity? This, I claim, is the question *below* the question of God's worthiness of worship.

One might offer a number of responses to this question: (1) God's existence may be arbitrary and without reason—a total *brute fact*; (2) God's own *unrelenting power* might plausibly justify God's own existence and thus God's worthiness of worship; (3) God's reason could be that God is *logically necessary*, something the very denial of which is logically contradictory; or (4) it may be that we are forced to finally throw up our hands and submit to *utter mystery*—we do not know and cannot know why it is that God exists.

Each of these four answers fails to ground a God worthy of worship; they also fail to illuminate what worship is (or ought to be). In what follows, then, I seek to dispel each of these answers with the help of a constellation

---

6. Kaufman, *Theology for a Nuclear Age*, 20.
7. Whitehead, *Process and Reality*, 5.

of echoing insights from John Leslie, A. C. Ewing, Keith Ward, Alfred North Whitehead, and Nicholas Rescher. I offer instead a fifth option differently expressed by these thinkers, one that has lasting roots in the Western tradition of philosophical theology: only that God whose very *reason for being* is founded in the creative supremacy of its own *Value* can be worthy of worship. Put differently, only a God whose Value is "creatively effective," or "ethically requiring" of its own reality (to use Leslie's phrasing), can persuade a human response rightfully called worshipful.[8]

Although these different voices do not consider "worship" in any detail, they do differently support the conclusion that God's existence "is founded on Value" (to quote Whitehead) and thereby that there is an axiological foundation for the existence of God, the world, and ourselves as worshiping beings.[9] The axiological foundations of God and the world, moreover, constitute worship in terms of what I call "ontological gratitude"—a gratefulness for existence—which if properly expressed, manifests itself in a value-creative life that aims to justify that existence. To conclude, I will offer a brief review and final statement of my claims.

Divine Necessity and the Query of Worship

What is or should be the fundamental basis of divine necessity? It is important to grasp some of the different ways God's necessary existence might be

---

8. Leslie, *Immortality Defended*, 18–19. Scholars have employed various terms in attempting to capture the notion that Value has an ultimate standing in the universe. What Leslie calls "axiarchism" is the view that the universe is ruled largely if not entirely by Value. He details how this view "has immensely influenced both religion and philosophy," including thinkers like Plato, Aristotle, Plotinus, Dionysius, Aquinas, Descartes, Spinoza, Leibniz, Berkeley, Kant, Hegel, Lotze, F. H. Bradley, Henri Bergson, Alfred North Whitehead, W. R. Sorley, Paul Tillich, J. A. T. Robinson, A. C. Ewing, and Keith Ward. See Leslie, *Value and Existence*; and his magnum opus, *Infinite Minds*. Nicholas Rescher uses "axiogenesis" for his theory, aiming "to explain reality on the basis of merit, fact on the basis of value." See Rescher *Axiogenesis*, ix. Frederick Ferré uses "kalogenic" to argue for the inherently aesthetic nature of actuality. Refer to Ferré, *Being and Value*. Peter Forrest speaks simply of the "Value Principle" or "Evaluative Understanding" such that we can explain many features of the universe, "including its suitability for life, by appealing to its value, including its aesthetic value." See Forrest, *God without the Supernatural*, 149.

In addition to these texts, see also Ewing, *Value and Reality*; Rice, *God and Goodness*; and Wynn, *God and Goodness*. For further historical considerations, see MacDonald, *Being and Goodness*. For my own contributions in dialogue with Whitehead, Ward, and Leslie, and with respect to a tradition better termed "axianoetic," refer to Davis, *Mind, Value, and the Cosmos*. For a shorter summary of the axianoetic tradition, see Davis, "God as Reason."

9. Whitehead, "Immortality," 98.

framed. We can then consider their adequacy or inadequacy with respect to the question of God's worthiness for worship. As shown above, there are at least five different ways of articulating divine necessity. These include (1) reasonless brute fact, (2) unrelenting power, (3) logical necessity, (4) utter mystery, and (5) axiological necessity. Let's take each in turn.

Reasonless Brute Fact

Richard Swinburne has argued that God *cannot not exist* due to the eternal necessity of the divine nature. For him, to say that God's existence is *necessary* is to insist that the "existence of God is a brute fact that is inexplicable—not in the sense that we do not know its explanation, but in the sense that it does not have one."[10] Indeed, an "ultimate explanation," he states, is a complete explanation whose ultimate terms have "no explanation either full or partial in terms of any other factors"; they are "ultimate brute facts."[11]

Now ask yourself: Can you assign any worthiness of worship to a brute and arbitrary fact, ultimately reasonless in its existence? If you sit with this for a moment, it does not take long to draw a negative conclusion. Leslie has argued unwaveringly against the claim that some divine reality, "reasonless" in existence, can be explanatory of anything.[12] Ward too has pushed back, saying that if "God cannot be accounted for," this simply "makes the divine existence and nature something which just happens to be the case."[13] Consider this again: Can you worship something the reality of which just "happens to be the case"? Ewing has rightly insisted that without an answer to the question of God's "cause," any talk of God simply collapses. Indeed, explanations referring to "something else which is itself unexplained is not a satisfying explanation."[14] Nor is it satisfying to worship. Whitehead too would warn us that pointing to some "ultimate reality which, in some unexplained way, is to be appealed to for the removal of perplexity, constitutes the great refusal of rationality to assert its rights."[15] Perhaps then you would agree that to worship something that *has no reason* is really to worship *for no reason*—and that can hardly help our inquiry.

---

10. Swinburne, *Existence of God*, 96.
11. Swinburne, *Existence of God*, 79.
12. Leslie, *Immortality Defended*, 83.
13. Ward, *Religion and Creation*, 195.
14. Ewing, *Value and Reality*, 156–57, 163.
15. Whitehead, *Science and the Modern World*, 92.

Unrelenting Power

If God's existence is not reasonless, or without explanation, perhaps God's reason is due to God's own limitless power. Could unrelenting divine power be the ground of God, the very source of divine existence? Suppose it were for a moment. To account for the eternal necessity of God's existence, it would apparently have to be a kind of eternally dominant Will-to-be. Certainly, no shortage of demands have been made throughout the theological tradition that we "worship" (or at least fear) that unlimited power that is most supreme, causally able, and—in its worst form—all-determining. We could perhaps think of certain statements by Calvin, for example, that should send chills down our spines. Not even the falling of a sparrow, nor yet the breaking of a branch that kills a passerby, escapes God's determination, he assures us. There does, however, remain a kind of logic to unrelenting divine power: if God's power is unlimited and utterly determining, it must determine not only God's existence (being essential to divine necessity) but also the existence of everything else. How could any derivative mode of finite existence escape such power if it flows from the very essence of God? The answer seems simple: it cannot.

Now consider worship in this scenario. Can you plausibly assign worthiness of worship to inescapable divine power? Can you truly worship such power? Perhaps you would agree with Whitehead that "the worship of glory arising from power is not only dangerous: it arises from a barbaric conception of God" and that "even the world itself could not contain the bones of those slaughtered because of men intoxicated by its attraction."[16] Do you not agree with Ewing that "the worship of power as such is not good but evil" and with Leslie that "the sheer power of any deity" cannot possibly "deserve worship"?[17]

Considered by itself, then, it would seem that the worship of brute power can only emerge as a *veneer for our fear of it*. Can fear and worship possibly live together? "The worship of God is not a rule of safety," Whitehead reminds us.[18] It must not be a result of our fearful desire to appease divine power in quest for preservation. Rabbi Kushner's comment thus rings true: "You can fear an all-powerful God, but you cannot love him."[19] When it comes to worship, you might even agree with Hartshorne: unbridled

---

16. Whitehead, *Religion in the Making*, 44–45.
17. Ewing, *Value and Reality*, 161; Leslie, *Value and Existence*, 25.
18. Whitehead, *Science and the Modern World*, 192.
19. Kushner, "Would an All-Powerful God," 90.

omnipotence is a "theological mistake."[20] May we not seek to worship mistaken divine power—either in heaven or on earth.

Logical Necessity

Divine power as classically conceived is said to be restricted by logic. God's power is able to do anything that is not *logically self-contradictory*. We have heard the examples often: God cannot make a rock so heavy that not even God can lift it. Not even God can make sense of a square circle. God cannot commit deicide. These impossibilities are no affront to God—it is often said. Of course, if God exists at all, then God is *logically possible*. Perhaps then it is not that God has no reason, or that power determines God's existence, but rather that God's existence is reasoned by *logical necessity*. Many thinkers continue to argue this.

But would a logically necessary God really be worthy of worship? Can you truly assign worship to matters of logic—say to the proposition that God's *nonexistence* is logically self-contradictory? Could worship possibly be a matter of *p* and *-p* or the grand fact that the sum total of your bank deposit of two checks cannot equal less than the amount of just one of them? You might worship such logic as it relates to money, but neither is money worthy of your worship.

Whitehead insists that "logic lies upon the universe as an iron necessity," but does it also lie upon God in terms of divine necessity?[21] Ewing answers no: he agrees strongly with Kant's objection to a logically necessary being—and perhaps we should as well. "There could not be any contradiction in something not existing," Ewing states, "because you must ascribe conflicting attributes to something if you are to contradict yourself, but if you merely deny the existence of something you are not ascribing any attributes to anything, so there are no attributes to conflict." "This seems to me," he concludes, "a fatal objection to the view that the existence of God is logically necessary."[22] If so, is it not also a fatal objection to worshiping such a God?

Utter Mystery

Maybe at last we simply toss up our hands and appeal to *utter mystery*. It is not that God exists without reason or through power or logic; rather, we

---

20. Hartshorne, *Omnipotence and Other Theological Mistakes*.
21. Whitehead, *Science and the Modern World*, 18.
22. Ewing, *Value and Reality*, 147.

simply cannot know why it is that God exists. Can this possibly satisfy our inquiry? Whitehead points to a shared "faith" exhibited in human pursuits of science, philosophy, and religion alike. This faith, he holds, is expressed through a fundamental "trust" that "at the base of things we shall not find mere arbitrary mystery."[23] In some sense, of course, we must all acknowledge the depths of mystery; but mystery is not to be worshiped—and we know this. Why worship something you do not know? To "worship mystery as such," Ewing insists, "is to worship something simply because we do not know what it is like."[24] On the contrary, true worship seems to assume some mode of knowledge or experience, however fleeting, that would justify that which is worshiped as *worthy* of worship. Worship presupposes insight into what that something is truly like. The bewilderment inherent in pure mystery may fill us with wonder, but it can hardly constitute what is "most worthy of worship."

Axiological Necessity

Where are we then? If the explanation for divine necessity is not inexplicable "brute fact," all-determining power, logic, or mystery—what remains? Is there another kind of necessity that might aid our inquiry into God's explanation and, therefore, God's worthiness of worshiped? Ewing is adamant there is:

> If we are to meet the demand of the human intellect that there should be a reason [for existence], we seem to need a reason of such a kind as will give an explanation of existence without making the non-existence of anything logically self-contradictory. There remains only one alternative, as far as can be seen, which might do this, namely an explanation in terms of values. In that case, God's existence will be necessary not because there would be any internal self-contradiction in denying it but because it was supremely good that God should exist.[25]

Consider these questions: Is not "Goodness" or "Value" a reason for something to exist? Could not God eternally exist precisely because it is *supremely valuable that God should*? Put differently, could God's own existence be "ethically needful" or "required," as Leslie argues, with a creative success

---

23. Whitehead, *Science and the Modern World*, 18.
24. Ewing, *Value and Reality*, 161.
25. Ewing, *Value and Reality*, 157.

eternally procuring God's existence?[26] This may sound odd, but it is actually at the heart of the traditional affirmation of God's necessity. Why, after all, could not "ethical necessity" or "axiological necessity" be a reality—and be so with a robust explanatory power every bit as "iron" as logical necessity? In a deep sense, it would be an explanation that is both *axia* and *logical* in nature. "How are we to give any plausibility to the traditional idea that [God] has in [God's self] the sufficient ground for [God's self]?" Leslie asks. He answers: "We must I think conceive this ground as having an ethical side to it; we must view God's existence as ethically required because [God's] nature is what it is." On Leslie's account, God's intrinsic goodness is what "makes [God's] existence ethically required."[27] This requirement, for Leslie, moreover, need not be *outside* God, thereby landing us in a kind of Euthyphro dilemma writ large, but rather can have "its sources *in* [God's] own tremendously rich nature."[28]

Ward agrees strongly with both Ewing and Leslie in this regard: the "best reason that something *should* exist," he states, "is its intrinsic value." He reaches back to Aristotle:

> But if there is something which, as Aristotle has suggested, cannot exist otherwise than as it does, the best reason for its existence would lie in its supreme goodness . . . To be rationally explicable, it has to contain the reason for its existence in itself. So a rationally explicable being is a necessary being which is supremely good . . . a supremely good necessary being is ultimately explanatory in that it necessarily desires its own existence as that which is most worthy of existence.[29]

For Ward, if the supreme goodness of God is what makes God "most worthy" of necessary existence, it must also make God most worthy of worship. "A God who is worthy of worship," he states, "must be so good that it could never conceivably be evil." What is more, this God must have "some power for good with which we could align ourselves, to help us to be good." Ward thus stresses that we "think again about worship" so that worship is the "natural expression of attraction, admiration, and awe," the "immediate and natural response to a vision of supreme goodness, beauty, and creative power, in other words, to a vision of God."[30] These statements are strikingly

26. Leslie, *Immortality Defended*, 2.
27. Leslie, *Value and Existence*, 6–7.
28. Leslie, *Infinite Minds*, 56 (emphasis in original).
29. Ward, *Religion and Creation*, 196. For a recent exploration of Aristotle's metaphysics of goodness, see Mirus, *Being Is Better Than Not Being*.
30. Ward, *Confessions of a Recovering Fundamentalist*, 46–47.

reminiscent of Whitehead's own: "The immediate reaction of human nature to the religious vision is worship."[31]

What about Whitehead's vision of divine necessity? He too looks to Value. Not only does he speak of the "necessary goodness" of the "primordial nature" of God as the abstract, necessary foundation of divinity, but he associates "the concept of God" directly with what he calls "the World of Value," wherein Value represents "the infinity of values" in their timeless eternity. In fact, he insists clearly that God's existence is "founded on value," on "ideals of perfection, moral and aesthetic."[32] Whereas Leslie insists that divine necessity is God's ethical requirement, we might say on Whitehead's account that divine necessity is God's aesthetic requirement. Indeed, "any system of things which in any wide sense is beautiful," Whitehead states, "is to that extent justified in its existence."[33] This statement can be applied to the "why" of the existence of both God and the world. Whether one emphasizes the ethical or aesthetic—and these must be intricately connected—both renderings express primordial Value at the base of things.

Evidence, Existence, and Worship

These statements by Ewing, Leslie, Ward, and Whitehead are not at all simple; nevertheless, they speak to something I think fully plausible. Perhaps, however, you remain unconvinced that such an axiological scenario could possibly be true. What is the evidence after all, and what does it have to do with worship?

Imagine with me for a moment. The evidence is the very existence of the world, your very own existence, and that of those around you. As Ewing puts it, "If God's existence is determined by values, the existence of everything ultimately is."[34] Consider whether or not your life has any value. Consider whether or not the world has any value. If your answer is yes, then have you not given a reason (and perhaps *the* reason) for the existence of anything—including God? If yes, are you not propelled toward affirming something like the reality of Supreme Value? Would you not have to agree

---

31. Whitehead, *Science and the Modern World*, 192.

32. Whitehead, *Process and Reality*, 345; Whitehead, "Immortality," 88, 97–98, 101–2. Although inherently related, the "aesthetic" is more fundamental than the "moral" for Whitehead: "All order is . . . aesthetic order, and the moral order is merely certain aspects of the aesthetic order." Whitehead, *Religion in the Making*, 91.

33. Whitehead, *Adventures of Ideas*, 256.

34. Ewing, *Value and Reality*, 158.

with Ewing that "if any being exists on account of its value, the most perfect possible being must"?[35]

Even if you disagree, I would ask that you at least play along in imaginative generalization. Consider whether or not the Value that *grounds God's existence* and *reasons the existence of the world*—and the *existence of yourself*—is "worthy" of worship. Can you possibly answer no without denying the value of yourself and your world? Is not the Value or Goodness *through which God lives*, and the Value or Goodness *which God is*, not worthy of worship precisely because it's the *ontological ground of your own*—the presupposed axiological condition without which no value finds actualization at all? Moreover, when faced with questions as to whether a God "worthy" of worship must be personal or impersonal, unilaterally controlling or relationally persuasive, unmoved or most moved, mutable or immutable, necessarily loving or freely loving—ask yourself what Ultimate Value or Goodness requires. Would Supreme Value ever be impersonal? Is it ever controlling? Is it ever unmoved? One's answers to these questions will no doubt depend upon the shapes and shades of their own experience and their own theological imagination.

Finding God's reason and worshipfulness in the supremacy of God's Value suggests answers to these questions. It is not insignificant that it would also offer a reason and purpose as to why creation—a world including you and me—should exist at all. If indeed the mystery of divine necessity has to do with God's *creative axiological depth*—what we might, following Rescher, call God's "axiogenesis"—then the telos of human existence, purpose, and worship might find proper illumination.[36]

The Challenge of Ontological Gratitude

What finally is worship on this proposal? With Rescher, I want to suggest that the ground and aim of worship emerges from nothing other than a *gratefulness for existence*. I call this "ontological gratitude." Worship as ontological gratitude is an expression of gratefulness as a response to the goodness of existence as it is rooted in the goodness of God. To use Rescher's words, such worship expresses itself as a "debt of gratitude in acknowledgment of unmerited benefits—and in specific, the benefit of existence" and the value-laden opportunities it affords.[37]

---

35. Ewing, *Value and Reality*, 158.

36. Rescher, *Axiogenesis*.

37. Rescher, "God and the Grounding of Morality," 135. Rescher here is speaking to morality rather than worship; but in my rendering, both coincide in ontological

Yet worship as ontological gratitude comes in the form of a robust challenge. Indeed, what we might call the *challenge of ontological gratitude* is to aim to lead lives that are actively aware, and exemplary of, the inherent connections between the Value *through which God lives*, the Value *because of which* the world and human beings exist, and the value-creation that ever constitutes the *horizon of human purpose*. Here, worship actively involves a desire to match (or to justify) the value of our *individual existence* (its very fact) with the value-creation possible through our own *human livelihood* (the way we live).

The purpose of a worshipful human life, I claim, is to *act* out of the Value of its individual existence *on behalf of* the Value of the world's existence. Perhaps, this is indeed the mystery of creation itself and the very purpose of God. "The purpose of God," Whitehead insists "is the attainment of value in the temporal world."[38] There is a divine "unity in the universe enjoying value and (by its immanence) sharing value," he tells us.[39] So too the purpose of human life is to *justify the value of our mere existence* by *sharing* in the attainment of further value *for the world's existence*. Differently stated, the purpose of your human life is to invest a fresh and valued goodness into the world so that if you had never existed, the world would have been *less off* than if you had. So too, on this vision, God's yearning for the world is that it be *justifying of God's existence* such that if this world had never existed, God would have been less off than if it had.

Essential to this approach is that the reality of God, which lives through Value also *receives* the value of the world through what Whitehead calls the "consequent nature." The task of worship as *ontological gratitude* is to find oneself in that current of life that *justifies* the Value of God's existence, *through* the Value of one's own, *on behalf of* the wider Value of the world, as it is *received* again by God. This process is nothing short of a divine-human adventure in the *creation of value*. "What is done in the world is transformed into a reality in heaven," Whitehead imagines, "and the reality of heaven passes back into the world. By reason of this relation, the [Value] in the world passes into the [Value] in heaven, and floods back into the world."[40] Whitehead, I believe, is correct: the very "power" of God's axiological existence is indeed the "worship" this existence "inspires."[41] Such worship rightfully comes from beings that might not have existed at all.

---

gratitude.

38. Whitehead, *Religion in the Making*, 87.
39. Whitehead, *Modes of Thought*, 120.
40. Whitehead, *Process and Reality*, 351.
41. Whitehead, *Science and the Modern World*, 192.

PART THREE: TO PLURALISM, AXIOILOGY, AND APOCALYPSE

Conclusion: The Axiological Foundations of Worship

The particular question as to God's worthiness of worship will remain central to process-relational traditions and, indeed, to all theological and philosophical lineages affirmative of the claim that Value or Goodness resides at the ontological core of divinity. I locate myself among these traditions and have sought to offer another imaginative consideration indebted both to sources within process-relational thought (Whitehead, Ward, and Rescher) and also those outside them (Leslie and Ewing). I have focused in particular upon the shared axiological convictions of these figures and asked some particularly far-reaching questions. I have not sought to immediately offer an answer to the question of God's worthiness of worship; instead, I have probed its foundations by looking to the question below the question.

Why is it that God even exists? What is the nature of divine necessity? What explains divine existence and the existence of anything at all? I remain convinced that the way in which one answers these questions will determine whether or not God is worthy of worship. Neither reasonless brute fact, unrelenting power, logical necessity, nor utter mystery can finally reach a God worthy of worship. While it is true that appropriate renderings of power, logic, and mystery do belong in one's conception of God, the utmost question of God's worthiness of worship can only be answered *axiologically*. These then are my final claims: it is the divine Value through which God lives, the Value because of which the world and human beings exist, and the Value which ever lures the finest of human purpose that is ultimately worthy of worship. This Value is ontologically gracious, such that human worship consists in value-creation flowing forth from ontological gratitude.

Bibliography

Davis, Andrew M. "God as Reason." In *T&T Clark Encyclopedia of Christian Theology*. Edited by Jana Bennett et al., London: T. & T. Clark, forthcoming.

———. *Mind, Value, and the Cosmos: On the Relational Nature of Ultimacy*. Contemporary Whitehead Studies. Lanham, MD: Lexington, 2021.

Ewing, A. C. *Value and Reality: The Philosophical Case for Theism*. Muirhead Library of Philosophy. London: Allen & Unwin, 1973.

Ferré, Frederick. *Being and Value: Toward a Constructive Postmodern Metaphysics*. SUNY Series in Constructive Postmodern Thought. Albany: State University of New York Press, 1996.

Forrest, Peter. *God without the Supernatural: A Defense of Scientific Theism*. Cornell Studies in the Philosophy of Religion. Ithaca: Cornell University Press, 1996.

Griffin, David Ray. *God and Religion in the Postmodern World: Essays in Postmodern Theology*. SUNY Series in Constructive Postmodern Thought. New York: State University of New York Press, 1989.

———. *Reenchantment without Supernaturalism: A Process Philosophy of Religion.* Cornell Studies in the Philosophy of Religion. Ithaca: Cornell University Press, 2001.

Hartshorne, Charles. *The Divine Relativity: A Social Conception of God.* The Terry Lectures. New Haven: Yale University Press, 1948.

———. *Omnipotence and Other Theological Mistakes.* Albany: State University of New York Press, 1984.

Kaufman, Gordon D. *Theology for a Nuclear Age.* Manchester, UK: Manchester University Press, 1985.

Kushner, Harold S. "Human Suffering and the Power of God." Interview by John B. Cobb Jr. The Center for Process Studies (1984). https://www.youtube.com/watch?v=EdO120vwAM8/.

———. *When Bad Things Happen to Good People.* New York: Schocken, 1981.

———. "Would an All-Powerful God Be Worthy of Worship?" In *Jewish Theology and Process Thought,* edited by Sandra B. Lubarsky and David Ray Griffin, 89–91. SUNY Series in Constructive Postmodern Thought. Albany: State University of New York Press, 1996.

Leslie, John. *Immortality Defended.* Malden, MA: Blackwell, 2007.

———. *Infinite Minds: A Philosophical Cosmology.* Oxford: Clarendon, 2001.

———. *Value and Existence.* APQ Library of Philosophy. Totowa, NJ: Roman & Littlefield, 1979.

MacDonald, Scott, ed. *Being and Goodness: The Concept of the Good in Metaphysics and Philosophical Theology.* Ithaca: Cornell University Press, 1991.

Mesle, C. Robert. *Process Theology: A Basic Introduction.* With a concluding chapter by John B. Cobb Jr. St. Louis: Chalice, 1993.

Mirus, Christopher V. *Being Is Better Than Not Being: The Metaphysics of Goodness and Beauty in Aristotle.* Washington, DC: Catholic University of America Press, 2022.

Rescher, Nicholas. *Axiogenesis: An Essay in Metaphysical Optimalism.* Lanham, MD: Lexington, 2010.

———. "God and the Grounding of Morality." *Quaestiones Disputatae* 5.1 (2014) 130–37.

Rice, Hugh. *God and Goodness.* Oxford: Oxford University Press, 2000.

Swinburne, Richard. *The Existence of God.* 2nd ed. Oxford: Clarendon, 2004.

Ward, Keith. *Confessions of a Recovering Fundamentalist.* Eugene, OR: Cascade Books, 2019.

———. *Religion and Creation.* Oxford: Clarendon, 1996.

Whitehead, Alfred North. *Adventures of Ideas.* 1st Free Press paperback ed. New York: Free Press, 1967.

———. "Immortality." In *Science and Philosophy,* 85–104. Paterson, NJ: Littlefield, Adams, 1964.

———. *Modes of Thought.* 1st Free Press paperback ed. New York: Free Press, 1966.

———. *Process and Reality.* Edited by David Ray Griffin and Donald W. Sherburne. Corrected ed. New York: Free Press, 1978.

———. *Religion in the Making: Lowell Lectures, 1926.* Cambridge: Cambridge University Press, 1926.

———. *Science and the Modern World.* 1st Free Press paperback ed. New York: Free Press, 1967.

Wynn, Mark. *God and Goodness: A Natural Theological Perspective.* Routledge Studies in the Philosophy of Religion 1. London: Routledge, 1999.

12

Power, Apocalypse, and the God of Love

CATHERINE KELLER

Eloi, eloi, lema sabachthani: the last words of the one whose enlivening teaching threatened power and resulted in his death. Whatever you do with it, however you work out your Christology (if you have one), there remains no single greater symbol of the powers that be, that were, that persist, than that crucifixion. Christianities of social justice have long been at pains to underscore that the crucifying power was the Roman Empire (not the Jews, not God). We stress that since then, Power with a capital *P* has taken the form of any number of powers, Christian or not, imperial or neoimperial, political and economic. Right, mutters John of Patmos in my ear: the enthroned beast of Roman power and the Great Whore of its global economy.

I don't mean to darken this volume with crucifixion and apocalypse. I will find a way back to the amorous God. Promise. But I can't get there without some meditation on those last words: "my god my god why have you forsaken me." At least according to the Gospels of Mark and Matthew, they are the last words. Luke offers much more reassuringly: "Father, into your hands I commend my spirit." John offers simply: "It is done." What is surprising is that Mark and Matthew retain the words of godforsakeness at all. It is such bad propaganda that by historical-critical criteria Jesus may really have said it.

And what those words signify, what they cry out, is that Jesus did not expect this outcome, that he feels abandoned by his *abba*. That he should not be experiencing this depth of pain, of humiliation, of disappointment. That *abba* could and should have made it come out otherwise. Or at least should have been there with him to comfort or strengthen. I will not discuss now the quick standard answer—that it *did* come out otherwise. Resurrection! That does not solve the problem here, of the actually unbearable pain. There of course the problem of theodicy takes hold: how could a loving god *let* this happen—let alone cause it? And right there lies the theological heart of the problem of power and the god of love. We can imagine what proportion of, say, Ukrainians, Israelis, Palestinians have recently felt that cry rise within them.

Let me suggest that without facing the forsakenness (which also means facing Jesus facing it), without grieving not just the specific unbearability but the sense of abandonment at the worst possible moment, every resurrection or restoration or renewal remains hollow.

Many of us in this volume find in process theology not just a key but a satisfying resolution to the problem of theodicy: to the question that David Griffin crystallized and answered so masterfully in *God, Power, and Evil: A Process Theodicy* nearly half a century ago.[1] And I'll say up front that I do too. This is the operative syllogism: if God is both all controlling and loving, and there is real suffering, there is no real God. But, if God's power is persuasive rather than coercive, then it does not contradict God's love: ergo, in the face of whatever traumas, God might just possibly exist!

And yet, it is nonetheless important—even among process theologians—to let that anguished godforsakeness surface afresh now and again. Otherwise our answer may become pat, abstract, detached from the fresh agony in our midst. The gospel of Godforsakenness expresses an existential anguish, not a metaphysical fact. So it has become clear to me in teaching—if I move too smoothly to and through the process theodicy, it feels to some no better than atheism. They suspect (though not saying so to the teacher's face) that it is process theology God has forsaken, or at any rate that it is process theology that has forsaken God.

So here is what I am wondering: How does forsakenness play in the big traumas of our time? That means right now, as I was writing, the trauma of war, with the nuclear threat coming into fresh focus. And it means, over a longer interval of now, of course, global warming. These are not apocalypses in the sense of the end of the world. The end of the world is at any rate not a biblical notion. I won't belabor that point, except to say I recently wrote *Facing Apocalypse: Climate, Democracy and Other Last Chances* to make clear that *apocalypsis* means not closure but disclosure, revelation—of a catastrophic human pattern pushing *not* toward a simple "The End," but toward worsening historical realizations set in "intensive contrast" to the greatest of earthly hopes.[2]

I was drafting this chapter soon after hearing understated, nonhistrionic President Biden use the word "Armageddon" to name the level of

---

1. Griffin, *God, Power, and Evil*.
2. Keller, *Facing Apocalypse*.

danger. For decades before and after, global warming can be relied upon to provide a good scientific illustration of the apocalypse. Apocalypse *not* as the End, I repeat and re-repeat. It is rather the disclosure of the Dragon/Beast/Whore trinity of systemic power bringing on planetary catastrophe—including such creepily resonant illuminations along the way as the burning of a third of the trees, the death of a third of the life of the sea. The Roman power that in the Gospels crucified Jesus gets coded in John's prophetic nightmare as the imperial power across sea and land; and it is empire mated with a planetary economy personified as seductive, in a vision of her twenty-eight luxury products for global trade.

Fundamentalist readings usually presume that if nuclear or ecological catastrophe happens, it is God's will. And a far wider array of Christians do assume that anything so huge must be somehow divinely willed, or they feel that if this all is not the direct will of God, God has let it happen—so that perhaps we have indeed been forsaken. And what is an honest answer to the despair? What Godforsakenness plays out here? And does process theology offer an adequate alternative—pastoral and political—theology?

Instead of leaping to process theology, it may be helpful to pause with another highly influential, politically progressive and ecologically oriented theology, that of Jürgen Moltmann. He takes us directly to the cross. As he writes in *The Crucified God*:

> When God becomes man in Jesus of Nazareth, he not only enters into the finitude of man, but in his death on the cross also enters into the situation of man's godforsakenness. In Jesus he does not die the natural death of a finite being, but the violent death of the criminal on the cross, the death of complete abandonment by God. The suffering in the passion of Jesus is abandonment, rejection by God, his Father ... He humbles himself and takes upon himself the eternal death of the godless and the godforsaken, so that all the godless and the godforsaken can experience communion with him.[3]

I find that Moltmann's theology remains existentially persuasive at a certain level: Jesus' being truly human means that the fullness of the incarnation requires that it partake of the fullness of human suffering. And that means a suffering unalleviated by faith, the worst kind of suffering, a traumatism that feels helpless and hopeless. This manifests for Moltmann how God's solidarity extends to the Godless, the Godforsaken. The divinity of Jesus forsakes the humanity of Jesus at that crucial moment, that cross-moment.

---

3. Moltmann, *Crucified God*, 414.

Surely process theologians agree that God is just as attentive to the godless as to the godly; and that the divine lure may indeed call to the godless precisely through their most acute vulnerability, precisely in their sense of godforsakenness. And that in so doing does not actually forsake them. But that in Christ God is deliberately entering into godlessness on the cross by revealing the absence of Godself: does that feel—if not simply self-contradictory—a bit too performative? God *playing* godforsaken so as to lure the godless? A gesture of indirect but still omnipotent control of the situation . . . ? And if we apply the experience of godforsakenness to nuclear Armageddon or climate apocalypse, then we might get the impression that God has also chosen to play out absence, abandonment, on a horrifically global scale. The very earth nailed to the neoimperial cross? Well, yes, but not as strategic divine abandonment for the sake of ultimate communion.

Nor would Moltmann, who has been a leader among Protestants on matters of ecology, disagree. He sharply distinguishes God's almighty power from the "idolatry of power in world history." So God in creation self-limits: "The limitation of God's unending power is an act of God's power over Godself. Only God can limit God."[4] But "in the relationship of love, free spaces for the beloved develop"—hence God's creative power already holds within itself a "self-renunciation" of power. This God "determines everything" and is "responsible for everything, so the Almighty is also the accused in the theodicy question." For as Kierkegaard argued, God has created independence in the creatures. Not to have done so would have expressed a controlling rather than loving power. "So God's almighty power is his goodness."[5] These are meaningful moves. Yet Moltmann's reliance on the notion of God's withdrawal, God's self-renunciation, seems still to leave the sovereignty of controlling power fundamental. For it is because the power is inherently all-controlling that it must limit itself, withdraw itself. So the specter of all-determining power lingers. There is no hint at the way creatures can limit God.

Here is where the process theodicy of persuasive (cooperative) rather than coercive power offers an indispensable clarity. It allows one to embrace Kierkegaard's insight, and Moltmann's as well, by taking yet more seriously that God's power *is* God's goodness. On this Tom Oord has written much and powerfully—that God's power cannot be control, or else it contradicts love itself.[6] So then the power in play is not intrinsically controlling and needing to be somehow renounced—in creation cosmologically, on the cross christologically. But the understanding of the one God in monotheism

---

4. Moltmann, *Living God and the Fullness of Life*, 44–45.
5. Moltmann, *Living God and the Fullness of Life*, 44–45.
6. Oord, *God Can't*.

did and does tend toward versions of almightiness (even if that word is a mistranslation of *el Shaddai*—the Breasted One). And so the experience of Godforsakenness on the cross (whether it is the experience of the historical Jesus or of his disciples) might indeed suggest the last gasp of an interventionist hope—on the part of one whose life had manifest the most profound cooperativity with the divine known in human history. This does mean from a process perspective that he was wrong? Not existentially: that affect would be absolutely real. No one feeling the forsakenness is wrong. If Jesus felt that forsakenness, it means he felt the depth of his own powerlessness in that moment. And if there never was an absolute boundary between Jesus and his abba, then perhaps he faces in dying the meaning of that intimacy: that his own suffering cannot be separated from God's.

It is for Protestant theology important that for Moltmann—quite independently of process theology—God is no longer the unmoved mover but one who both moves and is moved, who does suffer with us: com-passion. Only therefore does the space open for a sovereignty of love.

Or, is the very notion of sovereign love an oxymoron? So we call it instead the power of love. Of course, power in the political sense of sovereignty will never be fully free of some edge of control.

So then, following Tom Oord, why *not* name this love power "amipotence"?[7] It has power, this amity, this love—in the sense of potential, potentiality: the relevance of pure possibilities to the potential for their realization. In precisely Oord's sense of uncontrol. The term "amipotence" thereby carries the relevance of Whitehead's eternal objects, the content of the divine lure, in the appeal of the lure to the becoming occasion—that is, as the objects initially aim the creature emerging from its own past toward actualization, indeed toward a *better* actualization in interdependence with fellow creatures with whom it is empowered to collaborate.

Those possibilities rely on the creature for that actualization. And so process theology doesn't muck around with any ghosts of all-determining power. Indeed, David Griffin offered the strongest and clearest case to that point ever made—if I may make such a claim for a teacher of mine—that God lacks any monopoly on power, that God's power cannot be equated with all-power, with all the power there is, or with a power to control all that is. He reflects with Hartshorne that "the ideal or perfect agent will enjoy the optimal concentration of efficacy which is compatible with there being other efficacious agents."[8] As Griffin puts it, "such a view greatly alters the problem of evil. Even a being with perfect power cannot unilaterally bring

---

7. Oord, *Death of Omnipotence*.
8. Griffin, *God, Power, and Evil*, 268.

about that which it is impossible for one being unilaterally to effect."[9] To be a perfect agent means sharing the world with other agents, creatures whose actions make a difference in that world. For to be a being at all is to exercise power: as he cites Plato, "being is power." To be is to affect one's universe. To exercise power. Hardly powerlessness! "And it is impossible for one being unilaterally to effect the best possible state of affairs among other beings. In other words, one being cannot guarantee that the other beings will avoid all genuine evil. The possibility of genuine evil is necessary."[10] Griffin then underscores that this is not the same as saying that genuine evil is necessary. It is that the *possibility* of genuine evil that is necessary. (It took me a while to let that distinction sink in.) The creator has called forth not a world predestined to evil but a universe in which evil must be a possibility. To simplify that—some element of creative freedom is crucial to an actually good creation.

So then, on this basis, Griffin can offer a form of omnipotence—he calls it "C-omnipotence"—the C standing for "coherent" and "creationistic." This differs dramatically from the creationism that signifies God's absolute power over a world The God of absolute power created ex nihilo. Griffin's "C-omnipotence" signifies a creativity attuned to the creation, indeed tuned *ecologically* to *kosmos*, order: so it is from whichever beginnings an ecocreativity. C-omnipotence signifies the omnitude of power that a being in a world of beings—where being is power, not dominance—can have, can be.

And so when rhetorically it is key to affirm God's omnipotence—as it is in some Christian contexts—David Griffin lets us do it. Sometimes, of course, we may have the luxury of offering Tom Oord's "amipotence," and this does not counter Griffin's argument for C-omnipotence Amipotence can deploy its logic in relatively amicable contexts, where such vocabularic play may bear fruit. Either way, we can retain a syllogism in which God's power and God's goodness do not contradict each other in the face of real evil. This is not a coherence of mere logic—it is a liberation from the theodicical, yes, even theocidal, contradiction. It has, it emits, an amicable feeling. The liberation is affective and therefore effective. And so it lets God live. For us and in us, by whatever names and namelessness.

What then of the gospel Godforsakenness? Would Jesus have felt more God-trust at that gruesome moment if he'd had the benefit of process theology? Well, no I am not interested in committing such anachronism. Nor am I claiming that the affect of forsakenness can be once for all dispatched. But the alternative theo-logic of Griffin's process theodicy does really free us

---

9. Griffin, *God, Power, and Evil*, 268.
10. Griffin, *God, Power, and Evil*, 269.

from the illusion of a controlling, if not monopolistic, divine power. And I don't think that was Jesus' God or God's basileia to start with.

Godforsakenness can mean in the gospel and in process theology that the real evil in the world at certain moments intensifies suffering so fully that the possibility of the better world seems to vanish. Then divine power seems contradicted not by its own goodness but by the world's power. And when that contradiction cuts close, despair bleeds from the wound.

And yes, in the Christian story the despair is more than healed within a couple of days. But that Mark and Matthew actually retained that crucified outburst in their stories surely warns us never to repress the despair. Letting ourselves feel it may indeed be sometimes the condition of overcoming it.

I hope we let that Godforsakenness echo in our guts when we confront more instances of systemic power's evil, of imperialism armed with weapons of mass destruction, of neoimperialism melting the glaciers, warming the oceans, storming the shorelines, extinguishing the species, poisoning the earth, wasting the future . . .

Let the feeling of godforsakenness arise; perhaps without it we do not rise up. And then naming it lets you remember that it is in these cases not a supreme power withholding itself for whatever mysterious or just reasons. That perhaps the God forsakenness means not that God has in a particular instance abandoned you or your world—but that the world has in that instance forsaken God. Who may therefore be suffering with us if we too feel forsaken by world of God.

Nor is this to say that in forsaking god the world has turned atheistic. Rather, forms of both atheism and theism collude in vast systemic networks of ungodly power. Power political, power military, power economic. It is not to say that all modes of such power are incapable of good. But that superpower political and economic, beastly and seductive, is degrading the world—bringing on, yes, an apocalypse. Not the end of the world—but possibly the end of our world, of terrestrial civilization. *Apokalypsis* does not close down but discloses: through voices of the prophetic traditions—including, I believe, process theology—it reveals the mounting susceptibility of our precious little bit of the creation to discreation.

And to call our communities, Christian and otherwise, into creative activity on behalf of the creation itself—into the work that taps the hope of the new creation—is to call us into love. That love enlivens. It heals despair, not because it guarantees a final fix—but because it opens possibility. It stirs within us those pure possibilities—eternal objects—amipotent gifts of hope.

We live into the resurrection energy that is; we recognize that it is we who forsake God, we who forsake Jesus. Redemption is a radically entangled process. God cannot unilaterally save us from ourselves, our God-forsaking systems. Nor can we unilaterally save ourselves. But who are "we"? Some more than others? We as a species? Yes, but that is too abstract. The Godforsaking ones, more insidious when they claim to be Christians, are not the majority of humans. For power is concentrated in the hands of a small percentage of us, whose lives add up to a mockery of love. Those few make the needed transformation of the world improbable, not impossible.

Grieving our grief, feeling our godforsakenness—and feeling afresh our godrelatedness—we may always begin again. The alpha and the omega: it spells this very moment. Perhaps every moment. The alpha of ecocreative possibility spirals toward actualization in the omega of cosmic consequences. Dangerous and promising.

The possibilities keep coming, even if they fall on hard ground. There is no more process-theological a parable than the seeds and the sower. And it lets me return to the gospel. Each seed—a pure possibility for the moment—a lure—and it is altogether up to us to actualize it a bit, a lot or not at all. It is up to us to prepare the ground for such fruitfulness, up to us in openness to the sower, in a receptivity that takes in the past world and in concrescence lets something fresh grow for the future.

A future as collective as is the past, and so we cultivate, as process thinkers like Tom Oord and John Cobb and David Griffin have done so intensively, the potentiality of a better world. As I imagine each of you do, and in doing, create and strengthen networks that exercise influence in the world—that in multiple ways resist the power grids that threaten the future, that poison the potentiality with their toxic emissions, material and ideological.

The feeling of godforsakenness will not then permanently disappear, I suspect, for any of us. But its sorrow can be embraced in trust, *pistis*, faith— that what we call God doesn't give up on us or on our world, but takes it all in, along with all of us, in that "consequent nature." That term holds open the responsiveness of a God who can grow so much more from us, through us, if we keep tuning to the primordial possibility, the lure, the seed of this very moment, which means ever again self-emptying, in a kind of Zen *kenosis*: letting go this self that already is folding into history—not clinging to its expectations, its disappointments, its forsakings. But letting go is not forsaking. It is opening, dis/closing. The ground becomes more open. This *apokalypsis* is infinitely subtle. And yet it does not mean just a theology of the present moment, which would reduce the vision to a private piety. Or to a badly westernized kind of Zen, which turns indifferent.

And in this disclosure the old syllogism of theodicy, with the transmutation of omnipotence to C-omnipotence, a coherent creationism, indeed a cosmic ecocreativity that works for us, not against: if god is omnipotence C, the power is loving, the power is love, the love is powerful. So let me begin to end with David Griffin's conclusion to *God, Power, and Evil*:

> because God does not promote any new level of intensity without being willing to suffer the possible consequences; because God constantly works to overcome the evil in the creation with good, and in human experience does this by simultaneously seeking to increase our enjoyment of life and to enlist our support in the effort to overcome evil by maximizing good.[11]

Indeed, I see no reason not to let Griffin's omnipotence C translate in the present context into Tom's amipotence.

The divine willingness to suffer the consequences of every creature's process is inseparable from the divine enjoyment of it all—not a pleasure in the pain, like some divine sadomasochism, but a *feeling with*, com-passion, that folds the suffering of the evil into the potential for the good. Those poles seem to have materialized in the uber-intense contrast of godforsakenness and resurrection. Importantly, the New Testament doesn't leave it there, in an individual event, to be humbly emulated by subsequent individuals. Not that such enactments of the *basileia* ever lose their love-force. Yet the Testament ends appropriately, if disturbingly, with the earthwide spatiotemporality of the book of Revelation. The Apocalypse and the New Jerusalem may be perhaps imagined as two poles of a contrast in the Whiteheadian sense; even as a contrast in the divine vision—a vision holding the potentiality of Earth's history in tension with pure possibility, those eternal objects glittering like the gems of the bridal city's walls. And that vision swirls back into the world not in a final intervention but in an endless amipotence.

Bibliography

Griffin, David Ray. *God, Power, and Evil: A Process Theodicy*. 1976. Reprint, Louisville: Westminster John Knox, 2004.

Keller, Catherine. *Facing Apocalypse: Climate, Democracy and Other Last Chances*. Maryknoll, NY: Orbis, 2021.

Moltmann, Jürgen. *The Crucified God*. 40th ann. ed. Minneapolis: Fortress, 2015.

———. *The Living God and the Fullness of Life*. Louisville: Westminster John Knox, 2015.

Oord, Thomas Jay. *The Death of Omnipotence and Birth of Amipotence*. Grasmere, ID: SacraSage, 2023.

———. *God Can't: How to Believe in God and Love after Tragedy, Abuse, and Other Evils*. Grasmere, ID: SacraSage, 2019.

---

11. Griffin, *God, Power, and Evil*, 310.

Appendices

Prehending the Past

— Appendix A —
Two Conceptions of Power

Bernard Loomer[1]

The problem of power is as ancient as the age of man. The presence of power is manifest wherever two or more people are gathered together and have any kind of relationship. Its deeper and sometimes darker qualities emerge as soon as the omnipresent factor of inequality makes itself felt.

The presence and operation of power are not limited of course to the life of humankind. If the findings of those who study animal behavior are to be accepted, power is an indispensable element in the preservation of the group life of the species in the animal world. Power manifests itself in the creation of order. This order which is essential for the maintenance of animal life seems to be derived from the pervasive fact of the inequality of power. Perhaps to a greater degree than we care to admit, the principle of the relation between order and inequality may function in the organization of life at the human level.

If power is roughly defined as the ability to make or establish a claim on life, then the range of the presence of power may be broadened to include the notion that power is coextensive with life itself. To be alive, in any sense, is to make some claim, large or small. To be alive is to exercise power in some degree.

The principle involved may be extended still further to the level of metaphysical generality. If value is coterminous with reality, as it is in all metaphysical systems, then the discussion of power becomes correlative

---

1. Bernard Loomer (1912–1985) was an American process philosopher and theologian. Loomer was former dean and professor at the University of Chicago Divinity School and at the Graduate Theological Union in Berkeley. A leading proponent of empirical process theology, Loomer was known widely for his theodicy of "ambiguity" based upon a vision of divine "size" and "stature." For an introduction to his work and influence, see *The Size of God: The Theology of Bernard Loomer in Context*, edited by William Dean and Larry E. Axel (1987). —Ed.

with the analysis of being or actuality itself. In this most general perspective, to be actual means to exercise power.

The following discussion of power is not meant to be primarily metaphysical in generality. The focus is on the human involvement with power. But no idea is self-sufficient in its meaning. Ideas, like people, have their lives only in a community of relations. The understanding and justification of any important idea requires an explanatory and relational context within which the idea lives, moves, and has its being. This explanatory context includes the immediate neighborhood of other ideas closely related to the topic under discussion. This neighborhood expands until it embraces those notions which constitute the most general description of reality of which we are capable during any particular historical epoch.

It is presupposed and perhaps obvious that all understandings of power, and particularly the two views to be discussed, are grounded in conceptions both of the human self and, at least implicitly, of the ultimate nature of things. The possible truth of any conception of power is in part a function of the descriptive adequacy of the views of selfhood and the general nature of things that undergird that particular conception of power. If these more general understandings are inadequate, then the correlative concept of power will also be truncated or inadequate in some other way. By the same logic, a basic shift in the conception of power should have consequences for a change in our understanding both of the nature of the self and of the basic nature of things. As William James was fond of saying, "There can *be* no difference anywhere that doesn't *make* a difference elsewhere—no difference in abstract truth that doesn't express itself in a difference in concrete fact and in conduct consequent upon that fact."[2]

After all these centuries of the practice of power and of theorizing about its nature and function, what is to be said about it that hasn't been said before many times over? I contend that our lives and thought have been dominated by one conception of power. To anticipate the later discussion a bit, this long-standing tradition has on the whole defined power as the ability to produce an effect, or as the capacity to bring into being, to actualize or to maintain what has been actualized. At the human level power is understood to be the capacity to actualize the potentialities for good and evil of an individual or a group. The heart of this traditional view is the conception of power as the strength to exert a shaping and determining influence on the other, whatever or whoever the other might be.

It would simply be wrongheaded to deny that the tradition has identified one aspect of power. But this viewpoint is not only truncated. It is

---

2. James, *Pragmatism*, 49–50.

demonic in its destructiveness. Too often it is the basic criterion by which the status or worth of an individual or group is determined and measured. It is to a large extent the condition whereby the ineradicable inequalities of life lead to, or are transformed into, life-denying injustices.

The problem of power is not just a matter of the actualization of possibilities. It is rather a question of the level of individual and social fulfillment that is to be achieved or that is to emerge. It is a problem of the kinds of possibilities that are to flower and the kinds of contexts conducive to the emergence of these possibilities. The thesis of this discussion is that the nature and role of relationships determine both the level of human fulfillment that is possible and the conception of power that is to be practiced.

To put the point in another way, it could be said that our lives and thought have been dominated by one conception of the nature and role of relationships, and thus of one conception of power. This viewpoint is inadequate for the emergence of individuals and societies of the stature required in today's world. I do not mean to deny or castigate the role of power in the living of life. On the contrary. But I am concerned to set forth at least an initial version of a more humanizing conception of power. The problem of power is the problem of size and stature.

The rise of modern science and technology make this effort of reconception mandatory. In addition to improving the lot of modern people, science and technology have contributed to the rise and development of problems we have never had to face before in human history. These problems are of such magnitudes and complexity that the quality of the future of our planetary existence now confronts us as something more than just a theoretical or imaginative issue first detailed for us by the writers of science fiction.

The emergence of modern science and its operational offspring, technology, together with the evolution of that mode of thought called "historical understanding," have heightened modern man's sense of control and have led him to believe that he is responsible for the shape of history. This situation could constitute a rather grim illustration of Niebuhrian irony in that our very creativity may have resulted in the appearance of destructive historical forces too intractable for our capacities to manage or transform.

The development of science has opened Pandora's Box. Once opened it cannot be closed. The interests of scientists and the theoretical and technological consequences of scientific research have been such that, on the whole, science has become a major contributor to and servant of the traditional conception of power. The continued existence of science as a constructive force in human life presupposes that a sufficient number of members of our various earthly societies and religions take on a size never before required with such urgency. The traditional conception of power is inadequate to help us in our possible evolution toward this goal.

The problem of power is the problem of quality of our lives. Those qualities that make for the most complex and intense enrichment of life may not possess the greatest survival value. But they are not engendered by our dominant conception and practice of power.

The alternative conception of power is indigenous to process-relational modes of thought and action. This viewpoint has been elaborated most fully by Charles Hartshorne in his conception of God. In this discussion, as well as in other matters, I stand gratefully on the minds and shoulders of my very illustrious teachers and colleagues.

The two conceptions of power to be discussed involve a rather simple and obvious distinction. But the implications of this distinction are not simple. What follows cannot do justice to the possible fertility of this distinction. Neither type exists in its purity. To this degree, the discussion is more concerned with ideal types than with concrete instances of either type of power.

A sort of nonbiblical text and point of departure for this discussion is to be found in one of the definitions in Webster's *Dictionary*, which characterizes power as an ability either to produce or to undergo an effect. This is intriguing for two reasons. First, except possibly for certain scientific purposes, power as commonly understood is seldom defined as the capacity to suffer or undergo an effect. Second, the conception of power is characterized in terms of either/or and not in terms of both/and.

Linear Power

The first conception of power defines power as linear in character. Linear power is the ability to produce intended or desired effects in our relationships to nature or to other people. More specifically, linear power is the capacity to influence, guide, adjust, manipulate, shape, control, or transform the human or natural environment in order to advance one's purposes.

This kind of power is essentially one-directional or unilateral in its working. Briefly stated, linear power is the capacity to influence another, in contrast to being influenced. The influence may be direct or indirect, coercive or persuasive in nature. It operates so as to make the other a function of one's ends, even when one's aims include what is thought to be the good of the other. If the traditional distinction between the masculine and the feminine is accepted for the moment, the masculine being defined as active and the feminine as passive, then linear power is quite thoroughly masculine in character.

This is a one-sided, abstract, and nonrelational conception of power. Perhaps it would be more accurate to say that this form of power is non-mutual in its relationality. With respect to the one who is influenced, the relationship is internal. That is, he is altered by the relationship. With the respect to the one who is exercising this kind of power, the relationship is external. That is, theoretically he is unaffected by the relationship. In actual fact, the exertion of influence on something or someone else may involve some degree of reciprocity. Certainly, the exercise of power has some valuational effect for good or ill on the one exerting the power. But the main thrust of this kind of power is to produce a desired effect on the other in accordance with one's own purposes. Ideally, its aim is to create the largest effect on the other while being minimally influenced by the other.

It is apparent that the clearest illustration of this kind of power is to be found in the traditional Catholic conception of God, as Hartshorne has documented in systematic detail.

A.

In terms of linear power, we set forth our claims on life as individuals and groups against other individuals or groups with their opposing and competing claims. We make these claims and create our influence in order to actualize the values of life, including our status and sense of worth. The greater our capacity to influence others, the larger the claim on life we feel we are entitled to establish. Our more predominant power is our justification, our warrant, for our superior status and sense of importance.

Inequality is a categorical feature of our experience. We differ in energy, ambition, intelligence, emotional intensity, relational sensitivity, imagination, creativity, addiction to evil and other forms of destructiveness, and the capacity to love. We are strikingly unequal in power, in our capacity to influence others for good or ill, by fair means or foul. In this view, our size or stature is measured by the strength of our linear power. Our sense of self-value is correlative to our place on the scale of inequality. That is, our size is determined by our ability to actualize our purposes in the context of others with their competing aims. Our strength is measured by the amount of competing power we can resist, control, or overcome. It is evaluated by the amount of pressure others must exert before our claims are curtailed or before we must reach some compromise. The degree of our strength or the level of our size is relative to the degree of pressure we can handle or control.

The idea, that the relative strength of our linear power is too often the basis of our sense of self-identity and self-worth, is illustrated in the institution of athletics. The aim of sports is neither physical fitness, nor exercise, nor the rounding out of a balanced life, although these values may be its by-products. Sports is not primarily a matter of physical competition. Sports is an affair of spirit competing against spirit, expressed through the agencies of our bodies. The aim is to find or create our identity and place in the power structure formed in the arena of competitive games. The aim is to win, to achieve excellence. But, contrary to the idealists who find competition distasteful, we do not win by doing our best. We achieve the excellence of our best by striving to win. The conception of power as unilateral recognizes that our identity is largely a relational matter. We know who we are in the context of relationship, even the relationships of competition.

In answer to the inevitable question as to how well he shoots, the non-professional golfer may reply that he normally shoots in the high 70's or the low 80's. If he were more honest or fulsome in his reply, he would stipulate that he performs at that level of excellence when he is competing against players whose competence more or less matches his own. The club professional at the local golf course normally may shoot in the low 70's when playing against members of his club. If this same professional were to compete in a professional golf tournament held at his home course, he might do well to score in the low 80's. There is no such thing as a completely friendly game of golf unless the hierarchy of power has already been established and accepted by all the players.

I remember playing golf several years ago with the son of a professional golfer. We played several holes in desultory fashion, which means that the level of our play varied from fair to mediocre. He announced suddenly that, *he was going to play some golf.* He promptly proceeded to do so in rather excellent fashion. He was built in proportion to his tall height and he possessed a very enviable golf swing. I failed to match his level of play. In the middle of one fairway, he stopped walking and asked me if I knew why I wasn't playing well. In response to my negative reply, he offered the explanation that I had been trying to imitate his swing, that I had been playing his style rather than my own, and that I had lost my identity. His analysis was accepted as accurate, and I became aware once again of the difficulty of retaining one's sense of self-identity and self-worth in the face of the inequality of power, and of the possible crippling effect that too often accompanies the loss of one's own base.

I also remember being at a racetrack and watching a drama involving a very highly-bred horse. His pedigree was of the highest credentials. This horse apparently had not been winning his share of rich purses. Since it is rather expensive to keep a horse who is not paying his way, he was entered in a claiming race, which means that he could be claimed or bought. The interesting point is that all the other horses in the race, who were less highly-pedigreed, had run the distance of the race in times markedly faster than that of the horse who was the star of this little episode in the animal kingdom. But they had established their times for the race while running against a different class of competition than they were facing on this particular day. Suffice it to say that our hero won the race by the widest margin it is possible to have and still have it called a race. The inveterate gamblers could be seen nodding their heads wisely, and could be heard muttering something to the effect that class will tell.

I do not regard these illustrations as esoteric or applicable only to the field of sports. A much more complex illustration of the intricacies of power is found in a recent psychological study of the conditions of human courtship. The most decisive and interesting condition, as reported, consisted in the principle that if the woman did not affirm the man's self-image, then no courtship ensued or was possible. The man did not have to affirm the woman's self-image in order to have courtship occur. The dimensions and implications of this finding are too numerous to discuss here. The study came to the conclusion that the presence of this condition indicated the basic dominance of the man in courtship. I find this conclusion thoroughly ambiguous. The man is possibly dominant, but only if dominance is conceived of in terms of what I call linear power. A quite different conclusion is possible if a different conception of power is adopted.

B.

When power is defined in a linear fashion as a capacity to influence another, it follows factually as well as logically that the gain in power by the other is experienced as a loss of one's own power and therefore of one's status and sense of worth. At the human level, at least, and possibly with respect to nature itself, the other is often experienced as a threat or a potential threat to our ability to realize our purposes. The idea of being influenced seems to connote a loss or lack of power relating to our sense of insecurity. To be influenced by someone or something other is therefore experienced as a weakness, just as dependence on another is a reflection of our inadequacy or lack of self-sufficiency. Within this understanding of things, passivity is no virtue. On the contrary, it is a preeminent symbol of a lack of power.

In this competition of power, our relative strength or size can be ascertained by the degree to which the freedom of the other is curtailed.

The reduction of freedom is an attenuation of power. Consequently, in our struggle for greater power it is essential that the other be restricted in his power as much as possible, or that the freedom of the other be contained within the limits of our control—whether the other be another person or group or the forces of nature. We hesitate or refuse to commit ourselves to those people or realities we cannot control.

C.

As long as one's size and sense of worth are measured by the strength of one's capacity to influence others (and this influence always takes the form of shaping the other in our image), as long as power is associated with the sense of initiative and aggressiveness, and passivity is indicative of weakness or a corresponding lack of power, then the natural and inevitable inequalities among individuals and groups are the means whereby the estrangements in life become wider and deeper. The rich become richer, and the poor become poorer. The strong become stronger and the weak become weaker and more dependent. From a deeply religious point of view, and in the long run, this manner of handling the inequalities of life results in an increasing impoverishment for both the strong and the weak. Whether on a Marxist or any other basis of analysis, the divisions between us become more destructive of the family of man.

This link between linear power and sense of worth or status in the eyes of others as well as in our own eyes, is one of the important factors involved in the problem that has puzzled and preoccupied ethicists for centuries, namely, that we seldom relinquish our power voluntarily. We loosen our grip and make our concessions only when we are forced to do so by some competing group that has acquired sufficient power to bring us to the negotiating table, as the history of the labor-management conflict and the modern women's movement illustrate. Without interference from this competing group our power tends to become inertial and self-perpetuating. As Saul Alinsky used to insist: people in power will listen only when you have enough political "clout" to make them listen. We tend to run over or trample on or remain indifferent to those people whom we feel we can safely ignore.

This conception of power takes on a darker color if the fact of inequality is united with the restive quality of human freedom. More than any other contemporary thinker it was Reinhold Niebuhr who taught us that the human spirit, which is the unity of the self in its freedom, possesses a transcendent outreach. Man in his freedom can transcend in fact or in imagination any given or proposed limitation on what an individual may regard as desirable or possible with respect to his security or fulfillment. On the basis of insights which he attributed to Kierkegaard, Niebuhr grounded both creativity and sin in man's basic anxiety or insecurity. No amount of security with respect to the goods of this life can overcome man's anxiety. Consequently, man's spirit in its unbounded restlessness moves toward the indefinite or infinite.

This quality of freedom is manifested in every aspect of a person's life. This means that any impulse of a person may become insatiable. This is especially the case with respect to his desire for power. In this way our demands or claims tend to become inordinate. This inordinacy reflects the element of self-interest which infects every activity of a person. His claim to rectitude is pretentious, since the self is often the servant and not the master of its impulses. The children of darkness know all this full well since they recognize no law that transcends their self-interest. The children of light who do not take sufficient cognizance of the expansive character of man's freedom whereby an individual's or a group's self-interest may take the form of inordinate or unreasonable claims, believe that our impulses are manageable and amenable to rational control.

The expansive character of freedom means that we tend to overstate the legitimacy of our claims and they become pretentious. We are prone to overplay our strengths and to refuse to recognize the limitations of our virtues, and the result is that they become destructive. While freedom can manifest itself in the form of creative reconstruction, it can also, when combined with the omnipresent factor of inequality, lead to injustices beyond those that may flow from our natural inequalities. This situation may be one reason for the adversary proceedings in our law courts. For Niebuhr it led to his defense of the system of checks and balances in our form of democracy. As he put it, our capacity for justice makes democracy possible, our capacity for injustice makes democracy necessary.

D.

It is apparent that this conception of power is grounded on a nonrelational or noncommunal view of the self. The self lives in a society, but the society does not live in the self as part of its inner being. The self has relationships with others, but the self is not created out of these relationships. The others are not constitutive of the self. Society is a context within which the self operates. The self has relationships with other members of the society because society is the necessary medium for the fulfillment of the self.

In this view, there is a movement of the self toward others, but these others exist as means for the realization of the goals of the self. These others exist either as helpers or companions, or as obstacles, or as possible threats to the full use of the self's power to actualize its purposes.

Furthermore, the freedom of the self is in no sense an emergent from the relationships the self has with its society. Freedom is a power inherent within the self in its own individual being. In the same sense, the possibilities of the self are latent within the self in its own life. Society provides the occasions wherein and whereby these possibilities are actualized.

In this conception of power, the aim is to move toward the maximum of self-sufficiency. The self is to become as self-dependent as possible. Dependency on others, as well as passivity, are symptoms of weakness or insufficiency. Dependency may become a threat to the integrity of the self. The self is to live out of the strength of its independence. It should relate to others out of its strength and not out of its dependency. Communities may exist as cooperative societies made up of essentially independent and self-reliant members who share common concerns. The less fortunate members of a society, the handicapped and disadvantaged, are the beneficiaries of the charitable and compassionate feelings of the more fortunate, although they are to be praised and prized most honestly when they approximate as nearly as they can the self-dependency of the life of linear power.

This viewpoint has its religious dimension, of course, because the independence of the self may be ultimately qualified by the sense of its dependence on God the creator and sustainer. This conception of power is at home with Descartes' definition of a substance as that which requires nothing but itself (and God) in order to exist. The strength of the creative and influential power of the self is derived from itself and from God and not from other members of the society.

I suggest that a linear conception of power is a reasonably faithful interpretation of the official creed of the Republican Party in this country. I also believe that it is basically congruent with the traditional metaphysics of substantive modes of thought. This viewpoint on the nature of power is integral to that tradition of Christian theology which has been heavily influenced by this traditional metaphysical outlook. I believe that this conception of power in Christian theology has brought confusion to our understanding of the meaning of Christian character and personality.

To push this point a bit further, I think there is at least one strand of the New Testament interpretation of Jesus which illustrates this conception of power. In several passages it is emphasized that Jesus derived his power and size from God, and from God alone. This is the same power that the Gospel of John reports Jesus as prayerfully asking God to grant to his disciples. It is not recorded that Jesus ever acknowledged his indebtedness to his fellows for his stature or power. As recorded, the relationship was essentially one-sided. The people were the recipients of the influence of his love, his healing graces, and his teachings. In return they gave him his crucifixion. As Scripture has it, "I came to minister, not to be ministered unto."

E.

Partly because of the nonrelational view of the self that is presupposed, linear power tends to be somewhat abstract in its operation. Linear power is an expression of specialized concerns. That is, we deal only with those aspects of the human and natural environment that are relevant to our purposes. Our interest in others is highly selective. We are not concerned to deal with the full concrete being of the other—whether the other be a person or nature in its livingness or God.

This character of linear power is not merely theoretical in its import. The fact is that the aspects of people or nature or God which we neglect tend to revenge themselves on us. The energy of repressed or ignored dimensions of the other must be expressed somehow. The actualization of the expression may be shorter or longer in its process of becoming. If it be true that God is not mocked, it may also be the case that the concrete life of other people cannot be disregarded with impunity. In due season the harvest is reaped, for good or ill. Surely our contemporary revolutions involving blacks, Indians, women, and the underdeveloped nations furnish us with more than sufficient evidence on this point.

If individuals emerge from their relationships, as I believe they do, then the practice of linear power blocks the full flow of energy that could be productive of the emergence of greater-sized individuals from these relationships. Linear power also blocks the quality of the gift that others would give to us out of their freedom.

Lord Acton's principle, that power corrupts, involves what I am calling linear power. The practice of power, like the possession of great wealth, tends to corrupt its exponents because it helps to create conditions of estrangement. Unless qualified by compensating qualities, the exercise of power tends to alienate the possessor of power. It attenuates the sense of fellow-feeling. It weakens the communal ties that bind us to each other. It deadens our sensitivity to the fact that we are deeply dependent on each other and that we are creative of each other.

The biblical advice to the rich, that they should give their wealth to the poor, will not solve our economic problems. But it could remove one source of alienation. However, the moral of the principle that power corrupts is not that we should divest ourselves of all power or totally eschew the exercise of power. The total absence of all power is nonexistence, and the refusal to exercise the power we possess leads to destruction. The moral is rather that another kind of power is required. In this connection it is instructive to note the resentment toward the United States expressed by those European nations who were helped by the Marshall Plan following World War II.

F.

The point concerning the abstractive character of linear power can be expanded. The continued practice of this kind of power breeds an insensitivity to the presence of the other—again, whether the other be a person or nature or God. The sense of the presence of the other involves a feeling of the concrete actuality of the other, of being truly present to another, of being less concerned to shape and control the other, of letting the other be himself in his concrete freedom.

Perhaps this is one reason why most of the great religious figures possessed qualities that we have traditionally associated with the feminine. They were open to the presence of the other. They were open to being shaped and influenced by the other. Certainly, much of what it means to be religious is opposed to the purely masculine.

The practice of linear or unilateral power is antithetical to many of the deeper dimensions of the religious life. The habit of trying to shape and control our human and natural world in accordance with our own purposes makes it difficult to give ourselves in faithful trust to that which we cannot control and which could transform even our sensitivities. Having been nurtured to be insensitive to the presence of the other, in this instance, a concretely actual God, God becomes something abstract and remote. So we sometimes have recourse, in Christian circles, to the "living Jesus" in order to overcome our sense of the abstractness, the remoteness, and the emptiness of what in truth is a living, concrete presence. The purely masculine stance in life tends to substitute ethics for religion. Even this approach may become an ethics of ideals which, after all, are themselves abstractions. In this fashion we can shape ourselves in accordance with our own projections, and thereby maintain both our independence and the feeling of self-determination that accompanies our sense of controlling power.

It follows, somewhat inevitably, that a life lived in terms of linear power reduces the sense of the mystery of life, the mystery of the other in its freedom, including and especially the divine other. Or perhaps it would be more accurate to say that the sense of mystery impresses itself most forcibly on us when this kind of power reaches its inescapable frustration. The freedom of God and the freedom of man are not subject to human control. The strangeness of life and the hiddenness of its meaning cannot be responded to appropriately by a lifestyle of linear power.

G.

When love is contrasted with power, as it is usually done within the Christian theological tradition, it needs to be noted that it is the linear conception of power that is regarded as the antithesis of love. Again, when Jesus (and other christological figures) is described as being powerless, and as having renounced power as the world understands power, it is unilateral power that is at issue. In terms of this kind of power, Jesus and other religious leaders are at the bottom of the hierarchy of power.

The issue between love and linear power is not finally the issue between persuasion and coercion. The contrast consists in the direction of one's concern, with power focused in the self-interest of an individual or a group, and love concerned with what is for the good of the other. In some interpretations of love, especially Christian love, it would appear that love is as unilateral and nonrelational in its way as linear power is in its way. The interpretation of divine love, as being a concern for the other with no concern for itself, may be the ultimate instance.

It may be that love has been interpreted in this fashion as a compensatory device to counteract the one-sidedness of linear power. Love then becomes one side of the coin that carries the face of power on the other side. This involves the principle that the way to offset one extreme is to introduce a contrary extreme. It would appear that this kind of love, like this kind of power, needs an alternative conception.

H.

This is the basic conception of power that has been controlling in Western historical experience. It has been dominant in political and economic philosophies as well as in ethical and theological systems. Its preeminence in military thought and action is obvious. Its efficacious role in the ordering of social life is no less apparent. It is rigorously operative in certain embodiments of leadership as well as in the relations between the sexes. The American experience in the leveling of a continent and the partial reshaping of the face of nature constitutes one large national illustration of this kind of force.

Bacon's aphorism, that knowledge is power, refers in the first instance to linear power. It symbolizes a modern transformation in the function of knowledge. In the premodern world knowledge had practical applications, to be sure. Artisans, farmers, alchemists, doctors, seafarers, astronomers, and a few physical philosophers had knowledge of various natural structures and processes. Their practical grasp of the ways of things enabled people to carry out the necessary affairs of everyday life in a tolerable fashion. But, on the whole, the most important function of knowledge was to serve as a handmaid to understanding and contemplation. But now, knowledge to a large degree has been conscripted in the service of unilateral power and control, especially as this knowledge and control are shaped by the concerns of theoretical and applied science.

Scientific knowledge is specialized knowledge. This kind of competence and understanding and inquiry is essential. But unless it is related to other forms of knowledge and inquiry and to other dimensions of life in some integral fashion, specialized knowledge becomes a prime servant of linear power with its ambiguous and destructive consequences. Our universities have become major training grounds for the practice of this kind of power.

Karl Marx's contention, that the aim of philosophy should not be the quiescent understanding and acceptance of life as it is, but rather the transformation of nature and society, strengthened the instrumental relationship between knowledge and power.

One of the interesting implications of Marx's interpretation of the role of philosophic study is that the traditional conception of philosophy is essentially feminine in outlook. The unified understanding of the nature of things as they are in their being, to which we must conform, has been replaced by a dynamic interpretation of things in their creative becoming, with which we should cooperate, to which we can contribute, and over which many of us attempt to exercise greater control.

In being at least partially responsible for the course of history, by what star, if any, are we to be guided? As we try to plan and direct the evolution of human society and its pluralistic values and styles, by what are we to be shaped and transformed?

Relational Power

The second and alternative conception of power is relational in character. This is the ability both to produce and to undergo an effect. It is the capacity both to influence others and to be influenced by others. Relational power involves both a giving and a receiving.

The true alternative to the traditional role of the masculine as the active agent who influences is not the traditional conception of the feminine as the passive recipient of the influence. This is so even if it is acknowledged that the undergoing of an effect influences the producer of the effect. The audience does help to create the actor. But the true alternative to a masculine version of power is not a feminine version of power. This would merely be substituting "she" for "he." With respect to developing a more adequate conception of power, the solution does not consist of choosing between the alternatives of producing an effect or of undergoing an effect. This solution would involve the lifestyle of either/or, which is a strategy of choosing between equally one-sided truncations.

I do not propose or intend to ground the conception of relational power on the possible distinction and relations between masculine and feminine roles. With respect to the problem of power in relation to human sexual differentiation, I am not concerned to defend either traditional or modern versions of the roles of men and women, or to deny or affirm their distinctive natures, regardless of whether these differences are understood to be inherent or culturally derived. A relational conception of power is hopefully applicable however the differences and similarities between the sexes are defined. In fact, the problem of sexual differentiation is finally irrelevant to the principle of power conceived in relational imagery, even though sexual differentiation has a bearing on the specific dynamics of relational power involving the two sexes. I mention this context at some length in order to emphasize the point that the dominant conception of power is describable in terms of qualities that have been traditionally associated with the masculine.

Power as Being-Influenced

Without opting for a traditionally feminine version of power, it needs to be stressed that the conception of relational power, in contrast to power conceived as linear or unilateral, has as one of its premises the notion that the capacity to absorb an influence is as truly a mark of power as the strength involved in exerting an influence. We all know that it takes physical and psychic strength to endure an effect. The immovable object may be said to be as powerful in its way as the irresistible force is in its way.[3] Yet, in spite

---

3. There is the New England short story ("The Great Stone Face") about the influence of a mountain in the shaping of a human face. Beginning when he was a small

of this, we have persisted in attributing power only to the producer of an effect.[4] But the principle involved goes beyond this simple observation.

The idea that the capacity to receive from another or to be influenced by another is truly indicative of power is not derived from an arbitrary linguistic decision to extend the term "power" to include the receiving of an influence. The idea rests on more elemental considerations that revolve around the notion of size. The concept of size is taken as fundamental and decisive because it is the most basic criterion by which to make decisions and judgments concerning value. To reiterate an earlier point, the problem of power is finally a problem of value. The justification for any conception of power consists ultimately of principles (or decisions or presuppositions) concerning value.

The term "power" is a value term. It is indicative of worth or significance. Under any conception of power, to refer to a person or group as powerless is to reduce that individual or group on the scale of value. Under linear power the worth (or size) of an individual is measured by the range of that individual's ability to influence others. The correlative thesis of this section is that the practice of relational power both requires and exemplifies greater size than that called for by the practice of unilateral power. Since the capacity to receive an influence is a necessary component in the actuality of relational power, the principle of size is applicable to the experience of undergoing an effect. It is the factor of value or size that enables us to attribute power to the experience of receiving an influence derived from others.

Our readiness to take account of the feelings and values of another is a way of including the other within our world of meaning and concern. At its best, receiving is not unresponsive passivity; it is an active openness. Our reception of another indicates that we are or may become large enough to make room for another within ourselves. Our openness to be influenced by another, without losing our identity or sense of self-dependence, is not only an acknowledgement and affirmation of the other as an end rather than a means to an end. It is also a measure of our own strength and size, even and especially when this influence of the other helps to effect a creative transformation of ourselves and our world. The strength of our security may well mean that we do not fear the other, that the other is not an overpowering threat to our own sense of worth.

---

boy and persisting throughout his life, a certain man developed the habit of spending many hours looking at a stone face which the forces of nature had etched on the side of a mountain. Gradually over the years the man's face took on the character of the great stone face.

4. The scientific definition of power as the capacity either to produce or to undergo an effect seems to be an exception to this general practice.

The world of the individual who can be influenced by another without losing his or her identity or freedom is larger than the world of the individual who fears being influenced.[5] The former can include ranges and depths of complexity and contrast to a degree that is not possible for the latter. The stature of the individual who can let another exist in his or her own creative freedom is larger than the size of the individual who insists that others must conform to his own purposes and understandings.

The notion that being influenced may indicate a lack of sufficient self-dependence and that it may tend toward a neurotic dependence on others with its attendant lack of freedom contains a justifiable point of caution and limitation. This is the possible weakness of the strength of openness. But this contention has its counterfoil in the notion that the unqualified urge to influence or to dominate others may indicate a fundamental insecurity and lack of size. This is the possible weakness in the inner dynamics of the strength of controlling or unilateral power.

Under the linear conception of power the desire to influence another may well include a love for the other, where this involves a concern for what is thought to be for the good of the other. Or, to invert the point, a love for the other may indeed involve the desire to control the other in a direction that is felt to be for the other's good. But, under this conception of power, the good that directs the exercise of influence on the other has the limitations of a preconceived good. It often exemplifies the conscious or unconscious desire to transform the other in one's own image. It is of the nature of efficient cause to reproduce its own kind.

Under the relational conception of power what is truly for the good of any one or all of the relational partners is not a preconceived good. The true good is not a function of controlling or dominating influence. The true good is an emergent from deeply mutual relationships.

If power always means the exercising of influence and control and if receiving always means weakness and a lack of power, then a creative and strong love that comprises a mutual giving and receiving is not possible.

The Constitutive Role of Relationships

The foundation of relational power lies in the constitutive role of relationships in the creation of individuals and societies. The individual is a communal individual. He is a creature of contexts. He lives in society, and the society quite literally lives in him. He is largely a function of the relationships

---

5. The receiving of influence from another may result in the enlargement of one's identity or the creative transformation of one's freedom.

out of which he is born. He begins his pulsating, momentary existence as an individual from a set of complex impulses derived from the ongoing energy of past events as they objectify themselves into the present. This qualitative energy is carried by the relations or vectoral prehensions which largely constitute his life. His life is for the most part, but not completely, a gift from those others who make up the societal context in which he lives. Without these others he would not be. Or, as the former manager of the New York Yankees, the late Casey Stengel, said after his team had won still another baseball championship: "I could hardly have done it without the players."

This communal or relational conception of the self stands in marked contrast to the nonrelational or substantive view of the self. In this latter interpretation, which, like the linear conception of power, has dominated the history of Western thought, the self has relations with others, but its inner constitution is not composed of these relations. The influences of these others are not parts of the very soul of the nonrelational self. These others, through their objectifications of themselves, are not literally present within the self that is being influenced. In the nonrelational conception the self has its inner being within itself. Its essential life and the power of its being are derived from itself (and God). It lives in a context, to be sure, but this context is not part of the very warp and woof of its being. To put the contrast in another and perhaps more controversial fashion, in the nonrelational view the self has experiences, but the self is to be distinguished from its experiences. In the relational view the self doesn't have experiences. The self is its experiences.

The unilateral conception of power has endured in spite of the point, as noted earlier, that we all recognize it requires strength to absorb an effect. Analogously, the nonrelational conception of the self has endured in spite of the fact that thinkers in untold numbers have recognized what most of us are aware of, namely, that everyone and everything we encounter becomes part of the fabric of our lives. "Relation" in the internal sense is a way of speaking of the presence of others in our own being. It is the peculiar destiny of process-relational modes of thought to have transformed this commonplace but deep-seated observation into a metaphysical first principle.[6]

---

6. The methodology of historical understanding is thoroughly contextual in character. Every historical figure (or institution or movement) must be seen and understood contextually, because that individual lived his life in that particular context and in no other. All historical life is particular in its concrete existence. It is possible to interpret this methodology and its achievements in terms of a nonrelational conception of the self and society. In this conception a context functions so as to shape and limit an individual's possibilities which are relevant to that particular context. But a relational view of the self and society would seem to furnish a more adequate basis for grasping the significance of the work of historians. In a limited way an individual helps to give shape to his contextual environment, and that particular world shapes that individual.

In the relational viewpoint the individual begins life as an effect produced by the many others in the world of his immediate past; but he is not simply a function of these relations. He is an emergent from his relationships, and in the process of his emergence he also creates himself.

His life as a living individual consists of synthesizing into some degree of subjective unity the various relational causes or influences which have initiated his process of becoming something definite. His concrete life is constituted by a process of deciding what he will make out of what he has received. This is his emergent selfhood. What he makes out of what he has received is who he is. This is also his emergent freedom because he is his decision. His subjective life is his process of deciding who he is.

When selfhood has been achieved, the qualitative energy of the individual is released from the individual's self-preoccupation. Having been an emergent response to a complex set of causes, the individual now joins with others as a member of a complex set of causes to create the future, where the future may include another momentary occasion of the individual's ongoing historical life. In order to become an influence in the lives of others, the momentary individual must "die" as an experiencing subject and become an object to be experienced and received by other momentary subjects in their ongoing lives. Anything that can influence another reality can in turn be influenced at a later stage of itself by this other reality. This is the precise meaning of mutuality.[7]

In some such manner we feed upon each other. We are both cause and effect. We constitute each other in part. We are both self-creative and creative of each other, for good or ill, or for good and ill. We are dependent and yet autonomous. We are at once communal and solitary individuals. But the solitariness of individuality is lived out only in the midst of constitutive relationships.

In the relational, contrasted with the noncommunal conception of the self, possibilities do not inhere within the individual as latent entities waiting to be realized. In contrast to the traditional view which held that the acorn contained all the possibilities that were to flower later into the adult oak tree, the relational viewpoint maintains that possibilities are emergents

---

The individual lives in a context of others, but that context lives and has its being only within the individuals, and in the relations between individuals, who partly constitute the totality of that context. The context becomes part of the inner life of the individuals who live in that world.

7. In other words, the mutuality is not simultaneous. The presence of mutuality in the strictest sense requires a crisscrossing interrelationship of cause and effect in the successive stages in the ongoing lives of two or more individuals. For ordinary practical purposes this strict definition of mutuality need not be insisted on.

from relationships. A wife is not the occasion whereby a man actualizes husbandly possibilities that reside or subsist wholly within the confines of his enclosed selfhood. The husbandly and wifely possibilities of the respective partners are peculiar to and are created out of that particular marital relationship in which each helps to create the other. The more deeply mutual and creative the relationship, the wider the range of emergent possibilities for those participating in the relationship. The wealth of possibilities is not simply "there" as a present and completed fact, subsisting as a latent condition that is in some sense independent of the world of actual events. Possibilities are created or emerge as possibilities along with the advances that occur within the natural and historical environments.

Analogous considerations apply to the notion of freedom. The individual's self-creativity is an expression of the strength of his freedom. Or, more accurately, his freedom is a pervasive quality of his self-creativity. His freedom, like his self-creativity, is an emergent from his relationships. To this degree his freedom is not a quality that is derived solely from himself as though he were an independent, self-contained, self-derived, and self-sustained individual. The degree and range of his freedom is not wholly a function of his own resources. On the one hand, his freedom is derived from the unfathomable mystery of the emergence of his self-creativity. On the other hand, his freedom is in part an enabling gift from his society that is conveyed to him through his constitutive relationships. He is helped or hindered in achieving greater freedom by the enhancing or crippling relations in which he lives. The deeper his involvement in creative and transformative relations, the greater the possibility for the enlargement and empowering of his freedom.

Freedom has several dimensions, and all of them are emergents from the functioning of the constitutive relations in which an individual has his being. Certainly, one of the strongest components is that of transcendence, which is the capacity of an individual in fact or in imagination to transcend both society and himself. The intimate connection between transcendence and the expansive character of freedom was noted previously. Even though an individual's capacity to transcend his society is partly a gift from that very society, he often fails to acknowledge this indebtedness and acts as if he had somehow outgrown his dependence on that society. The tension between society and the freedom of an individual is abiding and irresolvable, to be sure. But in his pride an individual may come to feel that his freedom is wholly self-derived and a function of his own resources. He can imagine that he is essentially independent of all constitutive relationships. In this mood he tends to use his transcendent freedom to enhance his sense of self-importance and to strengthen his egoistic impulses. Almost inevitably he moves in the direction of a more consummate practice of linear power. In this fashion he becomes more fully estranged from his fellows and adds to the destructive consequences of our natural inequalities.

In terms of the relational or communal conception of the self, our constitutive relationships enable us to be free. In this sense we are related in order to be free, that is to actualize our highest possibilities relative to ourselves as unique individuals. But freedom does not stand alone as the one absolute or primordial value. Just as fundamentally, we are free in order to be more fully related. We are most free in all the dimensions of our freedom when we enter more deeply into those relationships which are creative of ourselves as people of larger size. The inclusive term is stature. Freedom and relationality are its essential components.

Power as the Capacity to Sustain a Relationship

From this perspective, power is neither the capacity to produce nor to undergo an effect. Power is the capacity to sustain a mutually internal relationship.[8] This is a relationship of mutually influencing and being influenced, of mutually giving and receiving, of mutually making claims and permitting and enabling others to make their claims. This is a relation of mutuality which embraces all the dimensions and kinds of inequality that the human spirit is heir to. The principle of equality most profoundly means that we are equally dependent on the constitutive relationships that create us, however relatively unequal we are in our various strengths, including our ability to exemplify the fullness and concreteness of this kind of power.

It is important to stress the point that in relational power the influencing and the being influenced occur within and are functions of the mutuality of internal relatedness. This kind of mutuality is to be contrasted with the mutuality of external relatedness that is involved in various instances of unilateral power, such as the mutual good of compromise and accommodation, or the mutuality of external cooperation and divisions of labor, or the mutuality of bargaining and a *quid pro quo*. In the context of relational power, giving and receiving, influencing and being influenced, producing an effect and undergoing an effect, are not only mutually dependent and interwoven. At times they seem to be almost indistinguishable and their roles appear to be interchangeable. Often the greatest influence that one can

---

8. This view of internal relations includes, of course, the presence of external relations. The communal individual is also solitary. All partners, especially marriage partners, as Gibran insisted, need "spaces in their togetherness.

exercise on another consists in being influenced by the other, in enabling the other to make the largest impact on one's self.

The principles of relational power mean that influencing and being influenced are so relationally intertwined that the effort to isolate them as independent factors would constitute an illustration of either one or both of Whitehead's famous two fallacies: that of simple location or that of misplaced concreteness.

If someone is to talk, someone else must listen. If one is to hear, someone else must speak. The actor in part creates the audience. The audience in its turn partly creates the actor. The drama is an emergent from the interaction between the actor and the audience. In this kind of mutuality of power, it is as blessed to receive as it is to give. In our kind of culture, where power is identified so strongly with the exercise of influence upon another, it is often more difficult to receive in such a manner as to enhance and further the relationship. One of the most difficult of all social graces to achieve is the ability to receive in such a way that the giver feels honored in the giving and in having the gift received, or in such a way that in giving the giver feels that he has received.

The art of receiving creatively the influence or gift of another is difficult to master because our sense of worth and power is identified so deeply with the direct act of creating, or giving, or exercising an influence on others. We have been nurtured to believe that dependence is indicative of a lack of worth. But in relational power the focus is not on any particular member of the relationship, or on one side of the relationship. The focus is on the relationship to which all contribute and from which all members are fed. The worth of the one who gives is partly dependent on the worth of the one who receives, or the worth of the giving is dependent on the worth that must attach to the receiving. Revelation, to be effective, must be received and made operative in the lives of those who are to be disciples. In fact, the cries and prayers of those who need and want to be redeemed in part call forth and create the messiah. The messiah's capacity to influence his people is in part derived from his being shaped by their need, although his response to their need may take a form which is other than what they want and think they need. The messiah who comes is usually not the one they had hoped for or expected.

In conceiving of relational power as the capacity to sustain a mutually internal relationship, the stress is on the primacy of relationships. These relations include, of course, those entities which are related. In the practice of this kind of power one must trust the relationship. The good is an emergent from the relationship. Except in a negative sense this process of creative emergence lies beyond our ability to direct or to command. The attempt to guide or control this process results only in obstructing the emergence or in restricting the worth of the relationship to the level of value which already exists. Those who are fearful of committing themselves to something they cannot control enhance the strength of the forces involved in the practice of unilateral power.

Those who conceptualize within the imagery of nonrelational or substantive modes of thought, and/or who find it difficult to transcend the traditional conception of power as linear, may also be uneasy with the conception of relational power. They may think that the practice of relational power is too nondirective or untrustworthy. They may feel that this kind of power is, for example, ethically sound only if one's concerns in the relationship are directed toward the other and what is for the other's good. But this possible response misses the whole point concerning the primacy and creativity of the relationship and the process of emergent good.

Being Present to Another

The primacy of relationships and the emergence of possibilities within relationships can be seen in looking at the phenomenon of being present to another, or being a presence to and for another. Being present to another, when this is understood nonrelationally as though we were dealing with independent individuals, can mean either that one discloses himself to another in a deeply personal way, or that one is so fully receptive to the other that the other feels that he is known and understood. When interpreted relationally the phenomenon takes on a different coloration.

The initiating disclosure of one's self to another enables and frees the other to receive the revealing of one's self. This reception in turn enables the revealer to be freer in his disclosure of himself. The active openness of the receptive mood of one who listens calls forth the disclosure of him who would speak. The speaking and the listening are creative of each other in the relationship. Also, through his listening the listener discloses himself to the one who speaks. In being heard, the one who speaks knows the one who hears. The two disclosures may not be equal in depth and range in that specific instance. Yet there is a mutuality of self-revelation. The knowing and the being known are mutually creative. Presence means that both knowing and being known are functions of the creativity of both the speaking and the listening. I would understand this to be the relational version of Buber's I–Thou.[9]

---

9. The fullest exemplification of "presence" would involve having each member both speak and listen in terms of the dynamics stated in the text. This situation seldom

There is an interesting contrast that sometimes develops in relations between at least some men and some women, although the point under discussion does not depend on the stereotyping of either men or women. The matter can be stated in a greatly oversimplified manner and without benefit of psychological or social contexts: women often seem to think that a man is not genuinely concerned about a woman unless he specifically asks her about her feelings, as she asks him about his feelings. Unless he inquires, she does not often volunteer information about her feelings. In the absence of his inquiry the volunteering of this information is tantamount to asking him to be concerned about the state of her being. She should not have to call his attention to her inner life. He should be sensitive to her nonverbal communication, as she is sensitive to his. Sensing something of the mood of her spirit, he should express his concern by asking her about her feelings and hopes.

A man, by contrast, thinks that a woman should evidence a concern for him and their relationship by initiating the process of her self-disclosure. She should communicate her feelings to him voluntarily, as he does to her, without first being asked about them. He should not need to keep reassuring her of his interest in her feelings and doings. She should assume that he does care, even though he doesn't always or even usually demonstrate his concern by the asking of questions.

Each perspective has its limited validity and value. But neither is normative or adequate. Each perspective, in itself, is focused on the self and not on the relationship. In brief, each point of view is to a large extent unilateral in its directional intent. There is a relationship, but it is a function of separate and diverse perspectives. It is not yet a relationship of mutual internality in which each asks and volunteers, in which the asking and the volunteering and the perceptiveness to nonverbal expressions are mutually creative within both partners. In short, it is not yet an association in which the relationship is the base and center.

Relational Power as Concrete

Relational power, in contrast to the abstractness of linear power, is concerned with the concrete life of the other, whether the other be an individual or a group. One of the important consequences of the major intellectual discoveries in the modern world, from Copernicus to Einstein, is our increased understanding of the detailed empirical processes which shape our thinking, behavior, and being. We are more aware of conditioning contexts,

---

occurs with full equality on any specific occasion.

histories, psychological dynamics, and relationships, which largely determine what we most concretely are.

The exercise of power must operate with an awareness of these elements. To do otherwise is to relate to each other inadequately in terms of abstract classes, or stereotypes, or groups looked at in a cross-sectional manner without reference to their peculiar histories. In this fashion we fail to deal with the inexhaustible and variegated richness, the confusing complexity, and the omnipresent and intertwined ambiguities present in the concreteness of individual and group life. Transparent clarity, cleanness, and the absence of ambiguity are found only in the abstractions of thought. Power, to be creative and not destructive, must be inextricably related to the ambiguous, contradictory, and baffling character of concrete existence. It must live with regenerative awe and wonder in the midst of the strange turnings that transform victory into defeat and defeat into victory; the humbling ironies and the intractable conditions within both people and nature that shatter the best laid plans and destroy the bridges of our hopes. It must be rooted in the relative chaos and mess in which we live out our days. In this respect, the concept of relational power is nothing more nor less than a recognition of what has in fact happened in our modern world. It is also a recognition of what is needed in order to respond creatively to what has happened.

As a capacity to sustain complex and mutually internal relationships that encompass more of the concrete lives of individuals and groups, the practice of relational power must confront the whole plenum of psychological and spiritual conditions that characterize the human spirit. This plenum includes the better and the worse, the good and the bad and their confounding mixture. It ranges from the balanced reasonableness of the mature to the excesses and deficiencies of the immature, and from the dependable goodness of sensitive souls to the demonic irrationalities of the deprived, the frustrated, and the depraved. Doubts, anxieties, inertias, resistances, and multidimensional forms of pride live in all of us.

In and beyond all these and countless other problematic states of the human spirit, along with their opposites, there are the many kinds and degrees of inequality that are present in all relationships. The fact of inequality is not just one consideration among many equally significant facts. It is a bedrock condition. The failure to recognize its decisive status has confounded many social and political theories and programs. It has been a major basis for the traditional conception of order. It is now one of the strong motivating forces which impel us toward the reconstruction of modern societies. It is an ambiguous factor in all lives. It is at once a basis for compassion and a reason to despair. It is at once a precondition of leadership and a major element in the drift toward social mediocrity. It is the presupposition of messiahship. The inequalities that are crippling and dehumanizing may be reducible in scope and influence, but the general condition of inequality seems not only ineradicable but necessary. It is a necessary component in the division of labor and in the variety of creative capacities. In this respect it is part of the meaning of human finitude.

In the practice of linear power many of these natural and cultivated inequalities inevitably result in obstructive and impoverishing structures of injustice. It is the hope that in the practice of relational power we may learn how to interrelate these inequalities so they may become mutually enhancing.

It is possible to have a reasonably well-ordered society (in both the large and small sense of that term) as long as we deal abstractly with individuals and groups. The practice of linear power can create this kind of society. It has done so throughout history. The price for this ordered life is the neglect or repression of many important dimensions of the human spirit. In moving from this well-ordered but repressive society to forms of social life which enable these dimensions of the human spirit to emerge in more concrete relationships, we must be prepared to live within conditions which are more complex, confused, and unsettling. The surfacing of repressed forces creates problems which did not exist previously. Roles are transformed. Habitual patterns of behavior and response are no longer appropriate or acceptable. Crises in the areas of personal, professional, and social identity appear. The established order in all areas of life is weakened. Traditional values, all too often grounded on structures of abstract relationships, are questioned. The total situation becomes disruptive and potentially disintegrative. It borders on chaos. The social consequences of the liberation of women and the changed consciousness of minority peoples and underdeveloped countries (among other factors) have brought us to just such a state of affairs.

This unstable condition holds great promise for the future. A wise man has said that "the great ages are the unstable ages." But not all unstable ages have been great milestones in the odyssey of the human spirit. The price for creative advance is enormous. The challenge may be beyond our strength. There is ground for hope and reason to despair.

It is clear that the continued practice of unilateral power is totally inadequate to the social task that confronts us. But the practice of relational power is an incredibly difficult art to master. This type of power requires the most disciplined kind of mutual encouragement and criticism. The creative openness of this type of relationship involves possibilities of the greatest advance and the greatest risk. It calls for the utmost of energy, patience, endurance, and strength. It can lead to the deepest joys and to the abyss of the agony of suffering. In it will be found both heaven and hell and the bitter-sweet amalgam of their co-presence.

Relational Power as Size

The ultimate aim of relational power is the creation and enhancement of those relationships in which all participating members are transformed into individuals and groups of greater stature. In this kind of relationship, the individuals (or groups) are neither swallowed up in the relationship nor are they absorbed into each other. Yet the relationship, which includes its members, exists only in terms of its members.

The aim of relational power is not to control the other either directly, or indirectly by trying to guide and control the relationship. The greatest possible good cannot emerge under conditions of control. The aim is to provide those conditions of the giving and receiving of influences such that there is the enlargement of the freedom of all the members to both give and receive. This enlarged freedom is the precondition for the emergence of the greatest possible good which is neither preconceived nor controllable. The commitment within relational power is not to each other but to the relationship which is creative of both. It is a commitment to the relational "us" and not to one or the other.

The elements of the structure of this highly involuted relationship can be stated very abstractly, although it must be emphasized that these elements operate relationally and dynamically. On the one hand, in exercising an influence within the relationship one makes his claims and expresses his concerns in such a style as to enable the other to make his largest contribution to the relationship. With this contribution the experiences of all the participants are intensified and broadened. In making one's claims and in exercising one's influence on the other in this fashion, the freedom of the other is recognized and respected. On the other hand, one is to receive the presence and influence of the other within the relationship in such a manner that the other is enabled to enter more freely and fully into the relationship. In being received in this fashion the one who influences may be more open to absorb the influences of others.

The structure of relational power, again defined ideally, is such that the claims of justice (from the perspective of linear power) are both included and transcended. From the side of the claimant, some portion of justice is obtained in the very making of the claim or in exercising an influence. But in making the claim relationally, that is by enabling the recipient to respond most freely and creatively, justice is transcended. From the side of the recipient of the claim, justice is also served in the very receiving and acknowledgement of the claim. But in receiving the claim relationally, that is by enabling the claimant to become more open to the relationship and to being influenced, justice is transcended. In this kind of relationship transcendence means that, all the parties involved both give and receive more than the requirements of justice demand or permit.

This is a description of the nature of the process of relational power viewed structurally and abstractly. It is also a description of relational power as operating ideally and without reference to the baffling and confounding realities which constitute our empirical existence. When looked at concretely and dynamically, the actual instances of relational power fall far short of this ideal structure. They are incredibly far more complex, ambiguous, and involuted. They involve all the contrasting qualities that are to be found in the endless variety of concrete individuals and social groups. They include the full plenum of conditions the human spirit is heir to. These qualities and conditions, which constitute the materials and contexts with which and in which the exemplifications of relational power must fulfill their ambiguous destinies, run the gamut from triumphant breakthroughs to crippling regressions, from life-restoring laughter to life-denying despair, from the beauty of the gracious heart to the debasing cruelty of the small mind and smaller soul.

Within this larger spectrum of the general human situation there appear to be at least two elemental factors with which the practice of relational power must wrestle in its struggle to create individuals and groups of larger size. These factors are at once the materials for creative advance and the grounds of frustration and persistent smallness of size.

The first is the fact of contrast, which often appears as conflict although not necessarily in the form of overt violence. Conflict more usually exhibits itself under the many guises of competition which infects all the dimensions of our social life. But contrast most generically refers to the inexhaustible differences of otherness. Contrast is the precondition of complexity without which the creation of a larger integrity is not possible. Without adequate contrast the intensity of experience may become too narrowly focused, and may lead to the crippling sickness of moralism or to the more virulent disease of fanaticism.

The second is the factor of estrangement which is the brokenness of life's essential relationships. The umbrella of estrangement encompasses the emptiness of the uncommitted, the heartless shrug of the indifferent and the insensitivity of the unmoved, the inertial smallness of the complacent, the errancy of the unfaithful, the demonry of the prideful and the absolutely certain, and the destructiveness of the hateful. The attempt to overcome estrangement is the "open sesame" to the experience of depth, without which the adventure of greater size loses its foundation of elemental simplicity.

Undergirding these two factors of contrast and estrangement and remorselessly immanent within all movements toward greater size, are at least four conditions which appear to be unalterable or categoreal in nature. The degree of decisiveness with which our grasp of these conditions permeates our understanding, and the manner in which we deal with them, define and shape the limits of our creative advance.

There are first, and most obviously, the inequalities of energy, vision, sensitivity, maturity, and the capacity and the love to sustain relationships. Inequality of some sort or in some degree is present in every relational situation. As noted previously, in the practice of unilateral power these natural and inevitable inequalities lead to destructive injustices. The strong become stronger, and the weak become weaker. This is a form of mutual impoverishment. In the practice of relational power, they create an imbalance that can be mutually enriching. Both the strong and the weak may become not only stronger but larger in stature.

There is, second, the puzzling fact of ambiguity, the interpenetrating mixture of virtues and vices. Virtues carried beyond their inevitable limits become demonic vices. An individual's weaknesses are the other side of his strengths. Like the biblical parable of the wheat and tares they grow together. They coexist within an individual. The evil cannot be cut out of a person's spirit without weakening the strength of his goodness. The evil can be lessened only by the transformation of the strength of his goodness. The passion that caused the individual to transcend the limits of his virtues, and thereby convert them into vices, is the same strength that gave rise to the virtues originally. The failure to recognize the depth of ambiguity in all matters of the spirit leads us to live moralistically, without compassion, and without adequate understanding of others or, more pitiably, of ourselves.

There is, third, the creative role of evil or brokenness in opening us to greater depths of experience. In the absence of problems or failures we tend to live our lives inertially. Dewey has suggested that we think only when our systems of thought and value break down, when we encounter dimensions of life we cannot handle. We often take the value and services of others for granted. Only when they have departed, leaving a vacant space against the sky, when it is too late to express our gratitude, do we come to acknowledge our indebtedness. An infidelity in marriage can lead to a deeper level of maturity in the relationship than perhaps was possible before. In the biblical parable of the prodigal son the deeply resentful older brother is given the possibility of a growth in stature in the face of the father's joyous welcoming of the repentant younger brother. The naughtiness of young children can call out depths within the parents which were not exemplified previously. The presence of evil does not lead inevitably to a greater good. Obviously, but the actualization of greater good seems to be grounded on brokenness in some degree.

Fourth, as Reinhold Niebuhr has reminded us, through all the ironies and strange turnings of the human spirit there persists the ineradicable dialectical condition wherein every advance makes possible greater destructiveness, and every gain brings new opportunities and larger temptations.

All of these categorical conditions are dimensions of a web of interrelatedness that constitutes the seamless context within which all human life is lived.

Relational power is the capacity to sustain an internal relationship. The sustaining does not include management, control, or domination. Rather, it involves the persistent effort to create and maintain the relationship as internal. This effort is carried out within the context of the factors and conditions previously described, and in the face of all the dynamic forces which operate to weaken or break the internality and transform it into the predominantly external type of relationship that is characteristic of the practice of linear power.

The discipline demanded by the effort to sustain internal relationships is at least difficult. Its cost is large and sometimes enormous. The price to be exacted involves the expenditure of great energy in the form of an active patience, physical stamina, emotional and psychic strength, and a resilient trust and faith. Above all, the cost is measured in the coin of suffering. The capacity to endure a great suffering for the sake of a large purpose is one of the decisive marks of maturity. In the Christian tradition the adequate symbol of the cost of sustaining an internal relation is the cross.

Within the conception of power as relational, size is fundamentally determined by the range and intensity of internal relationships one can help create and sustain. The largest size is exemplified in those relationships whose range exhibits the greatest compatible contrasts, contrasts which border on chaos (Whitehead). The achievement of the apex of size involves sustaining a process of transforming incompatible contrasts or contradictions into compatible contrasts and of bearing those contrasts within the integrity of one's individuality.

There are other less inclusive criteria which are applicable to the determination of size. Size may be ascertained by the degree of the concreteness of the other, including the other's freedom, that one can absorb, while attempting to maintain the relationship as mutually creative and transformative. This is especially the case when the freedom of the other moves him in the direction of indifference, refusal, or estrangement. Size may be measured by the extent to which one has enabled the other to be as large as he might become, and thereby make his fullest contribution to one's own life as well as to the lives of others. Size can also be determined by the freedom with which one's love of the other transcends the "in spite of" character of the traditional conception of love and moves toward an unqualified "because of."

In our religious tradition the "suffering servant" is an important symbol with respect to our topic of power. It may be used to refer to an individual or a people. The suffering servant has sometimes been interpreted as one who receives an influence without making any claim on his own behalf, as one who passively suffers the effect of self-centered or destructive unilateral influence. In this interpretation the suffering servant is one who exemplifies the purely feminine conception of passive power in contrast to the wholly masculine version of aggressive power. This is a contrast between two unilateral actions.

But from the point of view taken in this discussion, this interpretation is inadequate. The suffering servant is rather one who can sustain a relationship involving great contrast, in this case the incompatibility between love and hate. In absorbing the hate or indifference derived from the other, while attempting to sustain the relationship by responding with love for the other, the extreme of contrasts is exemplified. This contrast is an incompatibility, in fact an emotional contradiction. But by having the size to absorb this contradiction within the integrity of his own being, and in having the strength to sustain the relationship, the incompatibility has been transformed into a compatible contrast.

This is size indeed. This consideration highlights the principle that the life of relational power requires a greater strength and size than the life of linear power. The suffering servant, in returning love for hate, and in attempting to sustain the relationship as internal and creative, must be psychically larger and stronger than those who unilaterally hate. Without this greater strength and larger size, the suffering servant could not sustain the relationship. He would crack psychologically, or he would break the relationship and revert to the practice of linear power.

It follows from all this that a christological figure such as Jesus, who is to be found at the bottom of the hierarchy of linear power, stands at the apex of life conceived in terms of relational power. But a messiah of size cannot be created out of the weakness of a milquetoast. In considering the topic of size it needs to be noted, again, that inequality is present as an inescapable condition. Because of this inequality there is an unfairness to life. This quality appears to have something like a categorical status in our experience.

Our only choice is to choose between two forms of unfairness. In the life of linear power, the unfairness means that the stronger are able to control and dominate the weaker and thereby claim their disproportionate share of the world's goods and values. In the life of relational power, the unfairness means that those of larger size must undergo greater suffering and bear a greater burden in sustaining those relationships which hopefully may heal the brokenness of the seamless web of interdependence in which we all live. "Of whom much is given, much is expected."

It has been maintained that the contemporary world, which has been so decisively shaped by modern science, requires the presence of groups of people of adequate size. It is the contention of this discussion that the practice of linear power cannot create people of a size sufficient to cope with the problems we face. If the quality of terrestrial life is to attain a level which makes it worth the effort of living it, this achievement is possible only in terms of the practice of relational power.

But our situation is deeply problematic. The notion that the life of relational power calls for a stature which transcends the life of linear power does not mean, however, that relational power has greater survival capability than linear power. The higher forms of life may be less able to survive (as higher forms) than less complex forms of energy. The more sensitive the organism, the more it may need to be protected from some of the rougher and cruder aspects of existence. In terms of permanence, the stone far outdistances man. As Whitehead has observed, "The art of persistence is to be dead."

There is another dimension to our problematic situation. It is an issue that has troubled theologians and philosophers of history for centuries. Stated in terms appropriate to this lecture: can the life of relational power be sustained with sufficient strength in the face of perhaps overwhelming linear power? Those who live relationally are larger in stature and psychically stronger than those who live unilaterally. Nonetheless, can relational power become so efficacious historically that it may at least hold its own if it cannot overcome the destructive forces of linear power? The lives of those who live relationally may not be sufficiently efficacious or persuasive with respect to those who live unilaterally. In fact, the opposite may and does occur. The behavior of the larger may create a fury in the souls of the smaller and weaker that can eventuate in greater impoverishment and destructiveness. This principle is exemplified in the anti-Semitism which is an attitude of the weaker against the stronger.

Who shall inherit the earth? The Bible says it will be the meek. But surely this prophecy is not warranted if the meek are understood to be spineless doormats who live in terms of a unilaterally feminine conception of power. If the meek are understood to be living embodiments of relational power, if they are in fact members of a suffering servant people, then the proposition is surely interesting. It may even become true.

The earth belongs, or ought to belong, to those who make the largest claims on life. The largest claims are not made nor are they makeable in the form of linear power. They are made by those who attempt to embody most fully the life of relational power, for they are claims made not only for themselves but on behalf of all peoples.

The metaphysical depth and pervasiveness of the primary conditions which constitute the problematic context for the practice of relational power[10] point to a universe struggling toward creative advance. This problematic context confronts us whether we opt for linear or relational power. The god of unilateral power is not a tribal deity. On the contrary, it is a universal god. But it is a demonic god, an idol which is not large enough to merit our faith and devotion. The issue appears to be in doubt. But the faith which can live with that doubt is a steadfast and hopeful trust in both the goodness and the power of a relational God of adequate size.

Bibliography

James, William. *Pragmatism: A New Name for Some Old Ways of Thinking*. London: Longmans, Green, 1908.

---

10. Ambiguity, inequality, and the several dimensions of the inextricable relationships between good and evil.

— Appendix B —
Worship and Theodicy

David Ray Griffin[1]

Why This Issue Is Crucial for Process Theodicy

It might seem strange to have a separate chapter on theodicy and worship. Is this not what theodicy is all about? Has this issue, therefore, not been the topic of all the previous chapters? It is true that the basic question that motivates a theodicy is whether the evils of the world can be reconciled with a divine reality worthy of worship. There is a good reason, nevertheless, to have a separate chapter on this topic in a book on process theodicy. This reason is that the typical and fairly distinctive criticism of process theodicy is that it "solves" the problem of evil only by portraying a God who is not worthy of worship. The reason why this criticism is directed at process theodicy (and other similar approaches) in particular can be seen by reviewing the elements involved in the problem of evil. For a reality to be considered worthy of worship and thus to be called God, at least in biblically based cultures, this reality must be perfect in power and goodness. The problem of evil is generated by the fact that belief in divine goodness and power, when perfect power is understood as omnipotence in the traditional sense, seems to be rationally inconsistent with the acknowledgment of worldly evil. The reason for this apparent inconsistency is that a being of perfect goodness would presumably want to prevent all evil, and an omnipotent being would presumably be capable of preventing all evil. The various approaches to the problem of evil involve different judgments about which of the four

1. David Ray Griffin (1939–2022) was emeritus professor of philosophy and theology at Claremont School of Theology, emeritus professor of religion at Claremont Graduate University, and cofounder with John B. Cobb Jr. of the Center for Process Studies in 1973. He was the author of numerous books in philosophy, religion, and politics, and one of the most widely recognized and influential process philosophers of the twenty-first century. —Ed.

elements—rational consistency, worldly evil, perfect divine goodness, or divine omnipotence—to reject. What the typical criticism of a theodicy is depends upon which of the four elements it rejects.

A theodicy that rejects rational consistency evokes the charge not that it portrays a God unworthy of worship, but that it is irrational. Although in *God, Power, and Evil* I discussed three theologians who rejected rational consistency in an extreme sense by rejecting logical consistency (Barth, Brunner, and Fackenheim), none of my critics took this extreme approach. The issue of the importance of rational consistency in a larger sense does play a role in the present book, however, especially in relation to the positions of John Knasas, Alvin Plantinga, and Stephen Davis. Davis does not programmatically deny the importance of providing plausible explanations, but he seems to assume that admitting that he does not have plausible explanations for various types of evil does not seriously undermine the credibility of his position. Knasas tries to overcome the apparent inconsistency of saying both that God fully determines all worldly events and that some worldly events are truly free. The main question Plantinga's position raises is whether the human demand for rational consistency is met as long as no outright logical consistency can be shown, or whether this demand requires an explanation that goes beyond this minimalist conception of rationality to provide a plausible explanation for the coexistence of God and evil.

A second approach to theodicy is to reject worldly evil by saying that all apparent evils are, or might be, not genuinely evil from an omniscient standpoint. The main criticism this approach evokes is that it is incredible. As I showed in *God, Power, and Evil*, this approach was finally taken by most advocates of traditional all-determining theism, such as Augustine, Aquinas, Luther, and Leibniz. The fact that this approach is not of merely historical interest is illustrated by Nelson Pike in the present book, and also by Huston Smith, who, in a recent debate with me, says that "everything—the everything for which God is solely responsible—is exactly as it should be." Smith continues: "God's perfection, tied tightly to his omnipotence, precludes the possibility of any second-rate happenings—nothing that occurs would have been better had it been otherwise."[2] He thereby explicitly rejects the reality of what I mean by genuine evil: "anything, all things considered, without which the universe would have been better."[3] The main question this position provokes is: Can anyone really believe this? That is, can one consistently live in terms of the conviction that nothing that happens is really evil?

2. Griffin and Smith, *Primordial Truth and Postmodern Theology*, 162, 163.
3. Griffin, *God, Power, and Evil*, 27.

The third possibility is to reject the perfect goodness of God. This approach was illustrated in *God, Power, and Evil* by E. S. Brightman (who suggested that God has a nonrational, volatile, amoral nature, which is at odds with God's perfectly good will). This approach is illustrated in the present volume by Philip Hefner and (to be discussed below) Nancy Frankenberry.

The central criticism evoked by this theodicy is that it does not really provide a theodicy. The word "theodicy," coming from the Greek words for God and justice, means an attempt to justify the ways of God in the light of the world's (apparent) evils. This third approach provides an *explanation* for evil—by saying that the creator of the world is itself partly evil—but no justification. It does not defend God against the suspicion of being immoral or amoral, but simply turns this suspicion into an affirmation. In other words, this third approach, by rejecting God's perfect goodness, has not portrayed a divine being worthy of worship, and therefore in effect has not defended the existence of *God*. A book built around this approach would, like the present one, need a chapter on "theodicy and worship."

This question about worshipfulness also arises in relation to the traditional free-will theodicy (or defense). That approach provokes one or the other of the two previous criticisms. On the one hand, insofar as it acknowledges the existence of genuine evil, it evokes doubt that the God portrayed is fully good: if this God has coercive omnipotence, one wonders, why has this God allowed so many unspeakable evils? As we have seen, Davis says "I just don't know," and Plantinga denies the need to give plausible answers. On the other hand, insofar as this theodicy avoids this criticism by saying that everything will eventually work out for the best (Hick), this theodicy evokes incredulity.

The fourth possible approach is to modify the traditional doctrine of perfect power, so that it no longer implies that God can unilaterally prevent all genuine evil. This approach unambiguously retains worldly evil, divine goodness, and rational consistency (in more than a minimalist sense, insisting that a rational position must be plausible). But this approach typically provokes the response that it has reconciled God and evil only by portraying a God that is finite in power and therefore unworthy of worship. David Basinger, for example, indicates what he would say if all his other objections to process theism were overcome. Against the claim of process theists that the view that God cannot coerce is more adequate than the view that God can, he replies that many believe that "a god as 'weak' as the one affirmed by process theism is no god at all or, at least, a god not worthy of worship and thus see the coercive concept of classical theism to be more adequate."[4] Like-

---

4. Basinger, "Divine Persuasion," 332–47, esp. 345.

wise, the conclusion of Reichenbach's critique is that the God of process theism is finite in the sense of having less power than some conceivable being. (Reichenbach and Basinger both make this criticism even though they both, in their effort to provide an answer to natural evils, implicitly move toward this approach themselves, insofar as they adopt the position of F. R. Tennant.) The same point is made by John Knasas and Stephen Davis, and this point was the crux of John Hick's earlier criticism of process theodicy.[5]

This criticism has already been answered in previous chapters. The answer is essentially twofold. (1) The traditional idea of God is not really a conceivable idea and therefore does not provide a standard in terms of which to call the God of process theism finite, in the sense of imperfect—namely, inferior to some conceivable being. (2) Coercive power, far from being a necessary attribute of a universal, omnipresent being, is, like a voice, a beard, and a hand, an attribute that can characterize only a finite, localized being. This twofold answer, which has been developed at length in previous chapters, need not be elaborated again here.

There are, however, three other questions revolving around the concept of worshipfulness that have been raised. One is whether worship really presupposes perfect power. A second question is whether process theism portrays God as perfectly good. A third is whether worship really requires God to be perfectly good. I have already discussed the third question while responding to Philip Hefner in chapter 10. I will here, accordingly, respond only to the first two questions.

Does Worship Presuppose Perfect Power?

Peter Hare has asked whether it is not arbitrary to insist that a reality must be perfect in power to be worthy of worship. His question was evoked by the fact that I had agreed with critics of E. S. Brightman's deity that it is not worthy of worship. I had said that this conclusion follows not only from the fact that Brightman's God is not perfectly good, but also from the fact that, according to Brightman himself, his God had imperfect—that is, less than the greatest conceivable—power.[6] Hare uses my judgment here as a test case "of how fairly process theists judge other nontraditional theists," saying that it seems "unwise and unfair to consider 'greatest conceivable' a

---

5. For Knasas, see Griffin, *Evil Revisited*, ch. 4; for Davis, see "God the Mad Scientist: Process Theology on God and Evil," 18–23, esp. 22; and see Hick's criticism of my theodicy in Stephen Davis, *Encountering Evil*.

6. Griffin, *God, Power, and Evil*, 246.

necessary and sufficient condition of worshipability."[7] Hare believes it would be "fairer to consider the worshipability of power to be partly a matter of how far the power is from a monopoly and how far it is from the maximum in human power." Then, "instead of considering deities such as Brightman's unworthy of a theistic sort of worship" altogether, process theists should simply say that less strength of worship is appropriate to them than to the God of process theism, and that "the strength of worship appropriate to the process deity is the greatest strength of worship that is metaphysically and morally meaningful."[8]

The disagreement here seems to be partly semantic, and Hare's discussion points out an ambiguity in the term "worshipful." On the one hand, worship implies loving and serving the divine reality with one's whole heart, mind, soul, and body, and this unreserved devotion is not possible if the divine reality, in the worshipper's estimation, is infected with imperfection. On this basis, I said that Brightman's God was finite in a sense that makes it unworthy of worship. My main concern was to point out that, if the God of process theism be called "finite," it is not finite in the same sense as Brightman's, that of having less than the greatest power conceivable (within a given framework). That this was no idle concern I had indicated at the outset by pointing out that the only mention of the Whiteheadian position in John Hick's large book on the problem of evil was "the false suggestion that it is essentially the same as that of E. S. Brightman."[9] I had some support for connecting perfection and worshipfulness in Brightman himself, incidentally, in that he, concluding that God as a whole is not morally perfect, declared the object of worship to be the divine will, which is perfectly good.[10] In any case, I was here using "worthy of worship" in the sense of unreservedly worthy, and I agree with Anselm that nothing is thus worthy except that greater than which nothing can be (coherently) thought.

The term "worshipful," however, can also point to that which in fact does evoke religious devotion or commitment, and in this sense being worshipful is not an all-or-none matter but that matter of degree of which Hare speaks. I have at least implicitly used this notion by speaking of the basic religious motivation of human beings as the desire to be in harmony with the ultimate power of the universe. "To want to be in harmony with" is the basic form of worship, and this worship will be evoked by the power that is thought or imagined to be the supreme power of the universe. It need not

7. Hare, "Review of *God, Power, and Evil*," 44–51, esp. 47.
8. Hare, "Review of *God, Power, and Evil*," 47–48.
9. Quoted in Griffin, *God, Power, and Evil*, 11.
10. See Griffin, *God, Power, and Evil*, 246.

be assumed to be the greatest conceivable power, it must only be thought (or felt) to be, in some sense, the most effective power, at least in relation to matters of ultimate importance. And it certainly need not be thought to be perfectly good. The sun, the dialectical process of history, and the evolutionary process controlled by the survival of the fittest can each be "worshipful" in this sense of the term, they have indeed evoked overriding devotion from persons. Less than fully critical devotees may, in fact, believe that the deity in question is worthy of unreserved devotion. But the fully critical spirit will protest, saying that commitment of one's entire heart, mind, soul, and body is not appropriate if the object of devotion is imperfect.

This distinction between the two senses of the term "worshipful" seems to be implicit in Hare's discussion. He is using it in the latter, psychological sense insofar as he speaks of worship as a matter of degree. He implies the idea of being worshipful in the former, normative sense of the term in speaking of "the greatest strength of worship that is metaphysically and morally meaningful."

The one statement of Hare's on this topic with which I would take issue is his suggestion that worshipfulness should involve the question of how far the conceived power is from having a monopoly on power. If the idea of a being with a monopoly on power is, as Hare says, metaphysically impossible and morally repugnant, we should not accept it as a standard in relation to which to judge other ways to conceive the holy power whose existence we all at some level intuit. One difficulty with Hare's suggestion is evident from my discussion above about the sense in which the God of process theology has effected a self-limitation. By evoking the existence of beings with increasingly more power of self-determination, God has become increasingly removed from having a monopoly on power. Hare's suggestion would imply that, by creating living beings, and finally human beings, God had become increasingly less worthy of worship. It would be appropriate for us to worship God with great strength of devotion only if we, the potential worshippers, did not exist.

Is the God of Process Theism Perfectly Good?

Those who deny God's perfect goodness will, naturally, be critical of the notion that worship presupposes perfect goodness. Nancy Frankenberry, who wants to "collapse the ontological distinction Whitehead made between God and creativity"[11] and thereby, like Hefner, move toward a more monistic

---

11. Frankenberry, "Some Problems in Process Theodicy," 179–97, esp. 183.

worldview,[12] also like Hefner, cannot regard God as unambiguously good. She accordingly wants to challenge the "theological habit of connecting worshipfulness with moral goodness."[13] Because I have already addressed this question in the response to Hefner,[14] I will not treat it here, but will instead move directly to a related question raised by Frankenberry—whether the God of process theism (without her proposed collapse of the ontological distinction between God and creativity) portrays God as perfectly good. While her critique of the distinction between persuasion and coercion,[15] was meant to apply to process theology somewhat broadly, her claim about my theodicy in particular is that it does not salvage "a valid meaning of the goodness of God."[16]

Frankenberry begins her argument for this point by citing "Griffin's own admission that God is responsible for 'all of the evil of discord in the world.'" She comments: "This in itself is a major admission,"[17] seeming to

12. Frankenberry does not, however, mean to return to an all-determining, monistic theism. Her idea is that the creative energy provided by God to finite occasions is "not entirely determinative" (ibid., 183); she wants to avoid the conclusion that "our free acts are only apparently ours." She believes that this can be avoided "by a conception of creativity as that which becomes the creature's own in God's very giving of it moment-to-moment," so that it is not "so determinative that one can only conform slavishly to it" (ibid., 183). It seems to me that this idea makes sense only if the distinction between God and creativity is not totally collapsed. In any case, Frankenberry's attempts to work out this idea can be found in "The Power of the Past"; "The Emergent Paradigm and Divine Causation"; "The Logic of Whitehead's Intuition of Everlastingness"; and "Language about the Totality."

13. Frankenberry, "Some Problems," 187.

14. See Griffin, *Evil Revisited*, ch. 10.

15. Griffin, *Evil Revisited*, ch. 6.

16. Frankenberry, "Some Problems," 186.

17. Frankenberry, "Some Problems," 186–87. Frankenberry adds that my statement "ought to suggest, if anything could, that the doctrine of divine goodness is not the conclusion of an *a posteriori* mode of reasoning." Her position here is doubly problematic. In the first place, she makes this statement as if she were thereby making a point against my formal position. But I had said that my enterprise is not a "natural theology" in the allegedly neutral sense, calling it instead a Christian philosophical theology (See Griffin, *God, Power, and Evil*, 25–27). In particular, I pointed out that the idea that the divine reality, to be worthy of worship, must be morally good is a historically conditioned valuation that I share (ibid., 20–21, 23, 25–27, 275–76). The question is not whether one would, without that prior idea, be led by a survey of the world to the idea of a morally perfect creator. The question is: Given the idea of such a divine being, can we develop an account of reality that is more consistent, more adequate to the facts of experience, and more illuminating of those facts, than accounts starting from some other "a priori" preconception? My claim is that every worldview in fact begins with some "vision of reality" that functions in this *a priori* way, analogous to Christian faith. This point leads to the second problem implicit in her statement. She seems to think

imply thereby that my statement has already partly made her case against the unambiguous goodness of the process God. Why it does not do so was explained in the final section of the previous chapter,[18] in the discussion of the sense in which God can be responsible for discord or suffering without being indictable for it. Process theodicy asks: If the choice was either human-like beings who might treat each other very inhumanely, even engage in genocide, pollute the globe, and even build nuclear weapons with which to threaten all forms of life, or no human-like creatures at all, could we honestly say that God should have forgone higher-than-ape creatures altogether? Frankenberry seems to think my question was purely rhetorical, as she says: "But there are clearly two answers to this question." But that is what I had already said.[19] Although I do not think that God chose wrongly (assuming the truth of this picture of the options), I realize that others, especially those less fortunately situated, might well think otherwise. Certainly, some persons with strong ecological sensitivities have become misanthropic, deciding it would have been better if human beings had never been evolved.

Frankenberry, however, does not merely want the possibility of that answer recognized, she thinks it should, at least to an extent, be affirmed. She holds it against me that I do "not wrestle with those voices in our century who have been disposed to take Job's side of the case against God, and who, like Elie Wiesel, have been able to articulate a much more complex and agonized affirmation of the reality of God than has yet appeared in process theodicy."[20] But "to take Job's side against God" is to assume, with Job, the existence of a God who is more strongly responsible for the events of the world than the God of process theology. Frankenberry's comment thereby begs the question.

Likewise, the "more complex" affirmation of God that Frankenberry prefers is necessary only because she is suggesting a simplification of the Whiteheadian doctrine of God by advocating that the ontological distinction Whitehead made between God and creativity be collapsed. Whitehead's

---

that the view she advocates, which does not distinguish between God and creativity, and therefore does not regard God as unambiguously good, is somehow more empirical, more *a posteriori*, than the Whiteheadian view. She suggests that the divine reality is "revealed in concrete events for both good and for ill," so that we can look to see how good the world in its entirety is and say that "to that extent and no more, God is good" ("Some Problems," 189). But this view is no less an *a priori* idea than the view she rejects. In any case, her point here, even it were deemed valid, would provide no argument against the goodness of God as portrayed in my theodicy.

18. Griffin, *Evil Revisited*, ch. 10.
19. See Griffin, *God, Power, and Evil*, 309; Cobb and Griffin, *Process Theology*, 75.
20. Frankenberry, "Some Problems," 187.

famous statement, "All simplifications of religious dogma are shipwrecked upon the rock of the problem of evil," which Frankenberry cites,[21] is directly relevant here. In introducing this topic, Whitehead had pointed to "three main simple renderings" of the concept of God: the Eastern Asiatic concept of an impersonal order, which is the self-ordering of the world, the Semitic concept of a "personal individual entity, whose existence is the one ultimate metaphysical fact," and the pantheistic concept, which is the Semitic concept with the world as a phase within God. Whitehead suggests that we should not think of these "extremes of simplicity" as "mutually exclusive concepts, from among which we are to choose one and reject the others."[22] We should instead engage in that "complexity of thought" required to find some "mediation" between these concepts. Whitehead clearly meant his own doctrine of God to be a more complex doctrine in which that mediation is achieved, and which, among other things, would therefore not be shipwrecked upon the rock of the problem of evil. Frankenberry's proposal to collapse the distinction between God and creativity seems to lead back toward the type of simplification Whitehead wanted to overcome. One of the theses of *God, Power, and Evil* is that the complexity of traditional theology, with its notorious "scholastic distinctions," was due to the fact that it had not made distinctions soon enough, especially a distinction between the creativity of God and that of the world. If Frankenberry wants to collapse that distinction, it is not surprising that she should feel the need for a "more complex and agonizing affirmation of the reality of God" than those of us who believe Whitehead's distinction to be one of the greatest breakthroughs ever made in the history of philosophical theology. In any case, the proposal to modify process theism to make God more responsible for evil says nothing about the goodness of God in a process theism that has not been thus modified.

Frankenberry's main argument for the conclusion that the God of process theology cannot be considered morally perfect seems to be based on the principle that the God of process theology first of all promotes aesthetic value, meaning complexity and intensity as well as harmony of experience. She believes that looking at "aesthetic considerations would seem to lead to a more ambiguous and mixed estimate" about divine goodness. "Upon close examinations," she says, "this aesthetic order at concrete moments of

---

21. Whitehead, *Religion in the Making*, 74; quoted in Frankenberry, "Some Problems," 197.
22. Whitehead, *Religion in the Making*, 66–67, 74–75.

history can appear to be at best utterly indifferent and at worst implacably malevolent towards human good."[23]

How does Frankenberry's argument fare "upon close examination"? One problem with her statement is that it is about how the aesthetic order "can appear." No one doubts that it can appear as she describes it; but the task of philosophical theology, like that of natural science, is to try to discern the reality beneath the appearances.

If what she means, however, is that the aesthetic order really is as she describes it, then two responses are in order. First, process theology, being evolutionary, nondualistic, and nonanthropocentric, specifically rejects the idea that the world was designed for human beings in particular. To regard the world as reflecting a divine teleology is not to say that everything is

23. Frankenberry, "Some Problems," 188. Frankenberry seems to think that the use of the aesthetic criteria of harmony and intensity will somehow diminish the user's or reader's sense of the genuineness of evil. She says: "Surely one of the few conclusions to emerge with overwhelming clarity from the persistent theoretical and existential challenges to traditional theodicies is that 'explanations' of evil either by way of looking backward to a causal genesis, or forward to a teleological outcome, have the effect of negating or diminishing perception of the genuineness of the present evil with which we have to struggle. I suggest this applies also to the aesthetic criteria which Whiteheadians would have us recognize" (ibid., 193). This statement confuses explanations with criteria. To settle upon criteria to define or describe evil, and to distinguish its forms, so that you can know and communicate what you are talking about, is not to give an explanation for why evil occurs.

Furthermore, insofar as my theodicy, which employs these criteria, does show some *prima facie* evils not to be genuine evils, the purpose is to help us distinguish clearly between those *prima facie* evils that are genuinely evil and those that are not. This distinction is important in itself for practical purposes, and also serves to block in advance the inference that, because some *prima facie* evils turn out to be only apparently evil, this is likely true of all of them. Frankenberry's own discussion provides a nice example. Many people believe that it is evil that we all must die sometime. Frankenberry rightly points out that this eventuality is not an evil, because it could not be otherwise (Frankenberry, "Some Problems," 191). People who see that death is a natural, necessary feature of biological life will not waste emotion railing against the universe because they must eventually die, or waste time, energy, and resources trying to find a way to prevent eventual death. They will therefore have a more appropriate emotional relation to the universe, and will be more likely to devote their energies to trying to overcome *genuine* evils, such as the fact that millions of people each year die prematurely, often without even having had the possibility of a good life beforehand. Another example: my theodicy suggests that the possibility of intense pain is necessary if organisms are to have the possibility of realizing great values. Once this is accepted, people will not bemoan the fact that we are subject to intense pain. But this realization that the possibility of pain is not genuinely evil does not mean that the actual suffering people undergo is not genuinely evil, insofar as it has arisen from contingent factors. Through this type of distinction, we can hold that the world in its *basic structure* is *one of the best* of all possible worlds, while avoiding the enervating conviction that the world in its *concrete details* is *the* best of all possible worlds.

supposed to work together for human good. The divine purpose promotes harmonious intensity of experience in general. We humans generally benefit from this promotion, both directly and indirectly, but this promotion has necessarily had the possibility of resulting in forms of order and types of events, such as viruses, cancerous growths, earthquakes, and meteorites, that sometimes conflict with our welfare. To point out that the aesthetic order is not unambiguously favorable to human good is therefore to affirm, not to refute, one of process theology's basic points. Second, Frankenberry's statement is relevant only if we have already accepted her modification of Whitehead, collapsing the distinction between God's creativity and the creative energy of worldly beings (through which they can partially determine themselves and inflict themselves on each other in ways that run strongly counter to the divine suasion). As long as we hold to this distinction, the indifference and malevolence that characterize creaturely creativity cast no shadow upon the divine creativity. We can believe that Divine Creativity is always perfectly characterized by Creative and Responsive Love, with no admixture of malevolence or indifference. Frankenberry's counter-suggestion, that we must read indifference or malevolence into the divine nature, is to beg the question, which is whether we should collapse the distinction between God and creativity.

One of the reasons that I, as well as other process theologians, have given for regarding God as unambiguously good is based on the doctrine of God's "consequent nature," according to which God necessarily feels the sufferings as well as the joys of creatures along with us. I suggested that this doctrine is relevant to God's goodness in the light of the idea that God has lured the creation forward to heights where extreme suffering is possible. The idea that, because of the metaphysical correlations involving value and power, great values are not possible without the risk of great suffering surely provides the most important justification for God in this framework. But it is also helpful, I suggested, to reflect on the fact that God, in this theology, is no impassive spectator, goading the creation on to risk sufferings that will be the creatures' alone. Rather, "God does not promote any new level of intensity without being willing to suffer the possible consequences."[24]

Frankenberry seeks to turn this argument against the goodness of process theology's God. She constructs a damned-if-you-do, damned-if-you-don't argument around the question whether the "evil which lacerates the life of creatures . . . cuts deeply into the life of the creator." On the one hand, if it does not, then God as the "fellow sufferer" does not really "understand" the sufferings of creatures. I agree. On the other hand, she says, "if

---

24. Griffin, *God, Power, Evil*, 310; quoted in Frankenberry, "Some Problems," 188.

the lacerations are suffered more immediately by God . . . then the 'complexity' of the concrete nature of God may just as well spell the viper's tangle, and its 'intensity' reflect the full force of evil's perversity." In other words, "Whitehead's 'fellow sufferer' may be too deeply riddled with antagonistic impulses to be unambiguously 'good.'"[25]

Frankenberry has again confused two quite different things. This time the confusion is between aesthetic evil, or suffering, and moral evil, or perversity. This distinction, which was mentioned in the previous chapter,[26] has been emphasized countless times by Charles Hartshorne, among others. When a woman suffers during childbirth because, being naturally sympathetic to her bodily members, she feels the trauma experienced by her cells, we do not call her evil. When a father suffers in sympathy with the sufferings of his child, we do not call him evil, in fact, we would doubt his complete goodness if he did not suffer. We do say that suffering is evil, and that evil is thereby present in the sufferer. But this is evil *undergone*, not evil *intended*; it is *aesthetic* evil, not *moral* evil. To say that God suffers deeply is no basis for saying that God has "antagonistic impulses" unless one has already decided, with E. S. Brightman or Nancy Frankenberry, that God is the only natural locus of creative energy in the universe. Again, Frankenberry's criticism of process theology presupposes that the revision she would propose has already been made.

For a final point in her argument that I have not convincingly portrayed God as perfectly good, Frankenberry quotes the following statement from Robert Neville:

> If God's primordial decision regarding values and limitation in general is at root arbitrary, as Whitehead says it is, then it is only coincidence if God is metaphysically good, this being an arbitrary decision God makes in determining the metaphysical principles to which divinity must conform.[27]

Although this statement is used by Frankenberry to buttress her rejection of God's goodness, it is not at all relevant to her critique of my position. In a section entitled "The Notion of Metaphysical Principles Beyond Divine Decision," I argued directly against the view that Neville's statement enunciates. I not only presented Hartshorne's argument that the notion of a "primordial decision" is self-contradictory, because the eternal or primordial is necessary and therefore beyond all decision; I also argued that this position was

---

25. Frankenberry, "Some Problems," 188–89.
26. Griffin, *Evil Revisited*, ch. 10.
27. Frankenberry, "Some Problems," 190, citing Neville, *Creativity and God*, 11–12.

implicit in Whitehead's own thought, so that the revision is not *ad hoc* but makes Whitehead's position more self-consistent.[28] More recently, I have argued that, if one accepts the Whiteheadian view that all direct perception is sympathetic prehension, then the necessary goodness of God follows from God's omniscience.[29] This argument, it should be noted, proceeded from the side of Whitehead that Frankenberry most appreciates, his radical empiricism, it says that all our direct perception is sympathetic. God's perception of the world, by analogy, could not be indifferent or antagonistic. That argument is found explicitly in Hartshorne, and may be implied in Whitehead's enigmatic statement that God's "necessary goodness expresses the determination of his consequent nature."[30] This statement in any case shows that Whitehead himself, contrary to Neville, did not see his position as implying that God's goodness is at best a contingent truth.

I do not find, in conclusion, that Frankenberry has provided any good reasons to contend that the God of process theism, at least as portrayed in my theodicy, is morally not unambiguously good.[31] That contention would

---

28. Griffin, *God, Power, and Evil*, 297–300.

29. See Griffin, "The Holy, Necessary Goodness, and Morality"; and Griffin, "Nuclearism, Imperialism, and Postmodern Theism."

30. Whitehead, *Process and Reality*, 345.

31. I have not discussed Frankenberry's third criticism of process theodicy, which she evidently takes to be the decisive one. She says that "the real issue in this theodicy concerns the grounds for realistic hope" ("Some Problems," 194). My reason for not discussing this criticism is that, as I indicated in the first chapter (*Evil Revisited*, ch. 1), I agree with it. Process theology as generally presented, including the way it was presented in *God, Power, and Evil*, does not provide sufficient grounds for hope. This general agreement with Frankenberry does not mean, however, that I concur with all her related criticisms of process theism or with her proposals about how to reformulate it. For example, one of the dimensions of her criticism is that process theology does not provide grounds for hope that the future of humanity on earth will be better than the past, or for "any final or ultimate transformation as such of history or the cosmos or even of individual lives" ("Some Problems," 194). Although Frankenberry regards Whitehead's discussion of the way worldly events are "transmuted" in God as referring primarily to a redemption occurring in God alone ("beyond history," to use Reinhold Niebuhr's expression), she does recognize the fact, to which I had devoted considerable attention, that this transmutation in God becomes the basis for the next set of ideal aims directed to overcoming evil in the temporal world ("Some Problems," 193; cf. *God, Power, and Evil*, 302–7). Frankenberry's discussion of this point, however, is colored by her assumption, discussed in chapter 6, that God for process theology is not a "physical" agent and therefore only opens up new possibilities but does not provide any creative energy to support some particular direction ("Some Problems," 194). Not much historical transformation can therefore be expected. What we need, she says, are "redemptive concrete social energies, not just the assurance of unlimited future possibilities" (ibid., 195). Frankenberry's own proposal provides no help here, of course, even though her revision attributes "concrete social energies" to God, because the price

follow only insofar as Frankenberry's proposed collapse of the distinction between God and creativity is read into process theism; it therefore has no relevance to my position, which emphasizes that distinction. But the question of the perfect goodness of the God of process theism, as portrayed in my theodicy, has been raised from a different direction by Peter Hare.

The topic raised in earlier writings by Hare (and Edward Madden) to which I responded most fully was that of God's values. Having omitted harmony of experience from the criteria of beauty or aesthetic value, and having thereby assumed that aesthetic value could be achieved at the expense of moral and physical evil, Hare (and Madden) had declared the God of process theology, being concerned to promote primarily aesthetic value, to be not morally approvable. Hare (and Madden) had also interpreted some of Whitehead's statements about the transmutation of evil into good in God's experience to mean that the reality of genuine evil was ultimately denied.[32] My response on this topic in *God, Power, and Evil* was graciously called by Hare "an especially impressive achievement."[33] His point is that it takes careful interpretation and judicious emphasis to produce a tenable position out of the writings of Whitehead and Hartshorne, which contain some "seriously misleading things about God's values" that had dismayed and even outraged him. He says: "Griffin's careful account of the divine values of 'intensity' and 'harmony' seems to me such a tenable position."

A critical point, however, lurks behind this praise. Hare continues:

> It needs to be pointed out, however, that other tenable positions are possible even for those who accept a Whiteheadian-Hartshornean metaphysics as sound. Someone could consistently accept such a metaphysics and accept also a being of perfect power who has the values Griffin describes, yet legitimately refuse to worship that being. Such a person could grant that intensity and harmony are real values, but feel, for example, that the relative weight given by this deity to harmony in both the short and the long run is not sufficient to justify his worship. In other words, process theists should recognize that process theism can be legitimately regarded as good metaphysics but bad religion. We

she pays for this more robust view of divine power is the loss of God's unambiguous moral character. A divine eros that favors good no more than evil cannot provide a basis for hope for moral and aesthetic progress. A better basis for hope is provided by the God of process theology, who wills betterment unambiguously, who exerts more power than Frankenberry's portrayal suggests, and who can be thought to be even more effective, especially in the long run, than most portrayals of process theism heretofore have suggested.

32. For my discussion of their criticisms, see Griffin, *God, Power, and Evil*, 301–8.
33. Hare, "Review of *God, Power, and Evil*," 50.

should be suspicious of any attempt to show that one and only one system of moral priorities is legitimate. The fact . . . that a being of perfect power happens to have a certain set of moral priorities does not establish those priorities as worthy of worship by everyone. Worshipability is always an open question.[34]

I can agree with all these statements, but only by making some distinctions. I do not know if any real disagreement between us would exist once these distinctions are made.

The fact that "a being of perfect power happens to have a certain set of moral priorities" would not, I agree, make that set of priorities worthy of universal allegiance. No necessary connection exists between "being right" and "having perfect power." This is true at least if by power here we mean outgoing, creative, efficient power, as distinct from receptive power.

If a being, however, had perfect receptive power, meaning the power to feel sympathetically all the experiences of the universe, and this perfect receptive power were understood to be a necessary characteristic of the being, then a necessary connection with being right would exist. As pointed out earlier, this position involves the "ideal participant theory" that the very meaning of right and good is to be understood in terms of what an omniscient participant in the universe who is impartially and perfectly sympathetic to all other participants would prefer in particular situations. Although the basis for this account of the right and the good is present in the description of God as "the universal recipient of the totality of good and evil that is actualized," in contrast to "an impassive spectator deity,"[35] and in the endorsement of Hartshorne's position that the ideal of good belongs to God's necessary essence,[36] I did not develop this account in the book, so Hare cannot be faulted for not seeing it. According to this account, however, which I articulated only several years later,[37] the God of process theism is the ideal participant, so that God's values are worthy of universal allegiance, because they constitute the very meaning of right and good. It is not that God happens to have a certain set of valuational priorities, as Hare suggests; rather, because God is necessarily impartially and perfectly sympathetic to the entire creation, God's own values are part and parcel of God's eternal and necessary essence. God's preferences coincide with the very essence of goodness not because of coercive omnipotence, or even perfect persuasive

---

34. Hare, "Review of *God, Power, and Evil*," 50.
35. Griffin, *God, Power, and Evil*, 309–10.
36. Griffin, *God, Power, and Evil*, 297–98.
37. Griffin, "The Holy, Necessary Goodness, and Morality"; and Griffin, "Nuclearism, Imperialism, and Postmodern Theism."

power (this is no process version of "might makes right'"), but because of God's perfect receptive power.

Even on the basis of this understanding, I would agree with Hare's statement that "worshipability is always an open question," if it means that what persons in fact find worthy of worship is a contingent matter. Persons differ in this respect because of cultural, biographical, and temperamental differences. I had pointed out, for example, that many persons, because of cultural conditioning, cannot consider a being without coercive omnipotence worthy of worship.[38] But we can distinguish, as I did in that context, between this psychological question and the normative question of what persons ought to find worthy of worship. Likewise, a distinction exists between the values to which persons in fact give allegiance and the values to which they ought to give allegiance. This is Dewey's distinction between the preferred and the preferable. Although many give allegiance to the values of a tribal deity, all persons ought to give allegiance to the values that would be preferred by an impartially and perfectly sympathetic, omniscient being, because for such a being no distinction between the preferred and the preferable is meaningful.

All this is compatible, finally, with Hare's statement that process theism in general, and my formulation of it in particular, may be "bad religion"— that is, that persons might rightly refuse to worship the deity as described. It is one thing to state, in a purely formal way, that God's values are worthy of allegiance by definition (assuming that God is characterized by impartially and perfectly sympathetic omniscience). It is something else to state what God's values are, and therefore how, for example, the concerns for harmony and intensity are related. Every attempt to do this is extremely fallible, and should be formulated as a tentative hypothesis. Bias from one's religious upbringing, one's wider culture, one's race, one's social position, one's sex, one's temperament, and one's age, among other factors, will inevitably color one's attempt, so that no one's estimation of the divine moral priorities will be found universally acceptable. It may be, for example, that the Whiteheadian emphasis on the necessity of novelty for sustained intensity reflects a Western and especially modern bias. Also, I would now speak less of (momentary) "enjoyment" and more of (enduring) "character" in human life. We should therefore, as Hare says, be "suspicious of any attempt to show that one and only one system of moral priorities is legitimate."[39] This is especially true if one is speaking very concretely about particular moral values, but it is even true to an extent with regard to very abstract issues, such as the proper

---

38. Griffin, *God, Power, and Evil*, 258.
39. Hare, "Review of *God, Power, and Evil*," 50.

balance between harmony and intensity. We should never confuse the idea that axiological truth exists with the idea that *we*, with the help perhaps of our hero (be it St. Thomas or St. Alfred), have discovered and adequately expressed it.

The distinction Hare draws between process metaphysics and the religious vision advocated by process theologians is an important one. Process theology, to be sure, cannot be separated from process metaphysics and still be process theology. But the metaphysical position that is largely shared by Whitehead and Hartshorne does not imply any particular version of process theology; even less does it imply some particular form of religious practice. One who accepts the metaphysical position could be a Catholic, an Eastern Orthodox, an Anglican, a Unitarian, a Quaker, a Pentecostal, a Jew, a Buddhist, a Theosophist, or a devotee of Satya Sai Baba (although there would probably be some tension between process metaphysics and some of the historical doctrinal formulations of most of those movements). Even within the writings of Whitehead and Hartshorne themselves, one can distinguish between the strictly metaphysical vision and the cosmological vision, and between the cosmology and the even more contingent, culturally and biographically influenced, religious sentiments (both men were, for example, sons of Anglican clergymen). If the metaphysics could be consistent with different cosmological speculations, all the more could it be consistent with a wide variety of religious sentiments, emphases, and practices. One could well, then, look at the writings of any process theologian and conclude, "good metaphysics, bad (at least for me) religion."

I agree, therefore, with Hare's formal point, that a form of process theodicy that is superior to mine, either in general or at least for some persons, could be produced.

Conclusion: Living between Gods

Thus far I have discussed the relation between theodicy and worship in primarily philosophical terms. The central question, that about divine power, has concerned the kind of power we (intellectually) find worthy of worship. This becomes the philosophical question of the kind and extent of power that is the greatest conceivable.

But we are not only, or even primarily, intellectual beings; intellectual operations comprise only a fraction of the processes occurring in the human psyche. Emotional feelings and images are more fundamental, and more controlling. A more basic and generally more decisive question than the philosophical one is the psychological question of the kind of power that in fact evokes our religious worship. Our religious drive is to be in harmony with that power that we believe—or better, imagine and feel—to be the supreme power in the universe. If a theodicy solves the problem of evil intellectually, but does so in terms of a conception of divine power that does not fit our feelings and images about what real power is, about the kind of power that is in fact supreme in the nature of things, this theodicy will not fully satisfy. This theodicy, we will feel, will not have really portrayed God, the supreme power of the universe. A theodicy may fail psychologically, then, even if we find it impeccable philosophically.

Because we are social beings, psychological questions of this nature are largely sociological questions. The question of what idea or image of God in fact evokes a religious response from us is largely a question of the image or concept of God we have been conditioned by our social upbringing to associate with religious feelings. Because the dominant religion of Western culture has been Christianity, the crucial question for most of those in this culture is what notion of deity has been portrayed by Christianity. For the issue at hand in particular, the crucial question is what notion of divine power has been conveyed.

The central theological tragedy of Christianity is that, having originated with events that radically challenged the prevailing notion of divine power as controlling, unilateral, overwhelming force, it soon returned to and even intensified this notion.

Christianity takes as the supreme incarnation and revelation of God a man who taught love of enemies, forgiveness, and nonretaliation, and who died on a cross as the victim of the powers of this world. Christianity even adopted the cross of Jesus as its chief symbol, thereby suggesting that salvation comes through God's suffering love. The idea that God's agent of deliverance from evil would be one who was the victim, rather than the conqueror, of the coercive powers of this world stood in strong tension with the idea of God as the one whose "mighty hand" controls all earthly forces, including the coercive power of an imperialistic state. There is good reason to believe that many persons in the early centuries of Christianity had their religious sensibilities shaped by this new notion of divine power, so that it, not coercive omnipotence, evoked their religious worship. And this side of Christian teaching and imagery has continued through the centuries to work its influence upon the sensibilities and imaginations of Christians and others within its orbit of influence.

But from the outset this radically different understanding of divine power (which had roots within the Hebrew Bible and analogues in other traditions, such as Platonism) had to contend with tendencies to dilute it, and even to absorb it within the prevailing view of divine omnipotence.

Already within the New Testament we see the attempt to say that Jesus' death was the fulfillment of the divine plan, which means that God was in complete control all along. The fact that Jesus did not fit the preconception of a messianic warrior-king was handled by distinguishing between the first and the second comings. As Burton Cooper critically summarizes this rationalization: "in the first coming, Christ comes as the vulnerable one, the one who suffers for us; but in the second coming, Christ will show himself as the monarchial Christ, the one who comes with coercive power."[40] The result of this rationalization is that the revolutionary implication of taking a "suffering servant" as the chief incarnation and revelation of God is muted. In Cooper's words: "In principle, then, the life, death, and resurrection of Christ reshape our understanding of God's redemptive power. But instead, the redemptive action of Christ has been interpreted through the monarchial image of God's controlling unilateral power."[41]

This tendency was reinforced by several theological developments. The Greek idea that God is completely impassible, incapable of suffering, was accepted. The human and divine natures of Jesus were radically distinguished, with only the human nature being allowed to suffer; the divinity of Jesus was associated with his miracles and his resurrection, in which he was said to have demonstrated omnipotent power over the forces of nature. God's omniscience was said to be immutable, which implied that God knew the future down to the last detail, which led easily to the notion that God caused it. This latter notion was, in fact, explicitly proclaimed at least as early as the fifth century by St. Augustine. His doctrine of God's predestinating omnipotence, which exerted a very strong influence on Western Christianity, did not even have room for human cooperation with divine grace, as the Pelagians discovered. Although this Augustinian vision of the all-determining power of God was muted in the Middle Ages, at least verbally (as in Thomas Aquinas), it was reasserted in all its purity in the nominalist-voluntarist movement beginning in the fourteenth century, which was foundational for both the Protestant Reformation and (through thinkers such as Descartes, Pascal, Boyle, and Newton) the movement we call the "rise of modern science."

Although the two ideas of divine power have coexisted side by side, the idea of coercive omnipotence has been dominant. Persons in our culture have thereby been taught, in countless ways, to equate divine power, and therefore real power, with the power to control, the power to coerce, the power to destroy. The dominant image of the end of the world is that of

---

40. Cooper, *Why, God?*, 100.
41. Cooper, *Why, God?*, 103.

an apocalyptic event of overwhelming violence brought about unilaterally by divine power. It is no aberration, then, that the test site for the atomic bomb would be dubbed "Trinity" and that a nuclear missile would be called "Peacekeeper." Given these images and feelings embedded deep in our psyches, it is very difficult to feel that some other kind of power—in particular, the power of suffering, persuasive love—is real power, divine power, power worthy of worship.

Some philosophers of religion and theologians believe that this psychological problem is not their problem. The problem for philosophy of religion and theology, they believe, is the conceptual problem; the psychological problem is for others—parents, churches, psychotherapists—to handle. But that is, I believe, to take a too narrow, a too professionalized, view of the task of theodicy. As I suggested in chapter 2,[42] the task is to produce a plausible account of how God and evil are compatible. And plausibility cannot be limited to philosophical, intellectual plausibility isolated from the deeper currents of the human psyche. The theodicy is not plausible in the deep sense to persons unless they believe that the "God" thus reconciled with evil is really God, really the supreme power of the universe—unless, in other words, they find that this image or concept of God evokes their religious devotion. The psychological-sociological dimension of the problem cannot be ignored.

The essence of this dimension of the problem can be spelled out as follows. On the one hand, the image of God that still evokes widespread religious response in our culture is one that prevents an adequate theodicy and has many other deleterious effects as well. On the other hand, the idea of God suggested by process theism can solve the problem of evil, is intellectually satisfying in many other respects, and would have many beneficial psychological and social effects—in particular, I have suggested (in chapter 8),[43] it would induce a pacific spirituality. And yet it is widely perceived to be religiously inadequate, because it does not portray God as having the kind of power with which religious awe has been associated from childhood on.

To suggest a solution to this problem, with all its dimensions, would require a book in itself. In this conclusion I can suggest only the central idea of a possible solution. We need a generation willing to "live between Gods." By this I mean that persons would give up the idea of God that has hitherto evoked religious devotion, while committing themselves to a new idea of God that does not yet evoke this response, and perhaps never will, at least not as powerfully as did the old idea. This is likely because which idea of God evokes religious worship in us is heavily determined by early

---

42. Griffin, *Evil Revisited*, ch. 2.
43. Griffin, *Evil Revisited*, ch. 8.

childhood influences. But it is just this fact that requires the willingness to live between Gods. We need a generation—a generation of religious leaders, artists, and parents—who will work in terms of an idea of God that they themselves do not fully, except intellectually, feel to be God. They would teach this image—through symbols, stories, doctrines, and example—to the young people under their influence, with the goal that they, in adulthood, would have an understanding of God that is not only intellectually satisfying but religiously satisfying in the deepest sense of the word.

This program calls for tremendous psychic discipline. While recognizing that human feelings, images, and attitudes ingrained from childhood, and constantly reinforced by culture, are more powerful than recently acquired intellectual convictions, it nevertheless calls on persons to try to live, feel, think, teach, and worship in terms of a recently acquired idea of God that is found to be philosophically and theologically superior to the older idea, even though the new idea does not yet naturally evoke strong religious feelings.

The goal is to bring about a transformation such that the idea of God that intellectually seems *worthy* of worship will actually evoke worship. To some extent, this goal can be realized within the lifetime of a single person, and thus of a single generation. By a deliberate plan of reading, thinking, meditating, praying, teaching, sermonizing, worshipping, and acting, we can transform our sensibilities so that that which at first seemed intellectually correct, but only that, can come also to carry emotional clout. But to some extent such a generation will always remain between Gods. It will have lost the old God, and the new God will not be fully born. The full transformation can probably occur only in the next generation. We can portray the new image of God to our young in such a way that it will evoke stronger religious feelings in them than it ever will in us. At this time, our discipline, our sacrifice, will reap its reward. In this new generation, the gap between theodicy and worship, between intellect and emotion, which makes a fully satisfactory solution virtually impossible in our time, will be overcome.

Some may believe these psychological, even religious, reflections to be out of place in an academic book published by a university press. But the dualisms implicit in such a belief between the academy and life, between intellect and emotion, between theory and practice, and between reason and religion are some of the central dualisms of modernity that need to be overcome. The university will begin to realize its full potential for overcoming the existential, social, and global crises of our times when it overcomes these dualisms.

In any case, I have argued that process theism can provide us with a satisfactory solution to the problem of evil. I have suggested that the gap between such a solution and the position I presented in *God, Power, and Evil* can be bridged by reformulating some of the ideas more carefully, by filling in some omitted presuppositions, and by making some revisions, especially with regard to ultimate meaning and hope. In saying that such a solution can be satisfactory, I mean philosophically and theologically satisfactory: it can be seen to be self-consistent, adequate to and even illuminating of the facts of experience, adequate to the generic idea of God in our tradition, and expressive of the distinctively Christian suggestions about divine power in particular. Whether this theodicy is found to be *fully* satisfactory, in terms of other dimensions of the psyche, is, I have suggested in conclusion, finally dependent upon us—upon the kind of power we find divine, and therefore upon the kind of persons we are, or become. If we do find this idea of God theologically satisfactory, it is up to us to (help God) bring about the kind of persons who will find it religiously satisfying.

Bibliography

Basinger, David. "Divine Persuasion: Could the Process God Do More?" *Journal of Religion* 64 (1984) 332–47.
Cooper, Burton Z. *Why, God?* Atlanta: John Knox, 1988.
Davis, Stephen ed. *Encountering Evil: Live Options in Theodicy.* Atlanta: John Knox, 1981.
———. "God the Mad Scientist: Process Theology on God and Evil." *Themelios* 5.1 (1979) 18–23.
Frankenberry, Nancy. "The Emergent Paradigm and Divine Causation." *Process Studies* 13 (1983) 202–17.
———. "Language about the Totality." *Encounter* 44 (1983) 41–58.
———. "The Logic of Whitehead's Intuition of Everlastingness." *The Southern Journal of Philosophy* 22.1 (1983) 31–46.
———. "Some Problems in Process Theodicy." *Religious Studies* 17 (1981) 179–97.
———. "The Power of the Past." *Process Studies* 13 (1983) 132–42.
Griffin, David Ray. "Nuclearism, Imperialism, and Postmodern Theism." In *God and Religion in the Postmodern World.* Albany: SUNY Press, 1989, ch 8.
———. "The Holy, Necessary Goodness, and Morality." *Journal of Religious Ethics* 8 (1980) 330–49.
———. *Evil Revisited: Responses and Reconsiderations.* Albany: SUNY Press, 1991.
———. *God, Power, and Evil: A Process Theodicy.* Philadelphia: Westminster, 1976.
Griffin, David Ray, and Huston Smith. *Primordial Truth and Postmodern Theology.* SUNY Series in Constructive Postmodern Thought. Albany: SUNY Press, 1990.
Hare, Peter H. "Review of *God, Power, and Evil: A Process Theodicy.*" *Process Studies* 7.1 (1977) 44–51.
Neville, Robert. *Creativity and God: A Challenge to Process Theology.* New York: Seabury, 1980.
Whitehead, Alfred North. *Process and Reality.* Edited by David Ray Griffin and Donald W. Sherburne. Corrected ed. New York: Free Press, 1978.
———. *Religion in the Making.* Living Age Books. Cleveland: World, 1960.

Index

abba, 34, 186, 190
abortion, 127
Abrahamic traditions, 7, 70
aesthetic value, 175n8, 238, 243
Amida, 150, 161, 168
Anselm, 3, 16, 234
apocalypse, xxiv, xxvi, 186–89, 192, 194
archetypes, 82–84
Augustine, 231, 248
Aurobindo, Sri, 70–73, 76
axiological necessity, xxv, 176, 179–80
axiological, xxiv, xxv, 172–73, 179–84

being is power (Plato), 5, 6, 191
Bhagavad Gita, 70–73
Bodhisattvas, 146–52, 169
Bonaventure, 160, 163
Boyle, Greg, 16
Brahman, 71, 73, 168
Brightman, H. S., 232–34, 241
Buber, Martin, 16, 107, 219
Buddhism, 152, 161–62
Bush, George W., 129

Calvin, John, 35–36, 177
Caputo, John, 43n68, 52
Case-Winters, Anna, 35n47, 36
Cobb, John B., Jr., xi, xxv, 79, 193, 230n1
compatibilism, 36, 58
consequent nature (of God), 67, 105, 183, 193, 240, 242
contemplative yoga, xxii, 67, 69, 70, 72
Cooper, Burton, 248

cosmopolitics, 117–18
creatio ex nihilo (creation from nothing), 39n56, 41n60
cross (of Christ), xxvi, 4, 167, 188–90, 226

Davis, Stephen, 231, 233
Democratic Party, 126
depth democracy, 112
Dewey, John, 225
divine necessity, xxv, 173–79, 181–82, 184
divine trust, 51, 53, 55
Dombrowski, Daniel, xxiii, 94, 103–4, 106–9, 121–22
Dostoevsky, Fyodor, 4, 12
dream work, xiii
dualism, 80, 153, 250

eros, 79–80, 243n31
eternal objects, 82–84, 190, 192, 194
Ewing, A. C., xxv, 173, 175, 176–84

faithfulness, 18, 50–54, 61
Follett, Mary Parker, 104, 105, 107
founding fathers, 130–31
Frankenberry, Nancy, 231, 235–39, 241–42, 251
free will defense, 18, 36, 232

Gaia, 110–12
Gamwell, Franklin, xxi, 7
Ganesha, 158, 162

253

INDEX

Gautama, Siddhartha, 84, 144, 146, 150
genuine evil, 191, 231–32, 239n23, 243
God and creativity, 235–38, 240, 243
godforsaken, 186–94
Gore, Al, 129
great companion, God as, 21, 104
Griffin, David Ray, xi, xxvi–xxvii, 172, 187, 190–94, 230–251

Hare, Peter, 233–35, 243–46
Hartshorne, Charles, xi, xxi, 3–6, 8–10, 15, 17–18, 106, 109, 172, 177, 190, 200–201, 241–46
Hebrew scriptures, 31
Hefner, Philip, 232–33, 235–36
Hick, John, 233–34
Hitler, Adolf, 94–95, 121
Hobbes, Thomas, 101, 110, 118
holy mystery, 21–22
human development, 58
Hume, David, xxi, 4

ideal power, 3, 6, 11
ideal(s), 99, 106, 113, 117, 181, 208
idiolatry, 19, 101, 189
image of God (*imago Dei*) 16, 102, 105–6, 119, 121, 247–50
initial aim, 85–91, 125
integral yoga, 70, 72–73

James, William, 104, 198
Job, 27–28, 37, 52, 69, 237
John of Patmos, 186
Jung, C. J., 67–76, 78–91

Kaufman, Gordan, 174
Keller, Catherine, xxv–xxvi, 99, 102, 186–94
kenotic, 168
Kierkegaard, Søren, 98–99, 189, 205
Krishna, 71, 73, 161
Kushner, Harold

Latour, Bruno, xxiii, 94, 108–12
Leslie, John, xxv, 173, 175–77, 179–81, 184
Levinas, Immanuel, 107

liberal democracy, xxiii, 96, 103, 105, 125, 137
life of Christ, xx, xxi
linear power, xxvi, 200–210, 212, 217, 220, 222–23, 226–29
living between Gods, xxvii, 246
Locke, John, 97, 131
logical necessity, xxv, 176, 178, 180, 184
logos, 118
Loomer, Bernard, xxvi, 6, 164, 197–229
Lowe, Victory, 22

Mahayana, 76, 106, 145–48, 150–52
meaning crisis, 108, 109n61
Mesle, C. Robert, 172
Moltmann, Jürgen, xv, 20–21, 188–90
moral adequacy, xxi, 14, 18
moral value, 105, 115, 245

Nazi Party, 94–95
neoclassical, xiii, xxi, 3–4, 6–7, 109n63
neo-Kantian, 98–100
Neville, Robert, 144n3, 241
new orthodoxy, 49
Nicholas of Cusa, 160
Niebuhr, Reinhold, 125, 199, 204–5, 226, 242n31
nondualistic, 80, 239

obedience, 57, 73, 165
omnibenevolence, 4, 150
omniscience, 11–12, 106, 147, 242, 245, 248
ontological gratitude, xxv, 172, 175, 182–84
Oord, Thomas Jay, xxi–xxii, xxv, 24–48, 59, 189, 193
Original Face (Zen Buddhism), 68, 75
Orwell, George, 96
Otto, Rudolf, 80

panentheism, 118
Paul, Apostle, 31, 33, 35, 43–44, 51–53, 61, 112, 118, 159, 167–69
pedagogical power, xxiv, 143, 148, 149, 153–56
perfect power, xxvii, 19, 190, 230, 232–33, 243–44

perfection, divine, 3, 5–6, 10, 17, 19–20, 58, 166, 181, 231, 234
personalism, philosophical, xxiii, 94, 101–2, 106
Pike, Nelson, 231
Placher, William, 54, 59–60
Plantinga, Alvin, 231–32
Plato, xix–xxi, xxvii, 5–8, 14, 114, 175n8, 191
Platonism, 247
Prehend
Prehension, xxiii, 214, 242
primordial nature (of God), 84, 87, 181
problem of evil, xxv, 190, 230, 234, 238, 247, 249–50
process liberalism, xxiii, 119, 121–22
progressivism, 95
propositional feelings, 82–83, 90, 99
propositions, 82–83, 90, 98–99
psychological process, 68
Pure Land (Buddhism), 148, 150, 161
pure possibilities, xxiii, 129–30, 190, 192

Rawls, John, xxi–xxiii, 8–10, 94, 96, 103–4, 106, 121–22
real potentials, xxiii, xxiv, 129–30, 137
redemption, 70, 192, 242n31
relational power, xxvi, 15, 210–229
relational theists, 62
religious viability, xxi, 14, 16–18
Republican Party, 128, 206
Rescher, Nicholas, xxv, 173, 175, 182, 184
Roman Empire, 186

secularization of God, 112
secularization, 95, 102–3, 106, 112

Sermon on the Mount, 154
Sessions, William Lad, 62
Shakespear, William, 11
size (Bernard Loomer), xxvi, 164, 199, 201, 206, 212, 223–29
Smith, Houston, 231
Suchocki, Marjorie, 136
suffering love, xxv, 247

Tao, 158
teleology, 168, 239
Third Reich, 96
transmutation, 85, 88–91, 193, 242n31, 243
Trinity, 161, 169, 249
Trump, Donald, 10, 137n22
trustworthy, 50–51, 53, 56, 58–59, 61–62

United Nations Universal Declaration, 105
US Constitution, 134–36

Vervaeke, John, 109

Ward, Keith, xxv, 57, 173, 175
Watts, Alan, 162
Weber, Max, 108
Weimar Republic, 96
West, Cornell, 125
Wilber, Ken, 68
worthy of worship, God as, xxv, 172–75, 178–80, 182, 184, 230–236n17, 244–46, 249–50

Zimmerman, Michael, 80

www.ingramcontent.com/pod-product-compliance
Lightning Source LLC
Chambersburg PA
CBHW022002220426
43663CB00007B/922